29 DAYS

... to you becoming a great listener and communicator

A Simple Guide to Permanent Results!

Richard Fast

www.29daysto.com

29 DAYS ... *to becoming a great listener and communicator*

ISBN: 978-0-9865377-4-5 (softcover)
ISBN: 978-0-9865377-8-3 (ebook version)

29 DAYS™

1078 Westhaven Drive
Burlington, Ontario
·Canada L7P 5B5

www.29daysto.com

Book Design by Janice Phelps, LLC

How to Get Your 6-Digit PROGRAM ACCESS CODE

Your 29 DAYS program includes online access to your daily coach.

To gain access to your online coach you will need a special **6-Digit PROGRAM ACCESS CODE.**

If you purchased this program directly from the *29DAYS* website, your **6-Digit PROGRAM ACCESS CODE** can be found on your receipt.

If you purchased this program from another retailer, go to:

http://29daysto.com/listen

Enter the information required and you will be emailed your **6-Digit PROGRAM ACCESS CODE.**

**TO REGISTER FOR YOUR SPECIAL 6-DIGIT
PROGRAM ACCESS CODE PLEASE GO TO**

http://29daysto.com/listen

A BRIEF OVERVIEW ON HOW THE
29 DAYS COURSES WORK

If you were given a blank canvas and a set of brushes and paints to create a picture, the process of painting would be the same for you as for everyone, but the picture you paint would be uniquely yours. In *29 DAYS* we created a tried and proven process that will work for any number of people, but the discoveries, solutions and results that you uncover, will be as unique to you as your fingerprints.

In just twenty-nine days you will change the way you think! When you think differently, you act and perform differently, and twenty-nine days is all it takes for you to instill lasting, permanent change.

Your life is chock full of habits. Some good, some bad. Imagine what your life would be like if you could get rid of a few habits you don't want or acquire a couple you really do want? What kind of a person would you become? What kind of a life would you enjoy?

- How would you feel if you could become your perfect weight in 29 days?
- How would you feel if you could live the rest of your life without cigarettes in just 29 days?
- Would you like to adopt the habit of learning to save money in just 29 days?
- How about 29 days to become a great listener and communicator?

Humans are generally impatient. When we want a result we want it instantly as in, "Yesterday would be nice; I'll settle for today; and tomorrow is way too late!" In reality, instant results are almost impossible, which means we get side-tracked or bored and soon lose our passion for change. Thus, no change!

29 Days ... to a habit you want!, (a.k.a. "*29 Days*") breaks this self-defeating cycle. It guarantees results and it puts a time stamp on it. Can you wait twenty-nine days for a result that will dramatically change your life forever? If you think you can then this book is for you.

29 Days incorporates the latest technology to help you take control of the greatest asset you have: your thoughts. Here's how it works:

- Read the book *29 DAYS ... to a habit you want!*
- Choose the course that aligns with your desire for change (i.e. Quit Smoking, Lose Weight, become a Great Listener and Communicator etc.)
- Interact with your virtual "online coach" as he guides you, each morning and evening for twenty-nine days, through the necessary steps to permanent change and results.
- After twenty-nine days you will have either acquired a habit you really want, or you will have freed yourself from a habit you desperately want to be rid of.

The ultimate purpose of the *29 DAYS* programs is permanent change. Permanent change can only be achieved by changing your deepest thoughts. You will take small, simple steps that fit into your daily life. In fact, these steps will be so basic and easy, they will naturally and effortlessly become your new lifestyle. That is the *secret* to lasting change!

Change the way you think
and you will change your world.

ACKNOWLEDGMENTS

This book and the associated programs are the result of an enormous amount of effort from a great number of people. I want to express my gratitude and appreciation to:

Michele Bertolin, my wife and best friend for her tireless guidance and encouragement to get the endless ideas from thought to paper. Michele's efforts in co-writing *29 DAYS... to your perfect weight* speaks for itself. Thanks for always, always being there.

Gavin McDougald who continually donated his time, effort, feedback, and tireless enthusiasm to the myriad of details that are necessary to weave a book, a website and a series of programs into a cohesive whole. Your help, suggestions and guidance from the very beginning made this project possible.

Janice Phelps Williams, for her visual concepts, book design and her editing and re-editing with the patience of Job. Thanks so much for your attention to detail and your invaluable suggestions on improving the *29 DAYS* concept.

Thanks also to Jackie Bagatto, Tom Arnold, and Tibor Sarai for their advice, guidance, encouragement, and support for the ideas, format and philosophy of this *29 DAYS* program.

Then there are all the people who willingly participated as beta testers to ensure the viability, the daily interaction, messaging and overall concept that a twenty-nine day interactive coaching program really works. Your insight, suggestions and daily feedback were vital to creating effective, life-changing programs.

I also wish to thank the collective genius of Zig Ziglar, Maxwell Maltz, David Hawkins, Robert Maurer, Jack Canfield, Robert Ringer, Stephen Covey, Mark Victor Hansen, Deepak Chopra, Robert Fritz and Earl Nightingale for their inspiration, writing, philosophy and passion that are so instrumental in making our visit to this planet a better experience.

Book: *29 DAYS ... to a habit you want!*

Program: *29 DAYS ... to becoming a great listener and communicator*

PREFACE

Behavioral scientists claim that it takes as little as twenty-one days to develop a habit. Is this really true? Maybe ... it all depends on how *you* go about it! If you're going to try to change a habit using willpower, it might as well be twenty-one *years*!

All of us are mirror reflections of our thoughts, fears, beliefs and attitudes. If we cannot change those things, we cannot instill *lasting* results.

> *"We are what we think.*
> *All that we are arises within our thoughts.*
> *With our thoughts we make the world."*
> *~ Gautama Buddha ~*

29 DAYS is an interactive series of programs that serve as your very own personal coach. Each program is designed to eliminate an undesirable habit or add a positive one. These programs will change your thoughts, fears, beliefs and attitudes in one area at a time, and it will do it in a way that has never been done before, because it is different from any program ever created. It *does* come with some big promises, but it *doesn't* leave you on your own to figure things out. You will embark on an incredible journey of self-discovery.

> *29 DAYS* is designed to generate gentle, effortless, forward momentum – every day.

Throughout this book I have quoted a number of authors who have had a profound impact on my life and this philosophy. People like Zig Ziglar, Robert Maurer, Ph.D., Dr. Maxwell Maltz,

Earl Nightingale, Deepak Chopra M.D. and Robert Ringer are just a few of the giants in the world of self-help and motivational change who have positively impacted countless people.

29 DAYS sprang from two decades of my search for a *reliable* way to eliminate unwanted habits. With over twenty years of reading how-to material, attending seminars, and hiring a personal coach, I was still yearning for a better way to acquire good habits and forever eliminate the bad ones. I have attended a number of seminars that promised life-changing results only to be disappointed in the end because they failed to deliver the long-term success for either myself or the people I interviewed. In fact, most of the people I met at seminars would admit to attending four or five "life-changing" seminars a year!

On a personal level, I found the motivational books, videos and audio programs were wonderfully entertaining, informative, and helpful. In fact, the sources I referenced throughout this book have had a wonderfully positive effect on me. But in spite of all the positives, I knew there was one more step - a guided procedure of cognitive self-discovery - that was vital to complete the puzzle and instill permanent change.

So, after years of research, I have developed a simple, step-by-step process that will change your behaviors – permanently.

29 DAYS combines a number of philosophies, recent breakthrough discoveries of the human brain and the latest communication technology.

Each program will interact with you, twice each day for twenty-nine days, to positively change one significant area of your life at a time.

INTRODUCTION

Give a man a fish and you feed him for a day.
Teach a man to fish and you feed him for a lifetime.
~ Chinese Proverb

29 DAYS ... to a habit you want! is going to teach you *how* to fish. It has one purpose – to help you to independently make positive and permanent changes in your life.

Experience has taught us that if we want to make changes through willpower then those changes will be temporary at best. We also know that if the process is too difficult, it will seldom be followed. We further know that if we try to change too much too quickly, our *self-image* will never buy into it, which will result in nothing but frustration. And finally, a lot of detailed instructions that leave us completely on our own will also lead to a high rate of failure. There are certain principles and formulas to follow that will create the foundation for success and permanent results.

Many how-to programs have a lot of suggestions on how to muster willpower, set goals and repeat affirmations, and they will often work ... temporarily. They're much like diets. All diets will work if we can follow the instructions! But when someone goes on a diet, what is their goal? Is it to go on a diet? Is it to lose weight? The answer to both questions would seem to be yes. So if diets *always work* why do they have such a bad reputation? Studies show that 97% of weight-loss programs fail to achieve permanent results! In fact, most people will put on *more weight* following the completion of a diet because a diet is not a lifestyle change, it's a temporary and strenuous procedure that will eventually exhaust the dieter. The other problem with diets, and many of the "how-to" programs, is that they focus on the effect (weight, or the unwanted habit) instead of the cause (attitudes, fears, beliefs and self-image). It's the hole-in-the-bucket syndrome. If you have a hole in your bucket and you're trying to keep the bucket full of water, does it make more sense to find ways of continually adding more water to the bucket or would it be wiser to spend time and effort on repairing the bucket?

29 DAYS is not interested in helping you attain short-term results. These programs are designed to show you how to instill permanent change that will be with you for your lifetime. It's a step-by-step process that cannot fail if you really desire to eliminate a bad habit, or to instill a good habit.

29 DAYS programs are so effective because they actually don't tell you what to do, but instead they guide you on a twenty-nine day journey of self-discovery. This may be the first time in your life that your begin to uncover your deepest thoughts, behaviors and habits. 29 DAYS prompts you with specific questions, and then you begin to find the answers. These answers are so powerful and life changing because the answer you discover could only pertain to you, only you could find it.

Finding *your* answers is so exciting because now there's real meaning associated with it. The meaning goes to the core of who you are. There's no doubting the veracity or integrity of the answer because the giver is you. It's your answer. It comes with both meaning and understanding. When you discover the cause of your life-long habits and behaviors all on your own, you will at last get the 'aha.' What can be more empowering than self-discovery? Success breeds success. At last you've discovered the secrets to finding the answers to your problem. With this newfound awareness, you change the motor of all your thoughts and actions, you change the mightiest motor of all ... your mind.

All your habits have been programmed whether you are aware of it or not. The good news is that since you were able to install habits you didn't like, you're also able to install habits you desire.

To be successful at any undertaking, any undertaking at all, requires a certain set of rules that must be followed. No exceptions. These rules are the following:

- ✓ **You must have a specific goal.**
- ✓ **It has to be believable to you (self-image) or it will never see completion.**
- ✓ **You require a specific plan to attain your goal.**
- ✓ **You need a specific and systematic schedule to attain your goal.**
- ✓ **You should have the people and the support to help you achieve your desired outcome.**

The *29 DAY* programs incorporate all of the above.

You may wish to change a variety of things about yourself, but for simplicity's sake throughout this book we will use weight loss for our examples of permanent change.

Note: The same five rules listed above apply to any desirable change.

How Does It Work?

The programs are divided into four weeks with each week having a specific purpose. The four weeks are broken down as:

1. **Commitment and Awareness,**
2. **Preparation for Action,**
3. **Taking Action and**
4. **Staying the Course or, to put it another way, Permanent Lifestyle.**

Within these four weeks are the five steps necessary to attain any goal:

— Step One

Each program has a specific goal in mind. (Quit Smoking, Save Money etc.)

— Step Two

We will guide you toward the correct way to set your goal. Through this procedure you will lay down new mental (neuron) tracks that will harness untapped forces and build unshakable self-confidence. (This concept will be explained in detail later in the book.)

— Step Three

We will be in contact with you at least twice each day (via email) as we walk with you step-by-step toward achieving your goal. We do this through examples, stories, encouragement, prompting questions and generally changing the way you think about this goal or challenge. (This step is a scientifically proven process that will be discussed later in the book.)

━ Step Four

Each day you will be required to take a very simple step that will guide you toward completing your goal. This step may be as simple as writing your goal in your journal, reading something we send to you, noticing your tendencies and recurring thoughts, visualizing your goal for a few moments, or simply responding to us by email, which will indicate to your virtual coach that you have reviewed the information for the day.

━ Step Five

You and your program will combine forces to become "your daily coach." This unbeatable combination will help you to maintain your focus and commitment. All these steps are purposely designed to enlist the support of the most powerful force in the universe, as well as the one that's closest to home, your subconscious mind. With the blessing and support of your subconscious mind you can achieve anything that you can conceive.

29 DAYS is based on immutable scientific laws and a carefully structured process. Each day you will be guided and inspired toward achieving your specific goal through awareness and a gradual change in the way you think about this particular area of your life. You will quickly see that your mind, seemingly of its own volition, will be reviewing your goal over and over. By about day ten you will catch yourself thinking about your goal even when you weren't consciously focusing on it.

What is the key to real change? Instilling a new habit. Goals you thought were too difficult will be systematically broken down (by this program and your inner-thought process) into easy-to-follow steps so that in a surprisingly short period of time, you will have achieved your seemingly impossible goal. In keeping with the Chinese proverb of "How to Fish," *29 DAYS* will give you the know-how and the confidence to successfully "catch fish" or in this case – change the things you wish to change – and more importantly keep them changed all the days of your life.

So here's our promise: Using the *29 DAYS* programs and selecting the program that aligns with your desired change, you will successfully change that area about yourself, quickly, effort-lessly and permanently!

— THE BOOK —

29 DAYS ... to a habit you want!

— <u>PART ONE</u> —

Understanding the
Challenges to Change

CHAPTER ONE
What Is a Habit?

Before we dive into the philosophy and workings of *29 DAYS,* it's important to understand our definition of *habit.*

> Habit are things we do without conscious attention
> and without being aware of them.

To add to that, habits are those things we do that seem to happen almost of their own volition: like overeating, being negative, chain smoking or procrastinating. Have you ever described someone as being "habitually" late? But habits aren't limited to negative things. Many of our habits are desirable. How about a habit of always being complimentary, or looking for the positive in situations? How about the habit of being punctual?

How are new habits formed?

New habits are formed by thinking new thoughts and forming new pathways in the brain. Therefore, the more you think a particular thought and/or perform a particular action, the quicker you build up the pathway and create the muscle memory to support it.

> *"Our self-image and our habits tend to go together. Change one and you will automatically change the other. The word 'habit' originally meant a garment or clothing... Our habits are literally garments worn by our personalities. They are not accidental, or happenstance. We have them because they fit us. They are consistent with our self-image and our entire personality pattern. When we consciously and deliberately develop new and better habits, our self-image tends to outgrow the old habits and grow into the new pattern."*
> ~ Dr. Maxwell Maltz - Psycho-Cybernetics

CHAPTER TWO
The Philosophy of Permanent Change

In order for you to enjoy permanent change, you're going to alter the way you think – at least about one particular goal – because if you don't change how you think, you won't change.

The world we have created is a product of our thinking;
it cannot be changed without changing our thinking.
~ Albert Einstein

It doesn't matter if your goal is to lose weight, quit smoking, start an exercise program, stop being negative – or (start being positive), learn to save money or learn to be punctual, every desire for change is within your effortless grasp.

I suspect you're thinking "Yeah, right! I've heard this before. What's the catch?"

There's no catch. You simply must *want to change* and if you really want to change, I can absolutely promise success, and the input on your part is going to be minimal. In fact it may seem almost effortless.

It is a proven fact that our thoughts shape our world. Our beliefs affect the way we perceive the world and our beliefs always precede our behavior to reinforce our perception. In effect, our world is not so much experienced by what happens to us, but rather how we *interpret* and *react* to what happens to us. We've all seen children fall down and skin their knees, and we've also witnessed two drastically different responses to a skinned knee. One child will cry and scream and carry on as if he's just been put through the Medieval Inquisition, and another child will merely wince, wipe the blood and tears away and continue to play as if nothing happened. Same experience, two drastically different reactions.

So why would two children react so differently to the same experience? One child thought skinning his knee was a major catastrophe; the other child thought it was just a scrape. If you change how you think, then change will become effortless and permanent. What you think about becomes your truth. How you view yourself becomes your reality. Every thought you think helps to form your future.

In his wonderful book, *Creating Health*, Deepak Chopra writes:

> *… for any diet* to be permanently successful, you have to enjoy being on it. In fact you should not feel like you're on a diet at all. Everyone should eat a weight-controlling and healthful diet, not because he thinks it is good for him and will make him lose weight, but because he would honestly prefer not to eat anything else.*

> * You may substitute the word "change" or "habit" for diet.

BOOK

> ## Acquiring habits that are born of a change of attitude and thought, as opposed to willpower, is our goal.

(In the introduction we said that throughout PART ONE, we would use "losing weight" as our recurring example, but bear in mind that the "29 DAYS template" will work for any change you desire.)

If you think losing weight is going to be painful, difficult, and impossible, then it will be. If, on the other hand, you think that losing weight will be painless and inspiring, then that's what it will be. In other words it's not the experience itself, it's your attitude or view *of* the experience. If you have even the slightest doubt about this statement, all you have to do is look at the current fad of "piercing" that is popular within a segment of our society. To the vast majority being stabbed with a metal prong in the imaginative places that piercing is done would be considered, at the very least, borderline torture. But that being said, for those folks wearing the jewelry in those imaginative body cavities, it's an experience that brings pride and pleasure. It's all in how you view a thing.

This program will ensure that you view the experience in a pleasurable way. In fact we are going to ensure that it will be so painless, and the steps so manageable, that you may want to move faster than we suggest.

As you will see, our method is to give you first-hand experience, but at the same time we will work with you, guide you, prompt you and encourage you. While you are gaining the experience and learning how to change your habitual thinking, we're right there with you while you learn the fundamental steps of helping yourself. When you know how to help yourself, you can achieve any goal you desire.

Some Guarantees Deliver Everything They Promise ... but Ultimately Nothing!

I'll always remember the story my father told me about a so-called guaranteed solution to eliminate the hated potato beetle. My father was raised on an agricultural farm during the late 30s and early 40s. They had a large variety of crops, which included an assortment of fruits and vegetables. A nice selection of crops inevitably attracts the usual suspects. In this case it was the hated and feared potato beetle. If you thought that the third and fourth plagues of gnats and flies that Moses, Pharaoh and the Egyptians suffered through were horrific, that was a mere nuisance compared to the voracious potato beetle! A farmer could go to bed at dusk with a perfectly healthy crop and wake up to see his field stripped of leaves before breakfast. What makes the potato beetle so devastating is its proliferation and unmatched ability to develop resistance to virtually every chemical that's been used against it.

The local fruit and vegetable distributor was the life-blood of the community, for it was here that the neighboring farmers would gather to purchase fertilizer, seed, and the necessary range of equipment from ladders to tractors. It was the perfect place to trade stories, tell hard luck tales, gossip and to discuss methods of combating the potato scourge. As the suggestions, laments and woes of impending doom were being lobbed about, one of the farmers noted a small advertisement in the *Farmer's Almanac*. The ad claimed to have documented proof that this solution offered a 100% success rate in killing the pesky potato beetle. The ad said something to the effect that if you mailed $1.15 in either cash or a teller's check to *The Beetle Bug Solution* at the address listed below, you would be given the "secret weapon" that killed this scourge every time and without fail. It guaranteed that no potato beetle has ever, or could ever, survive this ingenious weapon. It was further promised that the solution would be mailed the very day your money arrived and of course this assurance was backed with an ironclad money-back guarantee.

Well, there was immediate skepticism to such a claim, but as these things are prone to do, the offer proved irresistible. After all, as one farmer pointed out, "What do we have to lose? If it doesn't work we're guaranteed our money back." That line of logic seemed to hold up under the weight of analysis as the farmers went their various ways.

The following day the neighborhood postman collected a satchel full of envelopes addressed to *The Beetle Bug Solution*. Well it wasn't two weeks later that the guaranteed solutions were delivered. When the anxious recipients tore open their packages it was a sight to behold. There in the little brown envelope was the secret weapon. They found two small blocks of wood and the typed instructions for their exact use. The instructions were short, succinct, and elegantly simple to follow. They read:

> To kill the potato beetle, place it on one of the blocks of wood, and before it can escape, smash down hard on it with the other block. It works every time!

As you can imagine, it took some time for the story to come out since no one wanted to admit they had been duped by such an obvious con. But eventually such a beautiful swindle had to be accepted for what it was, and the locals had a good laugh at their own expense. When someone suggested that "Something ought to be done about this kind of larceny," and that "The lying cheat who sold this malarkey should be locked up for a thousand years," an old wag elegantly pointed out, "The ad, the materials and the instructions did exactly as they promised!"

29 DAYS' Guarantees Are Not Sleight of Hand or Print
They're based on five key steps.

Let's review the five keys to success that were outlined earlier in this chapter. To be successful at any undertaking, any undertaking at all, a certain set of rules must be followed. No exceptions. These steps are the following:

1. **You need to have a specific goal.**
2. **You must find it believable or it will never see completion.**
3. **You need to have a specific plan to attain your goal.**
4. **You require a specific and systematic schedule to attain your goal.**
5. **You should have the people and/or the support to help you achieve your desired outcome.**

29 DAYS will teach you the simple techniques towards creating permanent change and lasting results. Once you've developed the "self-confidence" and "know how", you will be able to initiate change in every area of your life using the exact same formula. The only kind of change we want, the only kind of change that is really worthwhile, is the change that will have you walking to the river's edge with the confidence that you can catch a fish whenever you desire.

In other words instilling the confidence and the knowledge to make changes in your life that will literally stay with you *for* the rest of your life.

It's important to acknowledge the fact that a deeply entrenched habit has strong emotional bonds. People with a long history of low self-esteem won't transform themselves into highly confident individuals in twenty-eight days, but they can transform one area of their lives in twenty-eight days and thus begin to build the basis of a positive-belief-system and the crucial foundation that will transform them into a self-confident person.

Because our focus in *29 DAYS* is targeted toward specific goals, such as *losing weight, becoming positive, quitting smoking* or *saving money,* etc. you can be assured that you're tackling a manageable goal. Now imagine if you simply changed two or three habits each year. What kind of a person would you become in five years? Needless to say the change would be nothing short of extraordinary!

All of us were heavily programmed when we were too young to think for ourselves. Most of our thoughts about our capabilities, behaviors and what's right and wrong were instilled at a very early age, before we were even aware. You could spend years in counseling to uncover why you're afraid of achieving your goals, or you can simply overwrite the problem by changing your thoughts and beliefs about your capabilities, which is exactly what *29 DAYS* will do.

CHAPTER THREE
The Principles of Success

29 DAYS is based on *two* fundamental principles of success:

Principle of Success #1:

— **Patience and perseverance**

I bet you're thinking "Oh crap, this sounds hard already!" Stay with me, I know it sounds hard but in this application it really isn't. Although patience and perseverance are two distinct words, in our context they are practically interchangeable. Patience is not passive and should never be confused with idleness, in fact it's quite the contrary: It's active, it's concentrated strength, and it's perseverance. To persevere is to prevail. The basic application of patience and perseverance are crucial to your lasting success – and ironically – they are your quickest and most effortless path to permanent change.

Principle of Success #2:

— **The belief and support from your inner-self, which can also be summed up as simple self-confidence.**

Every successful undertaking in mankind's history has been built on patience and perseverance, *and* the self-confidence to not only undertake a task, but to continue at precisely the point when both patience and perseverance may be running low, you know, that point when everything seems to be going wrong.

In today's society of instant gratification and instant results, our patience and perseverance toward a new goal may be running low by the third day! That is exactly when *29 DAYS* will help to overcome self-doubt, negativity and impatience.

> *"A journey of a thousand miles must begin with the first step."*
> *~ Lao Tzu*

No truer words were ever spoken, *but* equally important are all the successive steps to complete the journey. *29 DAYS* will walk with you through the entire journey to make sure you fulfill your desire.

The Tortoise and The Hare

Do you remember the famous story of the Tortoise and the Hare? It's chock full of the principles of patience, perseverance and self-confidence.

Once upon a time there was a Hare who, boasting how he could run faster than anyone else, was forever teasing Tortoise for its slowness. Then one day, the irate Tortoise answered back: "Who do you think you are? There's no denying you're fast, but even you can be beaten!" The Hare squealed with laughter.

"Beaten in a race? By whom? Not you, surely! I bet there's nobody in the world that can win against me, I'm so speedy. If you think you or anyone else can beat me, why don't you try?" teased the Hare.

Annoyed by such bragging, the Tortoise accepted the challenge. A course was planned, and the next day at dawn they stood at the starting line. The Hare yawned sleepily as the meek Tortoise trudged slowly off.

When the Hare saw how painfully slow his rival was, he decided, half asleep on his feet, to have a quick nap. "Take your time!" he said. "I'll have forty winks and catch up with you in a minute." The Hare woke with a start from a fitful sleep and gazed round, looking for the Tortoise. But the creature was only a short distance away, having barely covered a third of the course.

Breathing a sigh of relief, the Hare decided he might as well have breakfast too, and off he went to munch some cabbages he had noticed in a nearby field. But the heavy meal and the hot sun made his eyelids droop. With a careless glance at the Tortoise, now halfway along the course, he decided to have another snooze before flashing past the winning post. And smiling at the thought of the look on the Tortoise's face when it saw the Hare speed by, he fell fast asleep and was soon snoring happily. The sun started to sink below the horizon, and the Tortoise, who had been plodding towards the winning post since morning, was scarcely a yard from the finish. At that very point, the Hare woke with a jolt. He could see the Tortoise a speck in the distance and away he dashed. He leapt and bounded at a great rate, his tongue lolling, and gasping for breath. Just a little more and he'd be first at the finish. But the Hare's last leap was just too late, for the Tortoise had beaten him to the winning post. Poor Hare! Tired and in disgrace, he slumped down beside the Tortoise who was silently smiling at him.

"Slowly does it every time!" he said.

There are a lot of life's lessons in this short story!

Let's take a closer look at our humble hero and notice the many qualities of character that allowed him to win.

- As noted, he's humble and he readily acknowledges the good in others:
  "There's no denying you're swift," he says to the Hare.

- He's knowledgeable and confident. He knows that everyone and everything *can* be beaten:
  "Who do you think you are? There's no denying you're swift, but even you can be beaten!"

  The Tortoise knows his history. He knows that it doesn't matter if we're talking about Muhammad Ali defeating the "unbeatable" George Foreman, Buster Douglas defeating the "unbeatable" Mike Tyson, The Duke of Wellington defeating Napoleon, the Allies defeating Nazi Germany, Jonas Salk and Albert Sabin defeating Polio, or ourselves overcoming an addiction or undesirable character trait, every seemingly unbeatable foe can be defeated.

- Our Tortoise hero is "human"; even *he* gets angry:
  "Then one day, the irate Tortoise answered back: Who do you think you are?"

- He willingly accepts a daunting challenge:
  "I bet there's nobody in the world who can win against me, I'm so speedy. Now, why don't you try?" Annoyed by such bragging, the Tortoise accepted the challenge.

- He's patient, determined, purposeful and *not* prone to discouragement or outside influence:
  "The Hare woke with a start from a fitful sleep and gazed round, looking for the Tortoise. But the creature was only a short distance away, having barely covered a third of the course."

- He has focus and staying power – perseverance:
  "The sun started to sink below the horizon, and the Tortoise, who had been plodding towards the winning post since morning, was scarcely a yard from the finish."

- The Tortoise knows how to harvest and enjoy the fruits of his labor:

  "Tired and in disgrace, he slumped down beside the Tortoise who was silently smiling at him. Slowly does it every time!" he said.

Like the Tortoise, when you combine the two fundamental principles (patience and perseverance) together with self-confidence, you will be guaranteed success, and you will find yourself reaching your goals quicker and with less effort than you would have ever thought possible.

If you ever catch yourself thinking that you're the overmatched-underdog, or that life has simply stacked too many obstacles against you, try to remember the story of the humble tortoise. History is abundant with "tortoise tales" of ordinary people winning against seemingly impossible odds.

— <u>PART TWO</u> —

Uncovering and Understanding
Our Greatest Foe: FEAR

CHAPTER FOUR
The Unlimited (or Limiting) Power of Your Inner-Self and Why We Fail

In all likelihood we don't change what we want to change because on a subconscious level the kind of change we are wishing for appears to be too hard and too painful. Our inner self-image refuses to buy in.

In 1960, Dr. Maxwell Maltz, M.D., a plastic surgeon, wrote the timeless classic, *Psycho-Cybernetics*. After thirty-five years of study and observation, he concluded that a person's actions, feelings, behaviors, and even abilities, are consistent with his or her self-image. In other words, you will become the sort of person you think and see yourself being. In Dr. Maltz's words he wrote:

I would argue that the most important psychological discovery of modern times is the discovery of the self-image. By understanding your self-image and by learning to modify it and manage it to suit your purposes, you gain incredible confidence and power.

This self-image is our own conception of the "sort of person I am." It has been built up from our own beliefs about ourselves. Most of which have unconsciously been formed from our past experiences, our success and failures, our humiliations, our triumphs, and the way other people have reacted to us, especially in early childhood. From all these we mentally construct a self (or a picture of self). Once an idea or a belief about ourselves goes into this picture it becomes "truth," as far as we personally are concerned. We do not question its validity, but proceed to act upon it 'just as if it were true'.

The self-image then controls what you can and cannot accomplish, what is difficult or easy for you, even how others respond to you just as certainly and scientifically as a thermostat controls the temperature in your home.

In short, your entire life is a perfect reflection of your self-image. Each of us will act in direct accordance with how we see ourselves. In fact, it's not possible to act otherwise.

As a corollary to that, I will say that willpower is tail-chasing. Creating a desired self-image is tantamount to success.

The *29 DAYS* programs are committed to shining a light into the dark recesses of our inner thoughts that have held us back because of a fragile self-image.

As you're going to find out, positive change won't be difficult because you are going to change the way you think about it. If you found change was difficult in the past it was only because you *thought* it was difficult.

In *Hamlet*, Shakespeare wrote: "*There is nothing either good or bad, but thinking makes it so.*"

So let's rephrase that Shakespearean quote: "If we *think* it so … it *will* be so."

The modern mantra of "no pain no gain" is often associated with a right of passage or badge of honor, somewhat like having your dentist skip the anesthesia when he's drilling for a cavity. It might make for some bragging rights, if you can stand the pain, but what's the point?

29 DAYS is not designed to avoid pain and heartache, because neither "pain" nor "heartache" will ever come into play. In fact, if this program ever *does* become painful, let *that* serve as a warning sign that you're *not* following the program properly. This program is about effortless and lasting change, not fleeting, teeth-clenched, short-term willpower.

How We Often Set Ourselves Up for Certain Failure: "The New Year's Eve Syndrome"

Let's look at a some "typical" examples of people who finally say "That's it, I've got to change!"

The tactic they employ is teeth-clenched, head down, smash-through-the-wall change – a sure recipe for failure.

SANDY – AGE 37

It's New Year's Eve. "After tonight I'm determined to change my life. I'm going into the New Year with a fresh start and a new attitude. I am certain that *I can* and *will* change. *I will* become a new person!"

Sandy is forty pounds overweight. She hates the way she looks and the thought of getting into a bathing suit and being seen in public causes her to break into a cold sweat. Sandy has always found great comfort in junk food, soda pop and long stretches flopped in front of the TV. But it's New Year's Eve and Sandy has hit the wall. She vows to herself that this is the year for positive change. She's going to join a womans' fitness club, throw out all the junk-food in the house, and buy a couple of "How To" books on getting into shape. She vows to start the New Year with a vengeance.

WHAT'S LIKELY TO HAPPEN: By about day three something will go wrong. Sandy's boss will reprimand her, or she'll imagine that she heard someone call her a "fat cow" or she'll pull a muscle in her new workout regimen, and wham, she'll be back on the couch with the snacks and clicker just as sure as sh--, God made little green apples!

WHAT DID SANDY'S INNER SELF SAY?: "Sandy my dear, I haven't said anything for three days about this diet and exercise stuff only because I was laughing too hard to speak. But now that we've both had a chance to come back to earth let's be serious. *You* join a womans' fitness club, and stop eating junk food? Come on, who are you kidding? Life isn't easy. Hey, relaxing after a long, hard day at work is *your* right. After all, so what if you're a few pounds overweight? People who are the "so-called" perfect weight don't seem any happier. We all have our vices. Life has to have some fun. There's more to living than just work and exercise!"

"Well, if you put it that way", Sandy replies to her inner self, "I suppose you're right. I guess I *was* being unrealistic. I'll get the snacks, you see what's on TV!"

JASON – AGE 28

Jason is a shy little wallflower. He's the kind of guy who goes to the beach and actually *does* get sand kicked in his face. For as long as Jason can remember he's been intimidated by loud, aggressive people. He hates contact sports and most sports in general. Jason's idea of a good night is reading the latest computer programming manuals or playing video games. But it's New Year's Eve and Jason is sitting at home, alone, in his parents' basement. As he sits watching the Times Square celebration on TV, he decides right then and there that he's reached the end of his rope. "No more Mr. Nice guy. If Jack Lalane can transform his life from a ninety-nine pound weakling, then so can I." Jason commits to joining a health club, hiring a personal trainer and getting pumped. At the same time he's going to join a martial arts studio, learn to fight and look like Arnold Schwarzenegger in nine months.

WHAT'S LIKELY TO HAPPEN: Jason might get as far as joining a club, and he may even begin a workout regimen – provided he goes so far as to hire a personal trainer. Jason will be so afraid of letting his trainer down he may actually stay with his workout schedule for a couple of weeks. But at some point between the martial arts classes and the gym workout, Jason is going to look in the mirror and see the same shy, skinny kid who absolutely hates what he's putting himself through. His subconscious will take over and he'll end up pulling a muscle or twisting his ankle and that will be his ticket to flee this madness.

WHAT DID JASON'S INNER SELF SAY? "Hey, whoa, slow down little guy, have you completely lost your mind? You are a square peg and that exercise stuff is a round hole! You are born to do gentle things. *You*, learn to fight?! With a video controller yes, with your fists … forget it. Hey why don't you worry about getting your own apartment? After all, you're twenty-eight years old and you're still living with your parents. You're just not cut out for that macho stuff."

LORA – AGE 33

Lora hates meeting people. Whenever she's introduced to anyone she never knows what to say. As for striking up a conversation with anyone of the opposite sex … forget it. On top of being painfully shy, she thinks her breasts are too small and her nose is too big. Lora is "celebrating" New Year's Eve alone in her apartment. As she thinks about the past thirty-three years of her life she decides it's time for change. Massive change. Starting tomorrow she vows that this is the year she's going to come out of her shell, and meet the man of her dreams. Right then and there she decides she's going to join Toastmasters, buy some sexy new clothes and throw off the shackles of feeling inferior. After all, she is woman … watch her roar!

WHAT'S LIKELY TO HAPPEN: Lora makes the call to Toastmasters and agrees to attend the first meeting as a guest the following evening. Lora spends the next day building mental images of awkward introductions and being forced to make impromptu speeches in front of complete strangers. That night she forces herself to attend the meeting and it's even worse than she had imagined. Everyone she meets asks her to say something about herself. She stammers and stutters and finally excuses herself to go to the washroom. On the way to the ladies' room she passes the coat rack and almost without realizing it she grabs her jacket and bee-lines to the parking lot. "What could I have possibly been thinking?" she asks herself as she's running to her car.

WHAT DID LORA'S INNER SELF SAY? "Lora, we need to get a grip on reality. You like meeting new people about as much as they like meeting you. It's a painful, awkward experience for everyone involved; so why don't you give yourself and everyone else a break and forget the whole thing. For your entire life the only place you've been comfortable is in the background. You're a good person just as you are. The world's got enough out going social misfits. You enjoy your own company so what's wrong with that?" After a nanosecond of thought, Lora agrees and retreats to her life of solitude.

Do any of these scenarios sound familiar? Not that *you* have ever made radical New Year's Eve vows like this … but perhaps you're familiar with some wild resolutions that *other people* have made?

Why didn't Sandy, Jason or Lora have the slightest chance of achieving their resolutions and goals? Because their hopes were one thing and their inner beliefs about their capabilities were something else.

Four basic reasons for their failure:
1. They attempted far more than they were mentally ready for.
2. They expected (wanted) change to happen almost instantaneously without properly preparing for that change.
3. They were acting out of desperation and fear, rather than from conviction, belief and the support from their inner-self.
4. They failed to enlist some form of external support.

29 DAYS will guide you to your goals by addressing each of the 4 causes of failure.

Most of us are like that rabbit in the *Tortoise & Hare*, speed is everything! We want results and we want them *now!* In fact, yesterday would be preferable.

Since we know that demanding instantaneous results is *one cause* of almost certain disaster, let's delve further into some *other causes* of failure.

CHAPTER FIVE
Fear and the Futility of Expecting Instant Results

Why Is Change So Difficult?

If we *know* what is good for us (lose weight, save money, be more positive, quit smoking) and we *know* what to do to affect the change (eat less, spend less, look for the good, don't light up) then why, why, why is it so difficult?

In a word, FEAR.

Our minds will seldom accept overnight change. Our brains* are hardwired to resist radical change; in fact as you'll soon see, it's a built-in survival mechanism.

If our minds will not accept instant change then how do we explain people who stop smoking cold turkey, or people who have never previously exercised suddenly begin a life-long workout program? What about people who suddenly change their diets and eating habits into a permanently healthy lifestyle?

Traditionally these "overnight" changes were either falsely interpreted or they are akin to an epiphany, a transcendence, or a "Saul on the road to Damascus" miracle awakening. Although we're all aware of examples of people's lives being suddenly transformed, such as a crippling addiction suddenly and effortlessly cast aside, or

Note: For clarification of terms, the brain is generally considered to be the physical anatomy and the mind is what the brain generates through its activity. Eastern philosophy and New Age thinking tend to suggest this view is backward. To them, it's the mind that is the source of thought, and the brain simply reacts to what the mind feeds it. In 29 Days, we use the words "mind" and "brain" interchangeably because either concept is acceptable.

someone achieving instantaneous spiritual enlightenment, in every case these spectacular events are neither predictable nor controllable.

To say that we're wired to resist change, and that our resistance stems from fear, does not discount the fact that many of us *have* managed to initiate radical changes in our lives – *when* and *if* we've hit the so-called "wall." You know the place, like our examples of Sandy, Jason and Lora, where you suddenly say, "That's it! I've had it! I'm never going to do that again!"

"So," you might reasonably conclude, "there goes your theory of *not* being able to make radical changes at will." Not so.

There's no doubt that radical, and instantaneous change does happen. It happens to people everyday, but is it something we can do on command? Is it something that we can do at will and with other, or all, areas of our lives? Can we sustain it? Can we make it a habit? The overwhelming evidence says no!

Let me give you a personal example of how I managed an "overnight" change.
I took up smoking when I was fourteen and by the age of sixteen I was a "committed" smoker. Within three years I had managed to ratchet my daily intake of cigarettes to two packs per day. By the time I was twenty-one, I was up to three packs per day – which at the time I thought must be close to the physical limits since there are only so many hours in the day, that was until I began waking up during the night to ... you guessed it, "enjoy" another cigarette.

Needless to say that over the years I had managed to "quit" a number of times. I often joked how easy it was to quit since I had managed the feat so readily. In reality it wasn't quitting, it was just a temporary suspension, that never lasted more than a few days. I was a bona fide smoker. In fact, I actually couldn't imagine life worth living without cigarettes. After all, if I quit how could I ever again enjoy talking on the telephone without the aid and comfort of a smoke? How could I ever enjoy a beer without an accompanying cigarette? Enjoying a delicious meal and relaxing in front of the TV would have been "empty" without the perfect finishing touch, a cigarette. These smoky pleasures permeated every area of my life, all day long and well into the night. I simply couldn't imagine living without them.

But like every seasoned smoker knows, it's a life sentence to slavery. Like all smokers I always told myself that I would quit before it was too late, whatever that meant. Even though it was less expensive to buy cigarettes by the carton, I never did because I always thought, "What happens if I buy a ten-pack carton and decided to quit with only a part of the carton used up?

I mean, what would I do with the other packs? What a waste. In fact, wouldn't I then keep smoking just to finish off the carton?"

Nobody ever accused a smoker's thoughts toward the addiction as rational!

As a smoker I loathed this part of my life. I was angry and disgusted that I was so controlled by my addiction to this utterly destructive habit. Then one day I decided that I would quit, but I also decided that I was definitely *not* going to try to quit *that* day. Instead I would look at the psychological bondage that I had tied myself to. Rather than trying to quit immediately, or trying to cutback as I had in the past, I actually forced myself to increase my daily intake.

Now remember this was many years ago, when smokers weren't looked on as the pariahs they are today. Back then you could smoke on airplanes, public transportation; aside from smoking in church, you could smoke anywhere you pleased and nobody gave it a second thought. So when I say I was going to increase my daily intake, I literally began to light one cigarette from the previous. Were there many times that I had just finished a cigarette and didn't feel like smoking another at that moment? Almost always. But I forced myself to smoke it anyway because if cigarettes are so pleasurable, why would I possibly deprive myself of *all* the pleasure I could garner?

With each cigarette I smoked I really thought about how much I hated it. I was "subconsciously" reprogramming my beliefs that smoking was "pleasurable" and "impossible to quit." This self-imposed torture of continually smoking went on for a couple of weeks, and as you can well imagine, it was beginning to seriously effect my immediate health. I was constantly fatigued and felt unwell. I knew that I was going to quit, I knew that I *had* to quit, but I let the entire fiasco run its course. I knew a change was going to happen, but I really didn't know how or when.

Then came the day. I can recall it as clear as if it happened yesterday. I was twenty-seven years old. I awoke one morning and it quite literally felt like someone was standing on my chest. It was a clear and unmistakable sign. The not-too subtle warning was accompanied by that deep knowing. It was one of those life-defining moments. Either I quit smoking or I would never see forty.

The knowing was so complete that when I got out of bed and looked at my pack of cigarettes I calmly threw them in the garbage, got dressed and went to work. I haven't smoked a cigarette in twenty-three years. Were there times in the ensuing weeks and months that I longed for a cigarette? Occasionally. In fact, years later I might be talking on the phone and the thought of "enjoying" a "pleasant cigarette" would pop into my mind, but the thought was fleeting and carried little substance. My freedom meant far more to me than anything else.

BOOK

To this day, I will still say that my greatest accomplishment was ridding myself of that vile, filthy, disgusting habit. For a long time I thought that I had broken my smoking slavery through willpower. Today I know that nothing could be further from the truth. What I had done was systematically change my thought process. I had slowly but surely began to see my habit and addiction for what it was. When I thought cigarettes were my friends I was completely under their control. When I changed my thinking to realize they were my biggest enemy *I* finally had control. It was then, and only then that I could stop smoking ... permanently!

Now, to underscore my point, even though I used to think that I had quit cold turkey, that's not really the case. Everyone who quits at some point has had their last cigarette. We might think that at that point, they had to quit, cold turkey. Technically this is true, but in reality there was a thought process that had to lead up to that point. In my case there was a particular moment when I said "That's it, I've had it!" but in order to get to that place where I could leave it behind, I had to spend a couple of weeks changing my deepest beliefs about smoking.

When people seem to change deep habits and addictions, 'overnight,' seemingly through the use of willpower, if you were to look closer you will likely find that there was much more involved than what appears on the surface. There are always exceptions but in all likelihood they're too rare to bother with. In fact, *if* one could manage such major change through the use of willpower, then by rights they should be able to transform themselves into a perfect walking, talking and performing human being overnight. The sad reality is that change through the instantaneous process of willpower has always produced dismal results.

The instantaneous attempts that are most common are fad diets, austerity vows to eliminate debt cold turkey, spur of the moment attempts at quitting smoking or drinking or gambling, or the assumption of a new personality by joining a social community.

There are always a few well-publicized success stories that fuel the belief that overnight change is possible and commonplace. These publicized stories often lead us to believe that if we can't initiate the instantaneous change we want, then we must be deficient in personal force or willpower. Nothing could be further from the truth!

> Your willpower will never be stronger than your subconscious mind, no matter what.

Mr. A – The Classic Overachieving Willpower Guy

Most of us know the classic Type A personality. The person who tries to run his life on the fuel of willpower. Type A people are aggressive, impatient, tense and hard driving. They are forever trying to beat a deadline, and relaxing is a foreign concept.

We may all know a Type A who by sheer will manages to quit a debilitating addiction, train for a triathlon, or perform some other life challenging task. This Herculian effort often produces eye-popping results, and it's even quite likely that many of us can think of examples in our *own* lives where we have achieved a goal through determination and massive overnight change. This kind of personal power can be a real confidence builder and an internal source of pride, but it's also very unreliable and can have some devastating effect on our confidence and self-esteem *if*, and inevitably in some area we will, fail.

If personal power was a sure formula for success, then it stands to reason that anyone who ever achieved success through personal power (stop a bad habit or start a good one) should simply be able to duplicate the same formula in every area of his or her life. By this reasoning, within a year or so, our "personal-power-individual" should (in his eyes at least) be totally pleased with every area of his life. As we've all witnessed, this formula may work on occasion, but for broad, long term, meaningful change, it's simply not reliable and will ultimately stack one more failed attempt onto a growing heap. In fact, successive failures can often lead to the debilitating attitude of, "Why bother? I never succeed at anything anyway."

If you happen to be an Type A personality, and you really can achieve your goals through sheer force of will, then good for you.

In the *29 DAYS* programs, our aim is to achieve our goals. *That, and only that,* is our measure of success. If we want to get from the country to the city our goal then is to arrive in the city. It doesn't much matter (to our ultimate goal) if we ride in a Chevy, a Rolls Royce or a bicycle for that matter, the aim is to get to the city. Our arrival – by whatever means - is proof of our success.

Getting back to our Mr. 'A', and his formula for success. We know him to be rather predictable, you know the kind … "I want everything yesterday, and I will get it *all*, even if I have to run through a wall or turn the world upside down to get it!"

For convenience sake, let's call our Type A personality "Arnold", and one day Arnold decides he's going to soften his aggressive personality.

Arnold's day isn't atypical. It is just another one of those days filled with tension and stress. But then late in the afternoon, after chewing out another employee, something happens to "lovable" Arnold. He has a quiet moment and he suddenly realizes that his demeanor and general behavior might actually benefit from some modifications and adjustments. As a result, he decides to try to mellow-out and soften his edges. Just like that!

Arnold realizes that being a bull in a china shop has its limitations and as a result, he decides he wants to modify his behavior for a better relationship with his family, friends and associates. As a result, he decides that starting the very next morning he will begin to enjoy a quiet moment, stop to notice the beauty of his surroundings, offer an uncharacteristic word of encouragement to his employees and take time out to reflect on life. All this will begin the following morning, through sheer force of will.

If you're imagining a Type A person right now, you're probably laughing at the notion. We simply KNOW that that type of behavior is completely foreign to a Type A personality and such radical, overnight behavioral change is highly unlikely.

If Arnold sincerely desires to be a more compassionate soul who takes time for simple moments and sincere communication, he *can* achieve his goal, but he must go about it in the right way. The cold-turkey, willpower approach will fail every single time and it will fail because Arnold will *never* sneak this one past his inner-self!

CHAPTER SIX
Simple Steps Will Sow the Seeds of Belief and Success

Arnold will fail in his attempt because his approach will never be accepted by his inner-self or subconscious mind. His inner-self will laugh hysterically at the very notion. Without the acceptance of his inner-self, any attempt at changing his "core" personality won't last.

For Arnold to make a sustainable personality change, he must take certain steps that will change his core beliefs.

These steps are fundamental to your success. They will work for any person, any personality and in any situation. They will work every time, and they will never fail provided the following conditions are met:

1. **You must sincerely want to change**
2. **You must be willing to change ... gradually (The Way of the Tortoise)**
3. **You must generate gentle, effortless, forward momentum every day ... for twenty-nine days — this will establish the strong foundation for a new lifestyle, and a new way of living.**

John Wooden, one of the most successful college basketball coaches of all time, beautifully phrased this process when he said:

"When you improve a little each day, eventually big things occur. When you improve conditioning a little each day, eventually you have a big improvement in conditioning. Not tomorrow, not the next day, but eventually a big gain is made. Don't look for the big, quick improvement. Seek the small improvement one day at a time. That's the only way it happens – and when it happens, it lasts."

Change Is Difficult because We Instinctively Fear Change

Man is a creature that craves familiarity, and as a result, we form habits and routines (some good and some not so good) that eventually feel comfortable. Have you ever noticed when you sit down to watch television you and your spouse always sit in the same place regardless of who gets there first? Do you have "your" side of the bed? Do you take the same route to the local grocery store or to work even though there might be alternatives that are just as easy or as close? Do you notice when a group of employees gather for regular meetings that within a short period of time everyone has their spot for successive meetings?

The old expression "better the devil you know than the devil you don't" holds true. Taken to an even greater extreme, how often have we read of mistreated children defending their parents? How about spouses finding excuses to stay in abusive marriages or people staying in jobs that they absolutely hate year after year? Even long-term prisoners who have yearned for freedom experience tremendous anxiety as their release date approaches. They've become so accustomed to their prison routine they experience genuine fear of change.

All changes, even positive ones, are scary. Attempts to reach goals through radical or revolutionary action will almost always fail because they heighten fear and cut off the cooperation of our subconscious mind.

The Keys to Goal Achievement

1. Focus or purpose: If you don't have a goal the odds are one-hundred percent that you will not achieve it. *29 DAYS* starts you off with an achievable goal and together we make sure it is gentle, measurable, and that you maintain forward momentum. This kind of progress builds unshakeable self-confidence.

2. Sincerity: You must want to achieve it. Don't confuse this with teeth gritted, iron will determination; in fact, it may be quite the contrary. At times you will want to move quicker than *29 DAYS* will suggest! But you mustn't force the matter. It's imperative to stay with the system.

3. Slow, consistent, forward momentum: Completely disarms the brain's fear response which will stimulate your inner-self, or subconscious mind, that bottomless well of all possibilities given to each of us at birth.

4. Self-monitoring system: *29 DAYS* will guide you each day through interaction and a measurement process as you literally begin to build your picture of progress and ultimate success.

5. Accountability: *29 DAYS* will ask you to participate every day whether that's something as basic as sixty seconds of meditation or spending several minutes reading the daily message, or simply acknowledging that it's your "reward" day.

6. Reward Yourself: That's right! *29 DAYS* recognizes your participation and progress and the importance that you should also recognize and appreciate your success. This is key to building that unshakeable self-confidence that is the foundation of all success.

   Too many people keep their nose so stuck to the grindstone that they wear themselves out even while they're making progress. They make themselves feel like failures even while they're successful. *29 DAYS* will be sure that you reward yourself for your steady progress and small, but life-changing victories.

— PART THREE —

Our Thoughts: The Source of All Good and Bad!

CHAPTER SEVEN
How Gentle Progress Bypasses Our "Hardwired" Brains

Examining Our Incredible Brain

When it comes to character traits and habits, it doesn't really matter whether we say our brain is hardwired from birth or we say to ourselves, "That's just the way I am" or "That trait runs in my family" it still comes down to the same thing – we are the result of programming – genetically, acquired or self-induced. Anyway we look at it, this ingrained programming can and must be bypassed.

Whether we're trying to remove a negative habit or make a positive change, the part that always trips us up, and the prime cause of our failure to make permanent changes in our lives, is that change activates fear. If we want to change, we must bypass fear.

Fear of change is part of being human. The kind of change that causes fear does not have to be catastrophic change to induce it. Fear can be caused by something as simple as ordering a brand new dish at our favorite restaurant (or NOT ordering that dish for the same reason) or taking an unfamiliar route to work.

> The key point is that
> CHANGE CAUSES FEAR
> and
> FEAR CAUSES RESISTANCE.

Fear of change is rooted in the brain's physiology, and when fear takes hold, it can prevent creativity, change and success. To understand this basic law of human nature, its causes and effects, we need to take a quick look at the source – our extraordinary brain.

Without our highly developed brain, mankind would have been lucky to survive a week in the harsh environment of planet earth. Because of our unmatched ability to think and to reason, man rules the earth, but without our brain we are completely defenseless. We cannot swim like the creatures of the sea, we cannot fly like birds, we cannot stand extreme temperatures like the polar bear, lizard or camel, we have no natural camouflage, we are relatively weak against a mammal like the gorilla or lion, and our ground speed is slower than almost all of our natural land predators. In short we cannot outrun, out-swim, hide from or overpower our natural predators, and without our brains man's the most defenseless creature on the planet.

Every psychological theory recognizes that we are made up of several different selves. Our brain has evolved over millions of years leaving us with distinct parts, each with its own function. To further complicate matters we have to coordinate our distinct brains along with two evolving minds: conscious and subconscious. That's a lot of orchestrating!

The Triune Brain

The "Triune Model" or three-part brain theory was developed by Dr. Paul MacLean, Chief of the Laboratory of Brain Research and behavior, National Institute of Mental Health.

The Triune model is based on three stages of brain evolution, the "Reptilian," the "Mammalian" and "Cortex." It is also commonly referred to as the R-complex, the limbic system, and the neocortex. Each of these stages represents a brain evolving over eons of time to the changing circumstances of its environment.

Each brain has its own function and each brain has a "natural tendency" to act in an isolated manner, behaving independently of the other two. Each have their own special intelligence, subjectivity, sense of time, space and memory.

How our three brains work and function

Understanding the basics of how our brains function, and how they relate to our current beliefs, and the way we interpret information can help us understand the process of eliminating negative habits or installing new positive habits. So with that in mind, let's take a quick look at the most extraordinary tools ever created – our brains.

REPTILIAN BRAIN

The reptilian brain may be as much as 300 to 500 million years old. Since it stopped evolving about 200 million years ago, this portion of our brain is essentially the same as in all reptiles. It is involuntary, impulsive and compulsive; it contains programmed responses that are devoted to self-preservation. This part of the brain does not learn from experience. It repeats its programmed behavior over and over. Its function is to watch for enemies and search for prey. Also, the same brain warns us of an approaching car or possible danger in a dark alley.

This brain evolved for survival. It controls basic life functions such as heart rate, reproduction, fighting, fleeing, feeding and breathing. It can be thought of as a life of easy choices: "Can I eat it?" "Should I ignore it?" "Should I run away?"

MAMMALIAN BRAIN

This brain evolved about 100 million years ago. We share this brain with all mammals similar to the way we share our reptilian portion with all reptiles.

For our purposes, we will combine the Reptilian Brain and the Mammalian Brain (the two oldest parts) and call it the subconscious mind.

The mammalian brain contains feelings and emotions. It is playful and the source of maternal care. Mammals will generally tend to their young whereas reptiles usually do not. The mammalian part of the brain provides us with feelings of what is real, true and important. It is the source of our emotions, family and social ties as well as feelings of responsibility, ethics and duty to others.

The mammalian brain, however, is inarticulate in communicating these feelings to the conscious mind. Important features are that the subconscious mind is the source of feelings and it derives its value system by combining both experience and its emotional impact.

THE CORTEX

The cortex represents the third stage of development, and it's what makes humans superior to all other creatures on our planet. This is the creative brain that is responsible for art, science, music, advanced communication, future planning and reason.

The cortex is the conscious part of the mind. An important feature of the conscious brain/mind is that it does not begin to develop until about age three and is not fully developed until about twenty years of age. This late development is why we have so many negative and counterproductive programs in our subconscious minds.

When the emotional part of our brains (subconscious) developed in our early years, we lacked the ability to filter out negative comments from parents, teachers, siblings and friends as well as the ability to select positive programs that would enhance our self-esteem. To compound the problem, we were not then, and even now, aware of most of these programs since we have no memory of them.

In contrast to the subconscious mind, which evolves its value system through emotions, the conscious mind evolves its value system through "rational" interpretation of experience.

The cortex (the conscious mind) will analyze problems and come up with rational solutions, often without the vaguest idea of what is taking place in the old brain, or subconscious mind, which is governed by non-rational feeling.

The old brain *can* bypass the thinking brain's control systems and act out of intense emotions that have been bottled up in the subconscious since childhood. The new brain (cortex), operating in present time, realizes that the person has strength, competence, and self-worth, yet the subconscious continues to trigger ineffective, inappropriate responses to life's challenges based on long-ago programming.

Let's evaluate your understanding of the three brains with this little test. See if you can connect which brain would be responsible for each answer.

1. You're sitting on the beach after a day of sunning and you're hungry. At that moment, what appears to be food, drops down in front of you.
   a. This looks great, and smells great. This might just be my lucky day. _____
   b. Chomp, chomp, gulp. _____
   *c. Is it really true? Is this really edible food?*_____
2. You're at home eating dinner and the phone rings. The caller says; "If you give me $1,000 I can turn it into a million dollars in less than six months"!
   a. If that's true, why are you wasting your time making these humiliating cold calls?
   _____
   b. Come over, I want to eat you. _____
   c. Sounds great. I'll get the money first thing in the morning.
   _____

3. A self-made billionaire, looking for investors, has a great idea for a new business venture.
    a. This sounds like a no-brainer. This guy has a great idea and he's rich.
    _____

    b. Forget the businessman and his past history. Explain the idea in detail. _____
    c. When can I eat this guy? _____
4. A politician running for office promises a "chicken in every pot and a car in every garage."
    a. Promises, promises. Let's talk reality. _____
    b. This sounds fantastic. You've got my vote. _____
    c. I'll eat both the chicken and the car. Can I eat the politician as well? _____

Let's see how you did.

1. a. mammalian   3. a. mammalian
   b. reptilian   b. cortex
   c. cortex   c. reptilian
2. a. cortex   4 a. cortex
   b. reptilian   b. mammalian
   c. mammalian   c. reptilian

With this simple picture of our three brains in mind, imagine them as three horses pulling a chariot. If we can get all three brains working in unison toward a common goal, our chariot will move quickly and efficiently to our directed destination. If, on the other hand, each horse is going in its own direction, our chariot will experience a great pull of force, but very little forward or positive direction.

This brings us back to our habits and goals and why positive change is often so difficult.

Fight or Flight? Ah, that Is the Question!

According to our two most primitive brains, everything is either agreeable or disagreeable. Survival is based upon the avoidance of pain (disagreeable) and the recurrence of pleasure (agreeable).

You're planning a winter vacation in the Caribbean so you and your cortex decide that you're going to go on a diet so you'll look your best in a bathing suit. That night however, you and your primitive brains decide to eat a large bag of potato chips.

You attend a how-to seminar and again, you and your cortex decide that you're going to make some serious changes toward enhancing your life. You're going to take up exercise, join a yoga class and take some night courses to increase your skills. Within a few days your primitive brain, or your inner-self, begin to send signals that any form of change is absolutely unacceptable! Soon the idea is all but forgotten.

Why do we self sabotage what we know is best for us?

There are two schools of thought on the culprit. One school of thought blames our self-sabotage on the ... amygdala (a-MIG-duh-luh).

The amygdala, an almond sized and shaped structure located in the mid-brain, can take full credit for man's survival as a species because it controls the fight-or-flight response. Its purpose is to alert the body for action in the case of perceived danger, but in today's world our amygdala is often nothing but a stick in the spokes of our modern lives.

The moment the amygdala detects even the slightest danger it seizes control. Earlier we said that man is a creature that craves familiarity and as a result, we form habits and routines that eventually feel safe and comfortable.

> Even things that pose a serious threat to our wellbeing
> such as overeating, smoking or excessive drinking
> will not raise an alarm once they're habitual
> because it doesn't register an internal alarm.
>
> This is a very important concept to grasp!

The amygdala always has its foot resting on the "gas pedal" and it won't hesitate to punch it down at the slightest hint of imminent danger. When the pedal gets pushed, "fight or flight" takes full priority, and all unnecessary functions such as digestion, thought processes and sexual desire are immediately shut down. As you can imagine, for many thousands of years, this automatic reaction to danger has allowed the survival of our species. If we were being stalked by a predator we were obviously in imminent danger. We wouldn't want our brain to stop and consider the percentages of survival, or consider alternate methods while evaluating the situation. We need to survive the next few minutes so that we can live another day to ponder how we can prevent a similar occurrence in the future.

The fight-or-flight response is still crucial today, but it hasn't fully adapted to our rapidly changing world. Although it's not *as* necessary in our modern world we still need the amygdala to safely cross a busy street, flee from a mugger, escape a burning building, overpower an intruder, or rise to some other life-threatening circumstance.

The glitch with the amygdala in today's world is that it's still ready to punch down the physical gas pedal of fight-or-flight even when we wish it would just stay asleep. The amygdala's goal is to make our lives predictable, because change could cause discomfort and anxiety, and change may invite unknown hazards.

Our amygdala can be aroused at even the slightest departure from our regular routines. Our mammalian brain wakens the amygdala at the faintest hint of fear, but that fear can be meeting new people, making a speech, starting a savings program, going to a job interview or starting a new exercise routine.

When alarmed, our amygdala stops other functions such as rational and creative thinking – thoughts that could interfere with our physical ability to run or fight. In fact, any time we attempt to make a departure from our usual safe routines, the amygdala alerts parts of the body to prepare for action – and our access to the cortex, the rational thinking part of the brain, is either restricted or shut down. In fact, it will even go so far as to send messages to you through such means as back pain, fatigue, minor accidents and mental confusion.

If you have the slightest doubt about this, consider the typical reaction we encounter when we're about to take a driver's test, give a speech, write an exam or tee-up a golf ball in front of a crowded club house.

Why would these situations cause our heart rate to increase, our palms to sweat, and our muscles to tense? It's our amygdala sensing fear, which starts up our fight-or-flight survival mechanisms even though it's the very last thing we need at that moment in time.

Fear restricts access to the cortex, which in turn can often result in failure. If we can bypass fear, we can access our cortex and usually enjoy success. Unfortunately the neural connections from the cortex down to the amygdala are less well developed than are connections from the amygdala back up to the cortex. Thus, the amygdala exerts a greater influence on the cortex than vice versa. Once an emotion has been turned on, it is difficult for the cortex to turn it off.

There is practically no limit to the imagined lions and tigers that constantly stalk us; only today they are paper lions and tigers disguised as losing weight, getting a new job, asking someone we admire on a date or meeting a sales goal.

There is a second school of thought that doesn't necessarily point any self-sabotaging fingers at the amygdala, but rather to an *inner child* or *rebellious side* that each of us carries around with us.

Dr. Eric Berne, author of *Games People Play* and creator of *Transactional Analysis*, along with other people in that field, talked about our "child," "adult" and "parent tapes" that are like three voices within us. One is the desirous child; one is the adult who is rational, intelligent, and educated; and one is the parent who tends to be punitive and moralistic.

The inner child is generally a spoiled, inconsiderate personality who demands everything immediately with no regard for cost. This child will violently rebel at the slightest hint of structure. This child is certain that any form of self-discipline will mean becoming a slave to routine, and a complete loss of freedom and fun. We can refer to this rebellious child as our inner demons or as discussed much earlier, our self-image. We all have inner demons. All of us have battled them. We also have the battle scars to prove their existence, those times when we do inexplicably dumb things and cannot say why any rational human being would have acted in that manner.

At any rate, it doesn't much matter whether we are blaming the amygdala, our inner demons, early life self-programming or our flawed self-image, it amounts to the same thing, we have inner challenges that must be overruled.

So what's the solution?

29 DAYS programs are designed to generate gentle, effortless, forward momentum – every day, while being careful not to arouse the amygdala or those inner demons. These small gentle steps engage the cortex, the rational thinking brain, while simultaneously laying down a new roadway for our subconscious thoughts. This new roadway is the superhighway that builds new habits and lasting results.

CHAPTER EIGHT
How Small Actions and Gentle Repetition of Thought Can Transform Our Lives

It's highly likely that you are familiar with the term, "Use it or lose it!" when people are referring to using ones muscles. But this statement is now accepted as fact when referring to our brains as well.

In December 1997, scientist Fred H. Gave, Ph.D. and his colleagues discovered a phenomenon called brain plasticity or neurogenesis. Their discovery revealed that when you stimulate your brain, no matter what your age, your brain will grow new connections that appear as tiny, thin strands — as intricate as a spider web — called DSPs (Dendrite Spine Protuberances). DSPs greatly increase the total number of connections in your brain along with your brain's capacity for achievement!

The term "plasticity" means adaptable, shapeable, changeable and capable of growth and transformation. For many years, scientists believed that we were each born with "hard wiring" in our brains, and that for the rest of our lives we were stuck with, and limited to, what we were given at birth. As it turns out, none of us are permanently "hard wired" at birth. This predetermined conclusion that science has believed for so long is a myth and our understanding of DNA has grown.

One of the pioneers in this field is cell biologist Bruce Lipton, Ph.D., who taught medical students before resigning to do research full-time. In his groundbreaking book called *The Biology of Belief*, Lipton establishes that your mental activity is strong enough to overcome the influences of early conditioning and programming that you unwittingly adopted through your formative years.

In another example of "use-it-or-lose-it" studies were done on Einstein's brain after his death. And yes…his brain was actually different from the average brain. Can you guess in what way, from the list below?

    a.   He had an extra large cerebral cortex.
    b.   His brain weighed one-half pound more than the average brain.
    c.   He had more interconnections among his brain cells.
    d.   He had superior blood flow to the brain.

The correct answer is (c). Studies of Albert Einstein's brain found that the only difference in his brain was that he had developed significantly more nerve cell interconnections than average. What does this mean? Although you can't grow new brain cells…you *can* continue to add new neural connections and brain power for your entire life. Every time you focus and stretch your mind…your brain creates entirely new connections. Literally, the more you use your brain (in certain ways)…the smarter you get!

This means that if we want to change, we can. No excuses! Telling ourselves "I'm too old," or "I'm too young," "I don't know the right people" or "I'm uncoordinated," has no basis in science.

Changing Our Internal Dialogue and Self Talk

We think approximately 60,000 thoughts a day. That means much of our thinking, or self-talk, is subconscious, under-the-radar of our consciousness. Self-talk is a powerful tool that can be either a positive or negative factor in our lives. To make self-talk work in a positive manner we need to make sure it is positive, specific and present tense.

Each of us make choices all day long, with many of these choices being made without our conscious awareness. Whether these choices are to sit in this chair or that chair, what to eat or what to wear, our choices result from our self-talk, an on-going dialogue that we have with ourselves. Very few of these subconscious thoughts even register with our conscious mind, yet they have great influence on our feelings and behaviors. This is why we often find ourselves doing things that we really don't want to do or, conversely, not doing the things that we know we should do.

Positive, specific and present-tense self-talk can overrule self-defeating negative thoughts because our subconscious mind will believe whatever we tell it… if we tell it with conviction. If your conscious self-talk says, "I should clean my desk," or "I ought to clean my desk," then your subconscious mind hears that you are NOT cleaning your desk. As a result, it doesn't move you toward cleaning it.

It's important to know that your subconscious mind sends messages to your motor functions, emotions, and other members of your physical and psychological network. If your subconscious mind believes that you are currently cleaning your desk, then that's what every part of your body will want to be doing.

Let's imagine that you're watching some re-run sitcom on television in which you have little interest. Let's also suppose that while you're watching the show you think that you really should be cleaning your desk. Since your subconscious mind believes what you tell it, if you repeat to yourself, "I am cleaning my desk," then your subconscious mind will focus your attention, physical and mental, on cleaning your desk. Both your body and mind will begin to go into a state of agitation and conflict until you actually go and clean your desk. As long as you repeat your positive, specific, present-tense self-talk message, you will feel compelled to clean your desk.

Your subconscious mind *will* respond to your message. Repeat it over and over and it will respond to your statement.

All the old excuses such as "I'm too busy, I'm too short, too old, not smart enough" can be overruled by dynamic, positive self-talk.

As you will see, *29 DAYS* will help you to use positive self-talk that will help you get past any and all of these old excuses.

> *29 DAYS* will help you cut a path through your old thoughts!

Imagine yourself as a forest fireman, whose job it is to set up two observation towers in the middle of a dense tropical forest. You're still in the rainy season and you can practically see the vegetation growing. In every direction all you can see is a wall of green vines, bushes, weeds, plants and trees. You are standing on the spot where you have chosen to erect the first tower. With all the lush growth around, it doesn't take you too long to cut down a number of trees and vines to build the first tower.

With the first tower completed, the real work begins. You need your second tower to be erected, due north, one mile away. This tower has to be built and functional in three weeks before the drier weather brings the inevitable forest fires. Using your machete, you begin to hack a small path through the thick growth. After two weeks of hacking and cutting you finally arrive at the spot where the second tower is to be built, and within a day your second tower is erected.

With both towers set up, your job is to go back and forth between the two towers, twice each day, for observation. As you set out to return to the first tower you can't help but notice that the path you had hacked out is getting thicker and thicker as you make your way back. In fact, aside from the small trees, it looks like it only took about one week for the vegetation to grow back to the thickness it was when you had first cut the trail. Moving a little faster than the first time, you manage to hack your way back through the new growth, and return to the first tower in less than one week.

It is now clear that you have two tasks. The first task is to keep your scheduled observation from each of the two towers, and the second job is to keep the path between the two towers clear enough so that you can quickly travel back and forth between them.

With your quicker return to the first tower, less than one week, you can now return to the second tower in less than two days, since you have quite recently cut down much of the larger growth. Before long you notice that each time you travel between the two towers your speed is increased, and the path is much easier to travel. Within a few days of traveling back and forth the new vegetation doesn't really get a chance to get started. With each trip your feet will crush and press down more of the growth. In fact, the more often you walk this path, the better and easier it becomes. If you travel it four times a day for twenty-nine days in a row it will be a lot more like a roadway than a pathway that somebody hacked into existence with a machete.

Brain scientists have discovered that the same thing happens in your brain when you fire off a thought. You create a new road of neurodes (neuron connections that fire together a thought) when you stimulate your brain by thinking a new thought. Repeating thought patterns strengthens the DSP connections of those patterns and lowers their firing threshold (resistance). Soon these new thoughts become the chosen path to travel.

I can't help but be reminded of Robert Frost's famous poem *The Road Not Taken*.

The Road Not Taken

Two roads diverged in a yellow wood,
And sorry I could not travel both
And be one traveler, long I stood
And looked down one as far as I could
To where it bent in the undergrowth;

Then took the other, as just as fair,
And having perhaps the better claim,
Because it was grassy and wanted wear;
Though as for that the passing there
Had worn them really about the same,

And both that morning equally lay
In leaves no step had trodden black.
Oh, I kept the first for another day!
Yet knowing how way leads on to way,
I doubted if I should ever come back.

I shall be telling this with a sigh
Somewhere ages and ages hence:
Two roads diverged in a wood, and I—
I took the one less traveled by,
And that has made all the difference.

This is the very reason *29 DAYS* programs can be so transformational. Each day you will create new neuron pathways that will soon become a brand new superhighway for your thoughts. Your old thoughts of "I can't lose weight," for example, will quickly become infested with thick brush from lack of travel. The new road of thought such as "What little thing can I do today to help me reach my weight-loss goal?" will become the path that you will begin to mentally travel, and it will happen without effort. You will discover that new empowering thoughts will pop into your head without any conscious effort on your part.

The key to making this happen, and the key to the power of *29 DAYS* programs is simply: repetition, repetition, repetition.

Automate Your Brain for Success – Your Reticular Activating System (RAS)

Brain scientists have discovered an automated system in the brain called the "reticular activating system" (RAS). The RAS is a group of interconnected neurons not located in any specific part of your brain, although it is part of your limbic (subconscious) system.

Every single impulse, whether derived from thought, touch, taste, smell, seeing or hearing, first passes through your RAS.

The RAS then sends signals to the proper area of your brain for interpretation. When something important is on your RAS, it sends a signal to the conscious level for your immediate attention.

Our conscious thought impulses travel about 125 miles per hour. Our subconscious thought impulses travel up to 800 times faster. If someone throws you a baseball and it's heading straight for your face, you don't consciously think: "Okay, I need to tell my hand muscles to open my catching glove, then tell my arm and shoulder muscles to rise up and reach out to catch the ball before it smacks me in the face" If you thought that slowly the ball would have hit you long before you could relay the proper instructions to the various muscles and parts of your body necessary to catch the ball.

One of the most important functions of your RAS is to recognize impulses coming into your brain and determine if it is related to fear, stress, danger, or anxiety. It instantaneously decides if it is something that requires immediate attention or not. If instead of a baseball being thrown at you it was a small child throwing a big plastic beach ball at your face, your RAS may very well choose to ignore it and let it hit you.

If the situation registers as dangerous however, it sends an impulse to your amygdala, which will send another signal out ordering certain hormones and neural transmitters to fire in your brain.

Needless to say this all takes place in a mere fraction of a second.

It is important to remember that your RAS functions at a subconscious level. Another important function of the RAS is that it can be utilized to your conscious benefit. It's the neuroscientific explanation for what the New Thought writers call the *Law of Attraction,* which has received so much attention in the popular book and movie titled *The Secret.*

The Law of Attraction says people's thoughts (both conscious and subconscious) dictate the reality of their lives, whether or not they're aware of it. Essentially, "If you really want something and truly believe it's possible, you'll get it." By the same reasoning, if you put a lot of attention and thought into something you don't want, it means you'll probably get that as well.

Our purpose in *29 DAYS* is not to debate the veracity of the *Law of Attraction,* but rather to point out a simple fact: You will notice that which you put your mind to. *29 DAYS* will very simply help you to keep your mind on your stated objective and goal. Our brain circuits take engrams (memory traces), and produce neuroconnections and neuropathways only if they are bombarded repeatedly (twenty-nine days) without missing a single day!

Have you ever learned a new word and then started to notice that word being used in conversation, on the evening news or in print? Prior to learning that word you probably weren't even aware of its existence.

Suppose you're planning a vacation to an exotic destination. Once again, you will suddenly begin to see ads in magazines, or catch snippets on the news, or overhear people talking about their experience at the very place you're planning to vacation.

If your brain recognizes that something is important to you, your RAS will send that impulse to your conscious level for your immediate attention. If you hold something in mind for a period of time – let's say twenty-nine days, it will be elevated by your RAS to be of paramount importance. If you add emotion to the particular subject of interest, it may well be with you for the rest of your life.

By this reasoning, *29 DAYS* programs will ensure your goals are your RAS's priority.

With this new goal or interest in mind, you will automatically begin to harness the incredible power of your subconscious mind. If you can focus your attention on what you want for twenty-nine days – just by thinking about it, visualizing it, meditating on it, speaking about it and pondering it, you will find solutions, tactics, information and energy coming from seemingly out-of-the-blue. Your subconscious brain will work twenty-four hours a day to help you achieve anything you put your mind to.

Please note, there are certain techniques that are necessary in order to properly set goals and to use visualizing techniques in order to positively harness the power of your subconscious mind. The techniques of visualization, goal setting, written affirmations, etc. and the steps in the *29 DAYS* programs will be discussed in a later section.

— PART FOUR —

The Principles of *29 DAYS*
... to a habit you want!

CHAPTER NINE
The Deceptive Power of Patience and Perseverance

In Chapter Two we said that there are two *Principles of Success*:

Principle #1 is patience and perseverance
Principle #2 is belief and support of our "inner-self."

As we have seen in Part Three, fear is the great obstacle to achieving change. I can think of no better example of the power of taking small steps than the example given by Robert Maurer, Ph.D. in his brilliant book *One Small Step Can Change Your Life*. Dr. Maurer is a practicing psychologist at the UCLA School of Medicine. In this book he tells the story of a woman who is woefully close to the end of her rope, but through his insight and guidance of incremental change she manages to completely transform her life.

Julie had gone to UCLA's medical center for help with high blood pressure and perpetual fatigue. While there she was interviewed by Dr. Mauer and a family practice resident. Julie's story was grim. She was a divorced mother of two who was trying to hold down a job and raise her kids. To add to her challenges she was more than thirty pounds overweight, her job was unsecure, she had no outside support and not surprisingly, she was battling depression.

It was obvious to both doctors that this woman had to make some drastic changes or she was headed for a physical and mental breakdown. When Dr. Mauer looked at the utter despair on Julie's face he knew he had to prescribe something that would actually work rather than what logic might dictate.

Dr. Mauer knew from years of observation, that to suggest she take up an exercise routine, change her diet and try to *will herself* to a healthy lifestyle would actually compound Julie's problems. This is the kind of advice patients like Julie get all the time and the usual result is that they ignore the advice and simply add a guilt trip to their compounding problems.

Surprisingly enough, even when we're living a life of despair and drudgery, familiarity with the life we know offers greater comfort than does change. Change of any kind can cause our most formidable enemy, fear, to to appear.

Julie's life was one of relentless pressure. After a long day at work she would pick-up her kids, drive home, feed them, bath them, put them to bed and then attempt to straighten out the house. Her only break at the end of her day was when she flopped on the couch in utter exhaustion, to watch a half-hour of television before putting herself to bed.

As Dr. Mauer had witnessed on too many occasions, a physician would prescribe an exercise program and the patient, in this case Julie, would think, "Exercise! You have got to be kidding? Do you have any idea what my life is like?"

The physician on the other hand is thinking, "Look, what's the problem here? Don't you care about your body and your health? If you don't do what I prescribe you're heading for serious trouble!"

The biggest problem is a lack of understanding. Julie is totally correct in her thinking because she is convinced she has neither the time, energy or inclination to add an additional half hour of strenuous exercise to her already overloaded day.

The resident with Dr. Mauer was absolutely correct in her assessment and prescribed solution. After all, if a person refuses to take charge of their own health, and lifestyle, then ultimately there's nothing anyone else can do.

Dr. Mauer, however had an 'aha' moment. He knew that he had to try something different in order to break this endless cycle of misery and failure on the part of the physician and the patient.

Just before the inevitable and dreaded aerobics prescription was uttered, Dr. Mauer jumped in and asked Julie if she thought that it might be possible for her to march in front of her television for just *one minute* each day? As the resident looked at him in disbelief, Julie's face actually brightened up and she replied that she could definitely give that a try.

When Julie returned for her follow-up visit she proudly announced that she had faithfully marched in front of her TV set every day for the prescribed sixty seconds. The fact that one minute of exercise would hardly make the slightest dent in affecting Julie's physical health wasn't important at this stage. What was important to Dr. Mauer was that she had actually done it, and she was eager for a slightly bigger challenge. In this short time between her first and second visit, her attitude had noticeably changed and Julie wanted to know what else she could do for sixty seconds a day!

Although it was still early, Dr. Mauer was thrilled with the initial results. Julie had opened her mind to new possibilities. Julie's new challenge was marching for an entire commercial break. Shortly after that, she was marching for two commercial breaks and before long she forgot to stop! Almost without realizing it, Julie had gotten herself to the point of exercising thirty minutes a day and incredibly enough, she was enjoying it!

Within a few months, she was not only embracing the concept of exercise, she was eager to take on full aerobic workouts. Before long she had restored her physical health, her mental health, and her self-esteem.

While working with Julie and other clients in similar situations, Dr. Mauer realized that small, almost embarrassingly trivial steps, were often the solution to dramatic wholesale changes. He realized that getting his patients to buy into the concept (change their fundamental thinking and lay down new neuron tracks) was an essential and crucial first step. Instead of suggesting that a client leave an unfulfilling job, he might ask them to spend a few minutes each day visualizing the "perfect" job. Using this simple, "one-small-step-at-a-time" approach, consistently produced spectacular results.

Dr. Mauer said that a large number of his patients intuitively knew what took him years of observations to conclude: Low-key change helps the human mind to side-step the fear that blocks our ability to achieve our desires. By taking steps that are so small they might seem laughable, we manage to defeat the thoughts of negativity that have always derailed our best intentions in the past.

Minor but consistent effort will cultivate an appetite for success and lay down new ways of thinking and ultimately, permanent results.

The Power of Principle #1

Julie's story is the essence of what *29 DAYS* is all about and why it is so effective. In almost any application, asking someone to march in place for sixty seconds a day would be dismissed as nonsense and an utter waste of time.

In Julie's case, it was probably the only thing that would have worked and the results were nothing short of spectacular.

In *29 DAYS*, we take into consideration that we are all at different stages of development on any given subject. That's why we like to make you your own interactive guide and coach. We will prompt you with a question, give you the proper guidelines in order to correctly answer the question, but ultimately you will come up with a solution that will be just right for you.

Example: Suppose you are the correct weight for your body structure and height, but like Julie, you need to start an exercise program. Our question would be the same to both you and Julie: "What small thing could you do to move you towards an exercise program that you would simultaneously follow and enjoy?" Same question, same guidelines but undoubtedly your answer and Julie's will be quite different.

In Julie's case the answer she may very well have come up with would be to begin by marching in front of the TV for sixty seconds each day. If you were already the correct weight for example, and your time demands weren't as onerous as Julie's, you might suggest that going for a walk in the evening might be just the thing to set you on the path toward beginning an exercise program.

The most important point to take from Julie's story wasn't where she was after thirty days. As anyone can see, marching in place for one minute a day isn't very far along towards establishing a meaningful exercise regimen. And that is precisely when most of us say: "It's no use, nothing is happening." In reality nothing could be further from the truth. On the surface it looked as if Julie hadn't accomplished anything, but below the surface she was establishing a powerful foundation of habit and confidence that wasn't based on the flimsy structure of willpower. After one month Julie had laid down new neuron tracks that were establishing a permanent habit. She was shocked to find herself exercising even when she didn't have to, and within a few short months Julie had graduated to full aerobic workouts!

Our goal in *29 DAYS* is to stay with you and keep your mind engaged and motivated. Keeping you focused for this length of time, while applying small simple tasks, will guarantee that you will step around fear while laying those neuron tracks that are so crucial to forming a lifelong habit. If you faithfully follow the program guidelines, in twenty-nine days your results will be as spectacular as Julie's.

CHAPTER TEN
The Hidden Power of
Support from Our Inner-Self

A True-Life Example of the Power of Principle #2

> You Are a Mirror of Your Inner Thoughts.
> As You See Yourself, So Shall You Be!

In his powerful book, *Over The Top*, Zig Ziglar relates the testimony of a seminar attendee who clearly had a transcending experience. This story is such a wonderful example of the importance of enlisting the support of our inner-self. The central figure in this story was "thin" the moment he *saw himself thin*, even though he had a long way to go to fulfill his goal. (Oops, plot spoiler!)

This story is about a man named Tom who attended one of Zig Ziglar's seminars. At that time he was pretty much down and out. In a letter he wrote to Mr. Ziglar he said that he was recently divorced, he had a job only because the boss was his friend, and at the time he had attended the seminar he weighed over four hundred pounds. He described himself as being financially, morally, spiritually and physically bankrupt; which pretty much covers all bases.

Tom said the seminar had no sooner started when he began to hear a bunch of self-empowering talk about how we can take charge of our lives and how we can change anything we want to change. He considered a quick exit but for one reason or another he ended up staying for the whole day.

As he listened to Mr. Ziglar talk he realized that he had been blaming the negative outcomes of his life on other people and outside circumstances. He was playing the victim-of-fate card. At some point during the day he understood that the moment he began to accept responsibility for his life, he also accepted his *ability to respond*. Tom had an "aha" experience. He finally saw that he had created the mess his life was in, and by extension, he also had the power to turn it around. It was a deep revelation and a moment of instant awakening. At that moment he made up his mind to re-evaluate his life.

The very next day he made some major life changes. He enrolled in a couple of university courses in psychology and joined a health club. At the end of the week he went to a clothing store and put a small downpayment on a bunch of clothes that would fit his body type if he weighed two hundred pounds less!

Tom said he was at last committed to change and the most significant thing he did was to *see himself* as a new person. He knew his new image of himself was complete when he caught himself staring at a store's front window one day. While he was absorbing the goods on display he saw a reflection in the window of some big guy standing right behind him. He spun around to see who it was and to his surprise there was no one there. Tom had simply seen his own reflection in the window, which he no longer recognized.

The reason that little episode is of such monumental importance is that Tom had made a complete transformation from the hopeless person who had attended the seminar just a few weeks earlier. Although he still weighed over three hundred and eighty pounds, he no longer *saw* himself as an obese person. He had changed the way he saw himself and the way he thought. He now saw himself at his ideal weight. At that point he said he knew, "and he knew that he knew" he was going to make it. What he was really saying is that he *saw his future*.

Tom had taken responsibility for his life, and because he was in control, he knew that no force on earth could stop him from achieving his goals.

In Tom's case he visualized himself as a new person. He saw himself in a new light. He saw a person who enjoyed total physical, spiritual, financial and emotional health. Within a short period of time, he had graduated with his degree in psychology and he began working on his doctorate. He eventually brought his weight down to just a little over two hundred pounds which is where it should be since he stands 6' 3" and has a large frame.

Tom changed his thoughts and the results were nothing short of extraordinary.

The Power of Principle #2

It was of particular interest to note that even when Tom weighed over 380 pounds, he *saw* himself as thin. At this point his goal, to lose the rest of the weight, was a *fait accompli*.

Once he had changed the way he saw himself (created new neural pathways of thought) nothing could stop his inevitable victory. He had effectively harnessed the power of his inner-self ... his conscious and subconscious mind.

Tom's mental makeover was much like Julie's in the previous story. Although Julie had physically accomplished very little in the first month, she had changed her thinking (new neural pathways) which led to greater and greater activity until within a few short months she was engaged in full aerobic activity. What Julie and Tom accomplished in the first month through patience, perseverance and the support of their inner-self, was everything they needed to carry them to their ultimate goals.

This is the essence of the power of *29 DAYS*. Our goal is not to look to the top of the mountain, which is our ultimate goal, but rather to focus on what we can do in the very short term that will build a highway to our desired achievement.

Picture yourself standing on a hilltop overlooking a series of neighboring hills. Since it's a beautiful day and you're in the mood for hiking, you decide to scale the closest since it's only a mile or so away. As you descend the hill and begin to cross the valley, you get a sense that this new hill is somewhat further away than you had originally anticipated. In fact, it seems like it might be several miles farther than you had first thought. At this point what would you logically conclude? That you're *farther away* from the new hill than when you started or that you are making progress but it will take longer than you expected?

This is a common scenario many of us experience when facing a new challenge or goal. We often misjudge what will be required, but then make a further mistake and assume that after weeks or months of effort, we're actually further away from our goal than when we started. But, like the hiker, we *have to* be making progress even though it may not initially appear to be so. When we find ourselves at this point of doubt, it's imperative that we keep our focus on the next task at hand, rather than looking at the top of the distant hill and concluding that it's actually moving away from us.

A great analogy to keep in mind is when you're driving your car at night. Your headlights will allow you to see only a few hundred feet in front of you, but that has no bearing on how far you can travel. You may travel as far as you wish without ever seeing more than a few hundred feet ahead.

29 DAYS strives to keep you focused on the immediate task at hand, because if you can do this without getting discouraged, your big goals will fall into place far easier and quicker than you will have dreamed possible.

BOOK

— <u>PART FIVE</u> —

Bringing It All Together

CHAPTER ELEVEN
How *29 DAYS* Will Help You To Achieve Your Goals in an Effortless Way

Tools and Techniques for Permanent Change

As we stated in the Introduction, all of us are mirror reflections of our self image; our thoughts, fears, beliefs and attitudes. If we cannot change those things, we cannot instill "lasting" change.

The reason positive change is often so difficult can be reduced to two basic human traits:

1. When we attempt to change something about ourselves, we want change to happen immediately, and if we don't see it immediately, we often give up and assume whatever technique we were trying simply doesn't work. We overlook the vital requisite of patience and persistence.

2. We try to change too much too soon through sheer force of will. Before long we find that we cannot sustain the requisite energy at that heightened level. We quickly get discouraged and return to our former ways.

The tools we will use to achieve success such as; *How to Write a Goal, Visualization, Asking Small Questions, Written Affirmations, Granting Ourselves Small Rewards,* and *Taking Small Steps,* work so well because they are strung together in a way that is effective without being overbearing.

29 DAYS programs can actually be everything that a hired coach can be and more for several reasons. It is very often human nature to want to do things by ourselves and for ourselves. Sometimes that can be good, and sometimes it can lead to frustration and capitulation. Have you ever had to fill out a form for a bank account or a mortgage application? If you have, you know what an unpleasant task that can be. "When were you born?" "Where do you live?" "What's your driver's license number?" … and on and on. Have you also had the experience of having to fill out a the same type of form but instead of you doing it all on your own, you had someone else ask you the questions and then fill in the responses for you? In this case you're still coming up with the same answers, but with someone else helping it seems so much easier. I don't know if it's because there are two people doing it, or if it's just more comfortable not to have to do it yourself, but with someone else's prompting the task seems almost effortless.

In our programs we want you to enjoy the same experience. We will prompt you with a question, along with the proper way to frame an answer, and you simply respond.

This Sounds Like a One-Size-Fits-All Solution!

Definitely not! It's true that questions we ask will be the same to each participant, but the answers and responses to those questions are personal to you. Each response will be as unique to you as your fingerprints. The process of setting goals and asking the right questions are universal. The answers you supply are not.

Your Personal Coach in *29 DAYS* is the *most supportive coach in the world!* How couldn't he/she be, it's ultimately YOU! In addition to being totally supportive to your success, your enrollment in this program can be kept as confidential as you wish.

The Importance of Privacy

Although it's completely up to you, the fact that you can take a program in complete privacy can also be an important factor toward achieving your desired results. In the case of Julie, if she had told anyone (including her amygdala) what she was working toward, she would have been ridiculed remorselessly. You can just hear the negative comments about the foolishness of sixty seconds of marching. At this early stage we may be very vulnerable and susceptible to the negative influence of others. Keeping our goals and our program to ourselves until we establish those strong inner beliefs, can be integral to our success.

CHAPTER TWELVE
How To Set a Goal, Visualizing a Goal

Earl Nightingale once wrote, "Happiness is the progressive realization of a worthy goal."

You feel truly happy when you are making progress, step-by-step. When you're absolutely clear about your goal, you do not have to know how you're going to achieve it. By simply deciding exactly what you want, you will begin to move unerringly toward your goal, and your goal will start to move unerringly toward you. At exactly the right time and in exactly the right place, you and your goal will meet.

> *Give me a stock clerk with a goal, and I will give you a man who will make*
> *history. Give me a man without a goal, and I will give you a stock clerk.*
> *~ J.C. Penney*

Your written goals must be described in a positive, personal tense.

Let's suppose your goal is to lose thirty pounds. *(As we said initially, we would use weight loss for our examples but this is the exact same process for saving money, quitting smoking, etc.)* Using the philosophy of *29 DAYS*, you're going to set a goal that you absolutely *know* you can achieve in twenty-nine days. Remember, your ultimate goal is much bigger than what you can accomplish in twenty-nine days. In fact, your goal is much bigger than losing the thirty pounds per se. Your real goal is to program yourself to enjoy a lifetime of health and inner-self-confidence without ever having to worry about your weight and what you eat again.

Your *29 DAYS* program goal might be to lose five pounds, and your lifetime goal might be to enjoy perfect health at your ideal weight of let's say 155 pounds. You now have an immediate goal and a lifetime goal.

Activate Your Subconscious Mind

29 DAYS will strive to keep you focused on your goal, not the process.

When a goal states exactly what it is you want to be, have or do, it then becomes easy to communicate precise details of your desire to your subconscious.

In his book *The Path of Least Resistance*, Robert Fritz talks about learning to become the creative force in your own life. On choosing to be the creative force he writes that many people get lost in the process. They spend their time and energy focusing on all the stuff they associate with getting to their goal rather than focusing on the goal itself. He writes:

> *Many people engaged in processes designed to bring them specific results have never actually chosen those results, either formally or informally. Some people who eat special health foods, take large doses of vitamin supplements, exercise assiduously, and avoid alcohol, coffee, tobacco, chocolate, bleached flour, red meat, and refined sugar have never made the choice to be healthy. Many people take healthful actions and still do not make the choice to be healthy.*

In other words, we often get so caught up in the process we forget to set our mission. Picture someone who decides to go on a diet in order to lose weight. Very often they dive into the program with reckless abandon and the probable result will be failure. Why? Their focus will be entirely on the process. They begin with an austerity program. They limit themselves to making, eating or ordering certain foods. They cut back on other foods. They focus on counting calories. They're thinking about their food intake all day long. They're totally focused on successfully completing the diet or losing the twenty, thirty or forty pounds. In order to speed-up the process they may even resort to exercising for a few weeks. Each meal becomes a major issue. They talk about it, moan about it and tell everyone the latest details. Can you see the holes in this process? Can you see how utterly unsustainable this is?

Have you ever seen someone who is busy from morning to night but never seems to accomplish anything? They're those frazzled, harried people who rush around with a slight scowl because life is always just out of reach. In many ways that is a mirror reflection of someone who dives into a process. What happens after they lose the weight? What happens when the process is completed? The person caught-up in this typical scenario fails to ask the big question; "And then what?"

If people would focus on an outcome, rather than a diet, the entire process takes on a radically different appearance. The procedure is more cerebral, more relaxed, more definite and ultimately sustainable. Making the choice for health and your perfect weight will gather the inner resources of the body, mind, and spirit. Using this method you and the unseen forces begin to work toward a mutual meeting ground. You align the energies toward your desire.

This is where the power of visualizations and affirmations and the subconscious forces come to your aid.

There are two ways to think about goals. You can write a goal for your conscious mind and you can also create a goal for your subconscious mind. There is a difference.

Conscious Mind Goals

Your conscious mind thinks in terms of time; past, present and future. If your goal is to lose thirty pound then a clearly written, conscious goal might be written like this;

I weigh 155 pounds on x date. This is a goal that is written in a positive tense with a specific time.

Subconscious Mind Goals

Your subconscious mind has no concept of time. It only functions in the present. Therefore when you communicate with your subconscious mind you will do so in the form of an affirmation. A goal for your conscious mind written as: "I weigh 155 pounds on x date," would become an affirmation to your subconscious mind that you would repeat as: "I weigh 155 pounds." The only difference is that you don't put a date on it. You relay this desire to your subconscious mind and it will find a way to achieve your goal.

You put the date on it for your conscious mind so that it becomes a believable goal for you. This aligns the believability your conscious mind needs to the positive, emotional feeling that fuels your subconscious mind.

As noted earlier, our subconscious mind is our success tool. Unfortunately we were never taught how to use it effectively. If you wish to eliminate a bad habit it is imperative to write your goal in a positive/positive way. In each of the programs we will walk with you step by step toward the proper way of writing and setting your goals.

Why Do You Want this Goal?

What is your purpose? What will achieving this goal do for you? What will it do for the way you feel, your self-confidence? How will it positively effect those around you? Will your increased confidence put you in a better state of mind, allowing you to be a better person to be around? Will it it effect your finances, your relationships?

You will think of many positive ways to achieve your goal. This exercise will give you enduring motivation. To succeed at anything, it's vital to know why you are doing whatever it is you are doing.

Are There Any Downsides to Achieving Your Goal?

Now is the time to be aware of any downsides to achieving your goals. You don't want to be well into achieving your goal only to have your amygdala, or inner-demons, come up with an excuse at the last possible moment in order to upset all the progress you've made.

If you know in advance of any "tricks" that might come up, and they will, you can address them as old news that's already been considered and dismiss these thoughts with a "Nice-try-but-it-won't-work" response.

Every time you write your goals or express your affirmations, you are impressing them deeper and deeper into your subconscious mind. At a certain point, you will begin to believe, with absolute conviction, that your goal is achievable. Once your subconscious mind accepts your goals as commands from your conscious mind, it will start to make all your words and actions fit a pattern consistent with those goals. Your subconscious mind will start attracting people and circumstances into your life that can help you to achieve your goal. Be clear about your goal, but be flexible about the process of achieving it.

In the *29 DAYS* programs we will reach out to you twice each day with tips, inspiring information, stories, encouragement – in short, all the things a good coach does. When you hear from us will depend on when you check your email. Reading your morning message is often the perfect time to spend thirty seconds reviewing your goal. If you review your goal twice a day, you will quickly create new neural pathways, new beliefs.

The more you review your goal, the larger, stronger and more often these neuron patterns will fire. These neuron patterns are new beliefs programmed into your subconscious by choice. Brain research has proven that neural pathways, used often, create the largest neuron patterns and fire the easiest. Stated another way, the more you think about something, the easier it is to think about it over and over again. This is how many of us have unwittingly reinforced our own negative behavior.

States of Mind

In order to access your subconscious mind most effectively you need to be aware of your various states of mind. The four states of mind are Beta, Alpha, Theta and Delta. Each of these states is distinguished by brain waves, which are determined by the amount of mental activity. When we are in our normal awake state we are in 'beta' which is characterized by a brain wave frequency of 14 to 35 cps (cycles per second). The beta state is by far the most erratic because it is constantly evaluating everything that is going on around us. This awareness is essential for conducting our daily affairs and our general survival.

The alpha state is characterized by a brain wave frequency of 8 to 13 cps. You naturally go into the alpha state a number of times during the day, but usually for only brief periods. You know you have been in the alpha state when you catch yourself daydreaming or staring off into space. I used to catch myself dwelling in the alpha state for long stretches of time when I was at church or school. The alpha state is referred to as the "meditative" state – a state of relaxed, focused concentration.

The theta state (4 to 7 cps) is similar to the alpha state but deeper and characterized by sudden intuitive insights or the "super learning" brain state. The theta is the brain state you were often in up to about six years of age. This is when the subconscious accepts and records everything without any filtering. This is why we often do things or behave in certain ways as adults that can seem inexplicable to us. These bizarre behaviors can often be attributed to early programing by parents, siblings, teachers and television long before we were consciously aware of it, and certainly before we were capable of filtering out the unwanted stuff.

The last state is the delta state (3cps and lower.) This is the sleep state in which there is no consciousness. Dreaming occurs in the alpha and theta states.

It is important to be aware of these various states of mind if you wish to have a greater influence on your subconscious mind and to be able to change your way of thinking.

You may have heard of the various studies that have been done on Indian fakirs or the participants in the annual *Phuket Vegetarian Festival,* where they are able to change their heart rates, body temperature or push unsterilized swords and spears through their bodies. There are dozens of grotesque but fascinating pictures on the internet showing the vegetarian devotees with various objects pushed through their cheeks and yet they're immune to infection and their wounds heal rapidly without leaving a single mark.

To achieve these amazing feats requires the participants to be in an altered state of mind. In order for them to control involuntary body functions they had to be in the alpha or theta states. Thus, the alpha and theta brain wave states are the doorways to your subconscious mind.

Suggestions and commands to your subconscious mind are least effective when your mind is in the beta state where your conscious mind dominates. Your subconscious mind however, will accept suggestions and commands much more readily when you are in the alpha and theta states. This is why affirmations and visualizations are so effective just when you are about to fall asleep or when you first wake up. Knowing that your subconscious is so receptive while in the alpha or theta state, repeating affirmations when in these states will focus your mind to fire with thought patterns reflective of your affirmations.

Incidently, the advertising industry is acutely aware of this phenomenon. When you're watching television do you have a tendency to let your mind go blank during commercials? You may actually pay attention to a commercial the first or second time you see it, but after repeated exposure you begin to consciously tune it out. Make no mistake, advertisers would much rather have you in this "tune-out" state (alpha) because then they are tapping straight into your subconscious mind. When you're in the beta state you might even think ... "What a ridiculous commercial! Who could possibly believe that?" The answer, your subconscious, that's who. That is precisely why advertisers will hit you with the same commercial over and over and over in a single show. They don't care what you consciously think, they want to lay down those powerful neuron tracks in your subconscious.

It's also not a bad idea to enjoy periodic daydreaming about things you desire and goals you wish to achieve. When you are in these receptive states (alpha states) you are super charging your subconscious.

When you first awaken each day, the subconscious is in the "alpha" or learning state and is most susceptible to re-programming. Then throughout the day your subconscious will bring to your attention anything which draws you closer to achieving your goals. At night while you sleep, your subconscious is still awake and active. What you focus on immediately before bed is what your subconscious will work on. Reviewing your goals before bed gives you the extra advantage of having your subconscious mind work on achieving your goals while you sleep.

This is why many psychologists recommend you do not watch the news before bed. Your subconscious will constantly be focused on events like war, murder or terrorism, negativity.

Your subconscious mind works like a massive computer that is never turned off. It will work tirelessly to bring you whatever it is that you focus on. Once your subconscious is locked on target, almost without your doing anything, it will materialize your dominant thought. Negative thoughts bring negative results. Focus on your goals and they will begin to materialize in your life, sometimes in the most remarkable and unexpected ways.

The belief that you cannot have what you want
creates a tension that is resolved by not having what you want.
~ Robert Fritz

Visualize Your Goal for Ultimate Success

"Imagination is more important than knowledge."
~ Albert Einstein

Visualization and Your Subconscious Mind

"Your mind and a computer have one thing in common: neither of them know the
difference between the truth ... and what you tell it."
~ Ken Blanchard

Many people's reaction to visualization is that it's a lot of New Age fluff. Not so fast!

Visualization is such a powerful mental tool because we can literally create the experience we desire if the actual one we want is not available. In fact, whether you know it or not, you practice visualization all the time.

Through our imagination and visualization, we can create a virtual experience. Science has proven that the human nervous system is incapable of distinguishing between actual experience and the same experience imagined vividly in complete detail.

Worry is a perfect example of how we create the synthetic experience. When we worry about something, what are we actually doing? We are projecting ourselves mentally, emotionally and even physically into a situation that hasn't even occurred!

If you think visualization doesn't work, or if it's just an overhyped self-help gimmick, let's consider the following: Have you ever heard of anyone who has worried so intensely about something that they've actually made themselves sick?

The fact is, if a person worries intensely enough about failure he will experience the same reactions that accompany actual failure! He will experience feelings of anxiety, inadequacy, humiliation and eventually physical ailments such as headaches and ulcers. As far as his mind and body are concerned, he has failed. And if he worries about a particular problem long enough, if he concentrates and visualizes failure intensely enough, he will fail.

If you think about it, worry is the *negative* use of creative imagination and visualization. It simply can not be anything else. Worry is nothing but a vividly imagined, negative, synthetic experience. It can't be anything other than *synthetic* because it hasn't happened!

The person who worries about failure is unwittingly defeating himself, while he's literally "creating" his own future. He's feasting on a banquet of negative data. If he spent the same amount of time visualizing success he would reverse the process. Instead of anxiety, apprehension and fear, he could develop confidence and self assurance.

Each of us, whether we realize it or not, constantly practice visualization and self actualization. Why not practice visualizing the person you most want to become, or the situation or outcome you most desire? This is the person you can be. Use your spare moments to concentrate on whatever it is you desire. Put more into the positive use of your imagination rather than devoting your focus and energy into worry. It really is that simple. Show me a worry wart who doesn't achieve his "negative outcome." The process of visualization, whether it be good or bad, works every time.

Each of us is the product of our thoughts and experiences. Through thought, we can control to an almost unbelievable degree our experience and environment. Whether we choose to direct our course through life, or not, is entirely up to us. The important thing is that we know that we can. We have that power.

Visualize Your Goal Continually

Visualization takes advantage of the latest neuroscience discoveries that suggest that the brain learns best not in large dramatic steps, but instead in very small increments. These small steps are likely a lot smaller than you've probably even imagined!

You possess and have available to you virtually unlimited mental powers. Many people are unaware of these powers and fail to use them for goal attainment. Your ability to visualize is perhaps the most powerful faculty that you possess. All improvements in your life begin with an improvement in your mental pictures.

Visualization activates the *Law of Attraction*, which draws into your life the people, circumstances, and resources that you need to achieve your goals. As it happens, you are always visualizing something, one way or another. Every time you think of someone or something, remember a past event, imagine an upcoming event, or even daydream, you are visualizing. Visualization is simply self-talk that uses mental pictures rather than words. It is essential that you learn to manage and control this visualizing capability of your mind and focus it like a laser beam.

Things to remember

- Your subconscious cannot tell the difference between truth and a lie, reality or imagination. This is why you can look in the mirror, see your overweight image but still say "I am fit and slim."

  Even if your conscious brain says B.S., your subconscious goes to work to create the "fit and slim" you.

- Your subconscious sees in pictures, images and patterns.

- Actions always come from the images (pictures) you create in your mind.

- The more you send an image down a neural pathway the clearer, easier and quicker it fires in the order you have visualized.

- Strong emotion attached to any visualization increases the ease in which your neurode pattern fires.

- It takes twenty-one to twenty-eight days to create a new habit.

A Real World Example of the Power of Visualization

As we mentioned earlier, Dr. Maxwell Maltz, M.D., wrote the timeless classic, *Psycho-Cybernetics*, in which he concluded that a person's actions, feelings, behaviors, and even abilities, are consistent with his or her self-image. In other words, you will become the sort of person you think and see yourself being. Change your vision and you will change yourself.
Dr. Maltz told the story of the time he was working with an ex-convict who was desperately trying to turn his life around. The man explained to Dr. Maltz that he felt magnetically drawn to frequent his old hangouts, but by doing so he knew he was playing with dynamite. Not only were his old friends a bad influence, but hanging with them was a direct violation of his parole conditions. Although the ex-con tried his best to avoid the usual people and places, at a deeper level he said he felt that this was just his lot in life. He was just cut-out to be a lowlife convict Dr. Maltz explained to him that if decided to think that; "I'm just a loser" or "I am what I am," he might just as well pack his up his kit because he was heading straight back to jail.

Dr. Maltz told the man that if he truly wanted to break his old thought patterns about being a loser who was destined for jail, that he should make two simple drawings. They could be stick figure drawings for all it mattered, but the man was instructed to draw one picture of himself standing in a jail cell and a sign above the door that read, *"That's Just The Way I am Prison."* The other drawing was to show a man walking away from the prison toward his family. The caption on the second picture was to read; *"I am what I decide to be."*

Dr. Maltz then told the man to make a few copies of these pictures and put them in places where he would see them for the next several weeks. He was to put them in his locker at work, his lunch pail, his car etc. so he would be constantly reminded of his options and direction in life. Each time he looked at the pictures he was to envision the life he desired.

Before long the man told Dr. Maltz that the two simple picture drawings had actually "drove him sane." Each time he thought of heading out to the pub to see his old friends the pictures and thoughts of his family flooded his mind. Before long he was pulled in only one direction, home.

After just one month the urge to associate with his delinquent buddies had all but disappeared. He had begun to make new thought patterns and new ways of thinking.

"I can zero in on a vision of where I want to be in the future. I can see it so clearly in front of me, when I daydream, it's almost a reality. Then I get this easy feeling, and I don't have to be uptight to get there because I already feel like I'm there, that it's just a matter of time."

"I set a goal, visualize it very clearly, then create the drive, the hunger for turning it into a reality. There's a kind of joy in that kind of ambition, in having a vision in front of you. With that kind of joy, discipline isn't difficult or negative or grim. You love doing what you have to do – going to the gym, working hard on the set. Even when pain is part of reaching your goal, and it usually is, you can accept that too."
~ Arnold Schwarzenegger

Remember, whatever you focus on is what
the subconscious believes you want.
What it believes you want, you'll get!

CHAPTER THIRTEEN
The Power of Focused Repetition

A habit is something that we do repeatedly and often without effort. Now, if only all of our habits were good ones! In order to create the good habits we want, we need to be sure our thoughts are consistently focused on what we want.

The *29 DAYS* programs will ensure that your thoughts stay focused on your goal. As for the rest … the laws of attraction and universal intelligence will play their part.

Affirmations

Before I understood how the subconscious mind receives and responds to our conscious thoughts, I thought affirmations and visualization to be nothing more than a bunch of New Age garbage.

The reality is that your subconscious mind *did* get programmed, and much of that programming went on before you were ever aware of it. In fact, most of the beliefs that you hold have been put there by someone or something else *without* your knowledge or permission.

So exactly how was this programming installed?

Excellent question and glad you asked. It was presented by outside influence (parents, teachers, television, friends) and installed by your subconscious awareness through the tools of affirmation and visualization.

We need to simply use the same method but install the programs of *our conscious choice* instead. It's that simple. So please do not think of affirmations and visualization as New Age hype, it's very real and very effective.

What exactly are affirmations and how do we make them work?

Affirmations are statements that you repeat to your subconscious brain to help you make positive changes. Affirmations are often viewed with a great deal of skepticism, because we have a tendency to think of affirmations as someone running about screaming "I am great, I am great," but that's a limited view. Our belief system is nothing short of a series of visualizations and affirmations.

If you give your subconscious new affirmations you begin to create new DSP connections (see Chapter Eight) in your brain that change, or at least overwrite, the beliefs and attitudes that were installed from previous "unwanted" affirmations.

A technique that is recommended by researchers in the field of brain science is to repeat an affirmation while looking into a mirror because a mirror generates emotion. When you generate emotion, you create stronger, longer-lasting neuron connections. Even if you know consciously that what you're affirming is false, it *will* generate emotion.

Suppose you wish to lose thirty pounds. If you stand in front of your mirror and say; "I am fit and trim," your conscious mind might be screaming B.S., but your subconscious mind says "okay."

Your subconscious mind will begin to go into action to create a fit and trim you. If you're skeptical about this technique, and many people are, don't forget, you are the result of your thoughts. So ask yourself, where did my thoughts and beliefs come from? Can you recall the time that you sat down and said to yourself? "You know, I think I would like to be over-weight." Of course not, but here you are (assuming you're overweight). Whatever your thoughts and habits are, they had to come from somewhere!

Throughout the *29 DAYS* program, and through the morning and evening interaction with you, you will find yourself repeatedly and effortlessly thinking about your goal, even if it's only a silent affirmation.

Each day you will be engaging the highly effective method of building new neural connections in your brain. Through the power of focus and repetition your mind will enthusiastically take over the process of change. With this concerted inner-support, you will be astonished at the ease and rapidity you make towards achieving your goal.

Character is not a thing of chance, but the result of continued focus. In fact it's the result of many unconscious affirmations. The easiest and most natural way to change an unwanted character trait is to select an affirmation which seems to fit your particular case. The positive thought will destroy the negative as certainly as light destroys darkness, and the results will be just as effective.

As stated earlier, we are the sum total of our thoughts. So if that is the case, how can we initiate so many good thoughts that they literally crowd out the bad? We actually can't stop the bad thoughts from coming but when they arrive we don't have to play host and entertain them. By using a ready-made positive affirmation we can begin to push the negative thoughts out. When a thought of anger, jealousy, fear or worry creeps in, just start up a counteractive affirmation.

The way to eliminate darkness is with light. The way to eliminate cold is with heat. The way to overcome evil is with good. When unwanted thoughts pop into your mind, simply affirm a positive affirmation and the bad thoughts will vanish.

And you shall decree a thing,
and it will be given unto you.
And light will shine upon your ways.
~ Job 22:28

CHAPTER FOURTEEN
The Power of Awareness

29 DAYS employs written goals, visualization and focused repetition. Each of these are powerful influencers in generating the forces to help us achieve our goals. Another tool in the drawer is how *29 DAYS* will keep you constantly aware of your goal, magically harnessing hidden, and inexplicable forces.

A recent Harvard University Study, published in a 2007 issue of *Psychological Science* tracked the health of eighty-four female room attendants working in seven different hotels.

The study found that those who recognized their work as exercise experienced significant health benefits. Cleaning hotel rooms is a physically taxing job. Each woman scours a hotel room for twenty to thirty minutes, cleaning an average of fifteen rooms a day.

The women were separated into two groups, one learned how their work fulfilled the recommendations of daily activity levels while the other, control group, went about work as usual.

Although neither group changed its behavior, the women who were conscious of their activity level experienced a significant drop in weight, blood pressure, body fat, waist to hip ratio and body mass index in just four weeks. The control group experienced no improvements despite engaging in the exact same physical activities.

The study illustrates how profoundly a person's attitude can affect ones physical well being and by extension, anything else we are focused on.

> Remember whatever you focus on
> is what the subconscious believes you want.

CHAPTER FIFTEEN
The Power of Questions

Anytime that you ask yourself a question you will get an answer. Which is why it is imperative that we ask ourselves positive, empowering questions. Our brains love to respond to challenges, and questions are challenges that request an answer.

If you ask yourself: "Why is my life so disorganized?," your brain might reply; "It's because you're a lazy slob!" *That* is not an empowering question. Suppose you changed the question to: "What small thing can I do to bring organization into my life?" Now you are beginning to ask a question that will bring you a positive, empowering answer.

We thrive on questions, not directives.

Whether a set of directives come from an authority figure, a book, a program, our parents, teachers or even *ourselves,* we will have a natural tendency to resist. When faced with directives we have a natural tendency to either tune them out or deeply resist them. In most cases, consciously or subconsciously, we resort to our basic instinct of fight or flight. If we're fighting the instructions, we push back and rebel. We may do this physically, verbally or just mentally.

If we resort to our flight response, we may appear to be going along, but we've tuned out the instructions or directives. We shut down any attempts at cooperation.

On the other hand, a series of innocuous questions will usually achieve the exact result we desire. We drop our instinctual fight or flight response, and instead we magically find an answer and a solution to our query that will be uniquely tailored to our own personal situation.

Using weight loss as our example, if you were to ask, "What small thing could I do today to

BOOK

lose weight?," the answer that you come up with will be perfectly suited to you. The answers you might come up with might be to substitute a piece of fruit for a slice of pie. You might say, "I'll take that elevator to one floor short of my destination and walk the last flight of stairs." You might say, "I'll take a parking spot at the far end of the lot and not only save my car from the inevitable dings and dents, but I'll enjoy the extra walk." It doesn't matter what the situation is, if you ask yourself, "What small thing could I do?" you will be amazed at the wonderful and creative answers your brain will supply.

These small steps are the secret elixir, the magic of achievement! Consider this: If you gain ten pounds a year, within ten years you are obese, but incredibly you may only be overeating by an average of less than one hundred calories a day. That amounts to little more than a tablespoon of oil, a third of a candy bar, or half a handful of peanuts. In point of fact then, packing on excess weight can happen in the most innocuous manner, and by the same logic, a tiny adjustment in the opposite direction will bring the weight down in the exact same way.

A Re-Cap of the Five Simple Steps

Step One

☞ Each day, for twenty-nine days, you will find yourself thinking about your goal. Far too often people work on a daily goal, and actually make measurable progress, but fail to notice, or recognize their achievement. A simple acknowledgement of achievement will reinforce your inner self-confidence allowing success to build upon success.

Step Two

☞ Each program will supply you with a visual measuring system to chart your daily progress. The program will allow you to choose an inspiring picture (from our library or preferably one of your own). On day one, when we begin, your picture will serve as a visual image that will help you to see your daily progress. Let's suppose it's a picture of a mountain. Each day when you have completed your simple task, you will respond to the *29 DAYS* program which will indicate that you have completed the day's request. This response will simply require you to click on a live "send" URL button, and we will be able to confirm your simple Action Step. When we receive your response, we will send you 1/29th of your picture in your evening message. Each day you will be sent another piece of the picture to serve as a visual reference toward the attainment of your goal. As you see more and more of the picture being completed, it will serve to stimulate your confidence and serve as an external mirror to the internal development of your desired goal. With each successive day your confidence will grow. Success breeds success until it will seem almost effortless.

Step Three

☞ *29 DAYS* programs give you the aid of daily support. Any athlete will tell you that accountability automatically improves performance. Just the act of reporting your progress to someone is helpful to staying on track. Very often we may want to keep our goals confidential. The program's interaction with you is restricted to interaction between you and your online coach. You will enjoy complete anonymity.

Step Four

☞ *29 DAYS* programs ensure that you reward yourself for your progress. So often we are so stuck with our noses to the grindstone that we wear ourselves out. Even though we are making positive progress we wind up feeling like failures. You can build your confidence by acknowledging and celebrating your small victories on a daily or weekly basis. Every seven days is marked with a reward that is the most effective of psychological motivators known.

Step Five

☞ Avoid getting burned out. *29 DAYS* is a powerful tool that ensures you avoid burnout. Together we will make certain that you are continually making forward progress, but at a pace that is both easy, measurable and enjoyable.

CHAPTER SIXTEEN
How Our Changing Wants and Desires Might Apply in the Real World

Keeping with our examples of weight loss, let's suppose you just love going to McDonald's, KFC or some other fast-food restaurant. Let's further suppose that you find yourself visiting "Ronald" or the "Colonel" twice a week, or eight times a month. Do you think that if you were to reduce your visits to oh, say, seven times a month, that it would make you feel greatly deprived? Highly unlikely!

Now the point is this. Let's say that during the course of one month you skipped just *one* visit to the Colonel and by visiting him just six times that month, instead of seven, it didn't leave you feeling the least bit deprived. Now suppose two months later you cut your visit to six times per month and so on until a year or two from now these "quick fix" outlets no longer even register on your radar. Your life and lifestyle in this area would have totally changed.

This new lifestyle is not about being a crusader, it's not about converting anyone else, or bad mouthing fast-food restaurants. It's simply a quiet change of desire that will be with you for the rest of your life. In fact, if you happened to go to a fast-food restaurant because you were out with a bunch of friends and that's where you ended up, so be it. You can eat a small portion, or choose something a little more healthful, *or not*, but now it's a once-in-a-blue-moon situation that will have almost no effect on your total health. The point is this, whether it's fast-food restaurants or some other weight-challenging problem, in a year or two from now you can see how easily you can change your lifestyle with a little focused thought and simple awareness, and, most importantly, you wouldn't feel the least bit deprived.

That is what permanent and lasting change is all about! And, it only takes twenty-nine days for you to think quite differently.

Now, if we can stack six or seven other small changes, such as drinking enough water, or enjoying a piece of fruit as much as an ice cream bar, then "suddenly" within a few months from now you will have a very different lifestyle. In fact, you will have magically changed your life in this area without teeth-gritted will-power. You will have simply started making different choices, and most rewarding is that these choices will have been made from an effortless point of "conscious awareness."

BOOK

CHAPTER SEVENTEEN
There Are No Shortcuts ... but *29 DAYS* Can Happen Surprisingly Quickly

In the *29 DAYS* programs we ask only two things – that you stay with this program for the entire duration and that you actively participate each day. We promise that if you do, you will be blown away by the results.

> Nothing of any value or meaning happens instantly.
> Everything worthwhile involves a process.

- Picture yourself as an electronics salesperson at a stereo shop. A customer walks into your store and says "I'm here to buy a complete stereo system for my recreation room. I have $4,000 to spend." You've got a luncheon appointment and you're pressed for time so instead of asking questions about the type of music he listens to and the size of the room etc. you reply; "You're in luck. We have just the equipment you need," and you start writing up the bill. Do you suppose the customer will hand over his $4,000 just like that? Highly unlikely. What is more probable is that you've blown an easy sale.

- Tammy's a young teenager who has a mad crush on her high school's star athlete. She is certain that her life would be utterly complete if only he would only ask her to be his date at the upcoming graduation dance. Then to Tammy's complete joy, he calls and asks her out to a movie. The next evening they go to a drive-in and Tammy's date tries to kiss her within the first twenty minutes. Tammy gets spooked and jumps out of the car.

- A world-class speed skater decides to "take-up" downhill skiing. She goes to the mountain and asks for some lessons from the resident ski instructor. She and the instructor start off on the bunny-hill where she is shown the basics of how to turn and how to stop. She quickly grows tired of the tedium and details and decides to ride the ski lift to the top of the mountain. Once there she chooses to go down a black diamond (a very difficult run) slope and she gets seriously injured.

- It's the second day of January, and aside from a slight hangover, Isaac is feeling ready to go. He's committed to fulfilling his New Year's resolution to pack on some muscle and lose some weight. Isaac goes to the gym for the first time in many years. He wants to get fit and trim as quickly as possible so he spends four hours pumping weights. The next day Isaac can't get out of bed, and on top of that, he's managed to pull a muscle.

Although these are just made-up situations, you can be sure that the world is chock full of stories just like these. Everything in life requires a process – whether we like it or not. If we can curb our desires for instant gratification we can have just about anything we can set our minds to, and we can usually attain it far easier than we ever imagined.

Enjoying life and achieving our goals doesn't have to be difficult. As we said in the very beginning, it's all in the way we look at a thing.

BOOK

CHAPTER EIGHTEEN
How Often Do We Play the Martyr?

I love the example that Zig Ziglar gives in his book *See You At The Top* about the pain, and sacrifice he went through while losing weight and getting physically fit. He tells about the "enormous price" he had to pay every morning by getting out of a warm bed into the cold and discomfort of running through his neighborhood. Since he traveled a great deal he would belly-ache endlessly about running in the heat of California or the cold of Winnipeg, Canada. Everywhere he went, and to all who would listen, he wailed about the sacrifice he was making in order to stay in shape.

He continues with his story that for a number of years he told his audiences that if you want to accomplish anything worthwhile you had to "pay the price." Then one day he was running on the grounds of Oregon State University. It was a beautiful, warm, spring day. He recalled how the ground was flowing effortlessly beneath his feet, he was breathing the fresh air and feeling about as good as one could wish to feel. Suddenly he knew he was having the time of his life. At the age of fifty he was in better shape than he was at twenty-five. He could run miles and miles without pain and drudgery. It was then, at that point, he had what could only be described as an epiphany. A deep and sudden knowing. The realization that hit him was this: You don't "pay the price" for good health – you enjoy the benefits of good health.

I cannot think of a more truthful or elegant statement.

You don't "pay the price" for good health – you enjoy the benefits of good health.

We have been so conditioned by our parents, teachers, media and "how-to" gurus that everything in life has a proportional cost/benefit ratio, the better the result the greater the cost. You don't pay the price for success, you enjoy the benefits of success. You pay the price for failure. You don't pay the price for a good relationship, you enjoy the benefits of a good relationship. In essence, once you get the method down, it's the journey, and the enjoyment of that journey (which is your life) that brings all the benefits together.

On a personal level, when I first started to exercise regularly there were times during the first few weeks when I genuinely hated it. But it wasn't long before exercise turned into one of the most enjoyable parts of my day. I may often feel stiff and tired when I start, but before long I'm in the flow and my exercise time often becomes my meditation time as well.

I've never met a habitual jogger who doesn't crave the daily experience of running. Oh sure there are days when our "running friend" may not feel like lacing up the shoes, but watch this person if they experience an injury and they can't run for a couple of weeks. They're as anxious as a caged animal to get back to it. If they had any temporary delusions about paying the price those thoughts quickly vanish and they come to appreciate how fortunate they are when they can let their body loose and feel the boundless joys of physical activity and a healthy body.

CHAPTER NINETEEN
Do the *29 DAYS* programs guarantee I'll reach my goal in twenty-nine days?

If I want to lose thirty pounds in twenty-nine days will this actually happen?

29 DAYS is not about making outrageous promises it can't deliver. *Could* you lose thirty pounds in a month? Perhaps, but that isn't the objective of *29 DAYS*. The objective is to transform the way you think. The *29 DAYS* program will provide you with the necessary frame of mind to not only achieve your goal, but to maintain your new way of thinking ... effortlessly and permanently.

I hope you are convinced at this point that together, with your desire and the right method, (whether that's quitting smoking, building financial independence or becoming a great communicator etc.) you can accomplish any goal you desire.

Our goal in *29 DAYS* is to help you change your lifestyle not to help you go crazy bending yourself out of shape in a supreme effort toward losing weight, creating wealth, quitting smoking or any other goal you may desire. A successful *29 DAYS* program will change your deepest thoughts and habits in twenty-nine days so that you can enjoy a new lifestyle in an effortless and lasting manner.

Do we want you to achieve your desired habit? Obviously, and you will. But our ultimate goal is to see you change the way you think about your existing habit so that you end the struggle once and for all. As we said right from the very beginning, *you* will change, when the way you *think* changes. If you follow a *29 DAYS* program faithfully, in twenty-nine days you will have changed the way you think. Once changed, you will never be able to go back to your old way of thinking.

If you can't believe that something is possible, then you aren't going to have it. But if you can have the smallest belief that it might be possible, you are already on your way to creating it. You cannot create something if you cannot picture having it. Live out your dreams in your mind; picture and feel yourself getting what you want; hear the words you will say to others and what they will say to you when your dreams come true. You will learn to make your imaginings so real that they feel as if you have already achieved them rather than like wishful and distant fantasies.

> *29 DAYS* will help you to create a vision, to daydream and fantasize, and then focus each day on the simple, concrete steps you can take to reach your goal.

You will always take the path of least resistance. The path of least resistance is small, effortless, daily contributions towards your goal. In the case of wanting to lose weight, is that not easier than the daily resentment of being overweight, uncomfortable and unhealthy?

Logically, small simple steps *is* the path of least resistance. The biggest problem that we have in not choosing this path is that we want change to happen too quickly, and as a result we usually get nothing.

CHAPTER TWENTY
Above All Else, Enjoy the Journey!

This seemingly self-evident concept is unfortunately often overlooked by many of us. Ultimately it doesn't matter if we are the ideal weight, have a billion dollar bank account, and we enjoy perfect physical health, if we don't enjoy living our lives everything else is pretty much moot.

In *29 DAYS* we hope you take these programs in the spirit in which they are offered. Your goals to improve your life should do exactly that ... improve your life and make it truly more enjoyable.

News Flash! Each and Every One of Us Will Eventually Die.

It's true that most of us readily accept the fact that everyone, aside from ourselves of course, will die. I'm always amazed at how-to gurus, health nuts and prophets-of-doom who warn us that if we eat at fast-food joints, indulge in alcohol, eat red meat, ice cream and refined wheat, that we will surely die!

Let's take that argument to the next logical plateau – if we don't go to fast-food joints, if we cut out alcohol and abstain from eating red meat and ice cream, and instead subsist on broccoli and tofu – does that mean we're NOT going to die?!

Look, we all know that drastically cutting animal products, coffee, alcohol and everything else we enjoy is going to be better for our system, and quite frankly, if you can read a "what-you-should-do" book and incorporate that into your life you certainly don't need this program. If, on the other hand, you're like the majority of us, you're not about to embrace the life of a Himalayan monk because somebody suggests this is the path to a long life. Hey, how long do you want to live anyway if all you're allowed to consume is water, vegetables and tofu? With a menu like that we'd all be happily looking for a made-to-measure casket.

Okay, so let's get this straight, these *29 DAYS* programs are *not* about austerity and sacrifice.

I'm reminded of the story of Zig Ziglar who is being interviewed by his doctor after he's had a complete physical. The doctor suggested that if Ziglar were a building he'd be condemned. At this point Ziglar jumps in and says, "I suppose you're going to give me one of those diets that says you can't have this, and you can't have that, and be sure to stay away from this, and oh man, you certainly can't have that!"

To Ziglar's surprise his doctor responded with the most wonderful words a "condemned building" could imagine. "No," the doctor replied; "You can have anything you want!"

Just as Ziglar was about to acknowledge that that was one of the most beautiful replies he could have imagined the doctor continued with … "Now I'm going to tell you what you're going to want!"

Now of course this is a humorous little story, but the point is "bang on" and it's in complete alignment with the *29 DAYS* philosophy, which is NOT about depriving you of anything you want, but rather our goal is to change the way you think and ultimately what you *really do want*.

The better choices that you're really going to want aren't going to happen overnight. If you feel that *29 DAYS … to Your Perfect Weight,* or any of the other programs offered, is making you feel deprived, then you and the program are not in alignment. The goal is to change what you truly want in a healthy and lasting way. In a surprisingly short period of time many things that you truly want are going to be great choices that lead to your desired new behavior.

This is going to happen at a very subconscious level which is why it won't hurt and why it's going to last.

In his book *Creating Health*, Deepak Chopra writes:

> *If we want to create health, starting this moment, then we have to start channeling the unconscious mind through habit. In my experience, any approach to new habits should follow these guidelines: the habit should be acquired effortlessly over a period of time, it should be guided by positive thoughts, and it should be consciously repeated, but always in a good frame of mind, never forced in as the enemy of a bad habit. Cultivated in this way, new habits condition the whole mind-body system to create health and happiness automatically.*

While the actions you take to fulfill your goal may appear small, what you will accomplish is not. You will be building powerful habits and inner self-confidence that will transform you and make your life infinitely more enjoyable.

To commit your life to deeper relationships, financial security, peak physical health or a rewarding career is to enjoy the fruit that life begs us to take. These are simple yet powerful goals that will respond to powerful forces one gentle step at a time.

We invite you to join us in one of the *29 DAYS* programs and experience the power and thrill of permanent, positive, life-long change.

— <u>PART SIX</u> —

Let's Begin

CHAPTER TWENTY-ONE
How *29 DAYS* Programs Work

Once you have chosen your program from our list of available programs, you will need to register at our website at www.29daysto.com and fill in the required information.

Information Required:
- your email address
- starting date (choose the Monday you wish to begin)
- your time zone
- choose a picture from our picture library to visually chart your daily progress/or preferably send us your own inspirational picture

Daily Routine:

Morning:

29 DAYS and your online coach will be with you twice each day. In the morning we will prompt you to fulfill your daily step, read an inspiring message from your coach, or do a small simple task, or possibly just think about your goal for thirty seconds, or visualize something you will enjoy with the achievement of your goal, or ask your subconscious a question, etc. This daily morning message will come with a reply box that you will click when you have completed the day's step.

Evening:

When we have received your acknowledgement email that you have completed the day's step, we will send you 1/29th of your picture, as well as an inspirational message, story or some advice that you can consider, or turn over to your subconscious mind to consider, for the evening.

The daily routine will slowly build on each successive day until day twenty-nine. Every seven days we will prompt you to give yourself a reward for your patience and perseverance.

BOOK

29 DAYS programs are based on four weeks, with each week having a target theme.

WEEK ONE: The first week is about commitment to your goal, and awareness of your present limiting habits and beliefs. Before you can neutralize the negative influences on your behavior, it is imperative that you become intimately aware of their existence. The first week you will focus on recognizing your habits, how and why you think the way you do, and to be absolutely certain that you are committed to change. This program is a four-part process with each week building on the previous week.

WEEK TWO: In week two you will begin to prepare yourself for action. You will begin to ask yourself simple but vital questions about how you might begin to make minor, but permanent changes to your behavior. These are changes that will almost seem too trivial to matter, but be assured, over time they will produce significant results.

WEEK THREE: By week three you will be wanting to take action. You will have spent the previous two weeks in decision and preparation. By day fifteen you will have a number of ideas and ways that you can tweak your lifestyle that will be relatively painless but will produce big results in a short period of time. And before you know it, it will be ...

WEEK FOUR: In week four you will be taking further action steps that will soon become habit. This week is really about driving home the concept that by maintaining the simple, yet painless changes you've made in week three, you are on the fast-track to a new life of effortless achievement and permanent results.

The daily changes you make in *29 DAYS* are small ...
the results are enormous

The Program

29 DAYS ... to becoming a great listener and communicator!

HOW TO USE THE *29DAYS* PROGRAMS

1. Be sure you have read *29 DAYS ... to a habit you want!* before you begin your program.

2. Register online to select your Monday start date.

3. Be sure you have your 6 digit **PROGRAM ACCESS CODE**. If you purchased your program from the 29DAYS website you will find your **PROGRAM ACCESS CODE** on your receipt. If you purchased your program from another party, go to:

    http://29daysto.com/listen

    ... and fill in your name and email address and you will be sent your 6-Digit **PROGRAM ACCESS CODE**.

4. After you register for your starting Monday, just follow the daily program in the morning and evening. When you activate your conscious and subconscious mind twice each day for twenty-nine days, you will create a powerful new way of thinking.

5. Do not skip ahead in the program. Follow each day and do the simple tasks as you receive them.

6. Enjoy! In just twenty-nine days you will have made a positive, and permanent change in your life

Introduction

There is no other skill, talent or habit that will have a greater impact on your life than your ability to become a "good" listener and communicator. Developing this single, and increasingly rare quality will transform every relationship you have. Although becoming a *great* listener and communicator is a lifelong pursuit, in just a matter of weeks you can learn to listen with empathy. You can become that rare individual who is able to *really* listen and communicate with another person. To listen empathically is to step into another's shoes and see the world through their eyes. To listen empathically means to touch another's heart, to validate their existence. One of the greatest gifts you can give another person is to truly listen and make them feel understood.

Our supreme ability to communicate is humanity's greatest accomplishment. It's the singular skill that sets us apart from all the other creatures on our planet. Human beings are the only animals that communicate with their own kind. Other animals signal to one another, as birds do as chimpanzees do, but they don't communicate in the sense where communing means sharing thoughts and feelings, sharing one another's minds.

Through our unique ability to communicate with empathy, sympathy or basic understanding, we share our common feelings. Without anything in common there is no communing and therefore the human community breaks down. Our level of enjoyment and success in this life depends upon our ability to communicate effectively.

On an individual basis, your ability to communicate effectively will set you apart from most other people. The quality of your friendships, the cohesiveness of your family relationships, and your ability to interrelate with every facet of your environment is a direct reflection of your ability to listen. No one is more valued, treasured, and appreciated than the deeply effective listener.

When I told a friend I was going to title this program *29 DAYS ... to becoming a great listener,* she was okay with that. Later when I told her I had changed my mind and I was going to title the program *29 DAYS ... to becoming a great listener and communicator*, she had a problem. In her opinion these were two different programs. She felt that she was a great communicator but not really a skilled listener.

I thought about what she said for a long time, and the more I did, the more I disagreed with her reasoning. I believe that listening and communicating are very much intertwined.

Communication *is* two-way dialogue. Have you ever suffered through listening to some windbag who refused to shut up, or cue into the blatant signals of the "listener" yawning and squirming? This guy bulldozed on for twenty minutes about his hemorrhoids or the cyst he had removed giving you a full run-down to the last detail. As a listener you fully understood every word, or "worse," if you're an exceptionally gifted listener, you might have pictured it all in vivid color! Was that communication? Yes! Was it effective communication? No! Effective communication is a two-way street.

The communicator in this case failed to clue into the fact that you weren't interested in the subject matter. In other words, the speaker wanted you to receive his communication (his story), but he couldn't be bothered to pick up your dis-interest.

If a speaker is lecturing, but not listening to his audience (picking up clues such as wandering eyes, cell phone texting or walking out), then how effective is his communication? Effective communication involves reading the listener's non-verbal responses. It's an active process that is vitally necessary for effective communication.

Even in conversation, without acute awareness of the listener's non-verbal cues, what results is one person talking, and the other person waiting for the speaker to pause so he can jump in. Unfortunately this is usually the level of conversation in today's world. As for communicating, we often think, erroneously, it's just a matter of clearly delivering our message. For communication to be effective, it's much deeper than that.

This *29 DAYS* program is designed to teach you the fundamental principles of listening and communicating ... both to yourself and others. You will learn to read between the lines, to see, hear, sense and feel far more than the spoken word. You will quickly understand that words are limited in their ability to convey feelings, meanings and emotions. Real listening involves far more than the auditory physical senses.

Most of us take listening for granted. We think listening is something we do as naturally as breathing. In fact, we often equate *hearing* to *listening* – always a mistake. Hearing is merely a cognizant registration of physical energy and vibration. Effective listening involves feelings, emotions, empathy and understanding. These are the human qualities that can totally transform your relationships as a spouse, father, mother, friend and business associate. Effective listening is a skill – which means anyone can acquire it. If you can learn to listen, *really listen*, you will rise to the top of any environment in which you find yourself.

There are very few emotional needs as necessary to the human spirit as the need to be validated and understood. By the same token there are few things as emotionally devastating as the empty void of not being heard, listened to or cared for.

The results of ineffective listening are everywhere:

- An inability to communicate keeps two loved ones from truly experiencing each other.
- An argument erupts with both sides spitting invectives without the slightest attempt at communication or understanding.
- You catch your mind wandering off while someone dear to you tries in vain to relay their deepest feelings.
- Your interactions with colleagues and associates is little more than a never-ending series of verbal noise and automatic reaction with more than seventy-five percent of it failing to register.

Communication is the very foundation of human experience. Our ability to communicate our deepest thoughts, feelings, and desires is one of the most valuable gifts we have. Unfortunately this gift is seldom used because it can often leave us deeply scarred. Few things can be more psychologically damaging than pouring out your deepest thoughts and emotions to someone and then realizing the other person isn't really listening. It's precisely why a sensitive ear is so valued. Many of us either don't know how, or we're afraid, to express ourselves. We drop veiled clues or skirt around our true feelings, desperately hoping the listener will clue in and invite us to open up and share what's weighing so heavily on our mind. Sadly, the desired communication seldom occurs because the intended listener never bothered to tune in or was completely unaware of the silent cry for a sympathetic ear.

Our modern lives and harried pace have reduced our attention span and listening skills to sound bites. We try to multi-task by attempting to carry on a conversation while checking our email. We like to think that we can effectively carry on several tasks at once when in reality all we're really doing is a number of things poorly and ineffectively. Ironically it's the very plethora of communication devices that can be blamed for communication's demise. Our lives

PROGRAM

are saturated with radio, TV, email, junk mail, faxes, pagers, cell phones, iPods, laptops, Facebook, YouTube, Blackberrys and now Twitter. We have the ability to be in constant communication without ever *really* communicating. We seem to be caught in an endless loop of limitless bits of trite information. The number of people who exhibit the art of listening is diminishing as it's rapidly becoming a quaint skill of a bygone era.

Not too long ago my friend Jeff was telling me a rather interesting incident that happened at their house. Jeff and his wife, Debbie, were in the kitchen preparing dinner when their eight-year-old daughter, Allie, walked in and announced that she couldn't talk to her best friend Janie because her "internet was down." To Jeff and Debbie it may not have seemed like a major issue, but to Allie this was clearly a problem. As she explained through several long sighs and exhales, the following day was school photo day, and she and Janie still hadn't figured out what they were going to wear. In the middle of texting back and forth, the internet cut out and now neither was sure of what they would wear for picture day!

If you're still trying to understand the problem, it seems Allie and Janie's preferred choice of communication was MSN. Jeff was about to suggest that Allie pick up the "antiquated" land-line device commonly known as the telephone, when it rang. Allie answered it and sure enough it was Janie. She began to explain that she was getting new carpeting installed in her bedroom and that her internet would be down for the rest of the night. Allie once again sighed heavily, and then to Jeff and Debbie's disbelief they heard her say; "Well, Janie, if you can't get onto MSN then I guess we can't talk. I'll see you tomorrow at school." Allie hung up the phone and sauntered off to watch TV.

I was telling my friend Glenn this story when he said, "I've got one that's similar to that." Glenn coaches a Peewee boys' hockey team. One day Glenn walked into the dressing room before practice to see the last three kids slowly getting dressed. Glenn couldn't help but notice that these kids would put a piece of equipment on, and then pick-up their iTochess or smart-phones and tap furiously for a few moments before returning to the business of getting dressed. Glenn didn't say anything as he laced up his skates, he just watched. This process of putting one piece of equipment on and then tapping the iTouch, and then another piece of equipment, followed by more iTouch tapping, went on for quite some time until Glenn finally had to jump in and ask what these boys were doing. "We're talking," replied one of the kids matter-of-factly. "To whom?" asked Glenn. "To each other," another boy replied, as if explaining the completely obvious to a borderline idiot. "Why not just talk to each other? You're all in the same room!" exclaimed Glenn. The kids just shrugged and said "It's more fun this way."

What is listening and communicating anyway?

It's the very foundation of civilization. In fact, without man's ability to communicate we would be foraging in the forest like other animals. Listening and communication is solely responsible for our relationships ... good and bad. If you think otherwise, try managing for even a short time without communication.

Listening, like many things in life, is not necessarily as it appears to our senses. There is *listening,* and then there is *effective listening.* Vast difference, especially in results. Our loss of being listened to in this modern era has left an undeniable hole in our lives. It leaves a sense of emptiness, a gnawing sense of being cheated of an essential ingredient to being human.

Have you ever suffered through the uncomfortable and somewhat embarrassing situation of talking to someone who was only pretending to listen, and to make it worse, they couldn't even bother putting much effort into their deceit? You know the type whose sporadic nods and uh huh's are totally out of sync while their eyes glance down at their smartphone or they scan the room for something of greater interest. Not only does it show appallingly bad manners, but it suggests some serious character flaws and bad upbringing. On the other hand, do you ever recall having a conversation with that rare person who shows genuine interest and concern for what you're saying? They listen with an intensity that makes you feel deeply appreciated, and that they genuinely care about what you're expressing. These people are not only rare, but they are treasured and cherished wherever they go.

Listening, true listening, is far more than being able to remember what the speaker said. In fact, surprisingly enough, being able to repeat back *verbatim* what the speaker said does not mean someone has listened effectively, it simply means the person heard the words. Effective listening means empathic understanding. Big difference.

Most people cannot bother to listen with the intent to *understand,* they listen with the intent to *reply.* They're either speaking or they're thinking about their reply. The essence of empathic listening doesn't mean agreeing with what the speaker is saying; it's being able to fully and deeply understand the speaker both emotionally and intellectually. To at least try to listen to another person is, at the very minimum, a common courtesy. To listen effectively is the very essence of humanness that in modern times seems to be vaporizing in front of our very eyes.

Becoming a good listener begins with desire. If you truly want to acquire the skills of communication and effective listening you can. You may never reach the point where you consider yourself to be a *truly great listener* – the better you are the more you realize you can improve -

PROGRAM

but you *can* become good at it ... really good. That's what this program will do for you. In just twenty-nine days your awareness and ability to listen and understand will radically transform your most valued relationships and your life.

When all the clutter and noise of modern technology are put aside, we are social beings that need and crave to be heard and understood.

In today's world, an effective listener and communicator will be as refreshing and life-giving as an oasis in a desert. In fact, effective listening and communication have often been called the lost skill or the forgotten art.

If you know a good listener consider yourself lucky. They are rare people who are held in high esteem by all who know them. With conscious effort, you can learn the skills to become one of these highly valued people. To master this skill is not necessarily easy, but it's the one communication skill that can catapult your life into a completely different dimension. When you take this program and follow the daily program for just twenty-nine days, you will be absolutely amazed at the complete transformation in every meaningful relationship you have in your life.

This *29 DAYS* program will interact with you twice a day, making each day a step closer toward your goal of becoming a great listener and communicator. It's a universal law of nature that we are the result of our thoughts and habits. The first part of this program is designed to help you become aware of listening in all its forms. You will become aware of listening to yourself as well as to others.

I will be your coach over the next twenty-nine days. I should add that although I'll be your coach, it's really *you* who will be discovering, and coaching your inner-self to the path of becoming a great listener and communicator. I'll just be hanging around to offer a little guidance and moral support. As outlined in the *Habits* book, you're going to learn how to do this all by yourself. Remember our motto from the Chinese Proverb:

> *Give a man a fish and you feed him for a day.*
> *Teach a man to fish and you feed him for a lifetime.*

Nothing of value can ever be created instantly. In fact, becoming a great listener is a lifelong pursuit. Like knowledge and wisdom, the more listening skills you gain, the more you'll realize how much more there are to acquire. That realization will only serve to inspire you. As you acquire the skills of listening and communicating, the instant payoffs will be so self evident and so inspiring you will instinctively strive to hone this most valuable skill.

When you commit to staying with us for the entire twenty-nine days, and commit to the daily simple steps, your life will be radically different by the end of the program.

Your program has been divided into four weeks, with each week building on the previous week. Each week you will be creating new neuron tracks/pathways, and embedding new ways of thinking and acting when it comes to communicating with the most important people in your life.

Here's how the Four Week Program works:

Week One – Commitment and Awareness Week

In the first week we want to establish two things - commitment and awareness. You will learn the various levels of listening as well as when and how you should use them. You will spend this week noticing the often over-looked world of listening. You will be astonished at how much information we assume and take for granted, and how often we mistake *hearing* for *listening*. Most importantly you will become acutely aware of listening to yourself. Awareness is the first fundamental of change. Through simple observation and awareness, you will begin to understand how much of your listening skills were programmed into you from your earliest years. Unless you have had focused training in listening, your present listening and communication skills are a result of habit. As you build awareness, you will simultaneously begin to build a strong foundation of commitment that will support you when you begin to put the first steps of proactive listening into practice.

Week Two – Preparation Week

Now that you have established a general awareness of listening, as well as an awareness of your own peculiarities and habits, you will develop your internal resolve toward acquiring the skills of effective listening. You will begin to ask yourself simple, but vital questions toward change. These are the beginnings of minor, but permanent changes to your listening and communicating behavior. At first these changes may seem too trivial to matter, but over time they will produce significant results. By day ten or eleven, the daily reminders and your growing desire and awareness will already be forming powerful new neuron tracks. These new thought patterns will begin to produce deep-seated lifelong changes to your listening habits. When you begin to notice how some simple changes to your daily listening habits can have such a powerful affect on those around you, your self-confidence and excitement will start to soar.

PROGRAM

Week Three – Taking Action

By now you'll be wanting to take action, and that is precisely the time to take it! You will have spent the previous two weeks in awareness and preparation. By the beginning of the third week you will have a number of ideas and ways that you can begin to practice what you've been discovering. By day fifteen you will have begun to view the entire process of communication in a very different light. In fact, you will have already been making subtle changes to your communication habits ... possibly without even being aware of it. As you begin to practice empathic listening you will see results in just a few days and in some cases immediately. The positive results and the inner feelings that will result will be all the inspiration you will need for week four and beyond.

Week Four – Staying the Course

Week four is not only a continuation of week three's skills, but it will serve to further enhance your newly formed habits, thoughts and listening ability. This week is about driving home the concept that by maintaining awareness, and the basic practices of empathic listening, you are on track toward a new life. In fact, after you have taken the entire *29 DAYS* program, it will no longer be possible for you to return to your old listening habits and patterns.

The gift of our attention, and true understanding, is one of the rarest, and truly greatest gifts we can give both to ourselves and to other people. In just twenty-nine days you can learn this skill and give this gift to the most important people in your life.

To listen empathically is a rare talent to possess, and a treasure to receive.

Enough talk already. Let's get started!

PROGRAM

— <u>WEEK ONE</u> —

COMMITMENT AND AWARENESS

DAY ONE
Awareness Is Vital
To Fundamental Change

DAY ONE - A.M.

Welcome to *29 DAYS ... to becoming a great listener and communicator!* Commit to this program for the next twenty-nine days and you will find it to be a life changing experience. The positive effects on both yourself and those around you will be far greater than you might possibly imagine.

As you can see from the title, this week is all about awareness. Over the next seven days you will become acutely aware of listening and communicating and its numerous intricacies. Most of us are poor listeners because we have never been instructed in the art of listening. Effective listening and communication are skills that anyone can learn.

For today and tomorrow you are going to respond to two listening assessment questionnaires. The purpose of these questions is to help you assess your present listening skills and habits.

Today's assessment is simply titled *How Would You Respond?* Please put a check beside the response that you would *most likely* choose in the given situation. None of the choices may be ideal, but choose the *one* that would be closest to your natural response. There are no right or wrong answers. Please be as honest in your choices as you can. If you were put into any of these situations ...

HOW WOULD YOU RESPOND?

1.   You're at home watching TV when the phone rings. You pick up the phone to hear your best friend, a newlywed, with exciting news. "Hey guess what? I just got the promotion I've been after! It comes with a raise, profit sharing

PROGRAM

and a company car. The only problem is I have to move out of town to the big city. I'm not sure how well I'd fit in there."

_____ a) "Are you kidding? Take the job. It's what you've been after for the past two years. You'll love city life."

_____ b) "I can't believe you wouldn't jump at this opportunity. You need to be more confident in yourself."

_____ c) "What city is the job in? What concerns you about moving?"

_____ d) "Congratulations on the opportunity, but it sounds like you've got some concerns about moving."

2. Your wife was having lunch with one of her friends and she comes home in a melancholy mood. "I don't know why I bother getting together with Joanne. All she ever does is brag about who she knows and how much money she's worth. She's not even remotely interested in my life."

_____ a) "It sounds like you don't feel very valued as a friend. Are you considering ending your relationship?"

_____ b) "You need to be more assertive. You should say what's on your mind. Don't worry about it, you've got lots of other friends."

_____ c) "If I were you I'd blow her off. Why should you sit and listen to her honk her horn all the time?"

_____ d) "If you make a point not to see her anymore what are the ramifications?" How will it make you feel?"

3. Your close friend tells you that her boyfriend has just asked her to marry him. "I've been waiting for him to ask me for over a year. Now that he has, I'm not so sure. I think I really love him but he has such a violent temper. Sometimes he frightens me."

_____ a) "Are you kidding me? You need to be a little more aggressive. If you're afraid now you'll feel a lot more frightened when you're married."

_____   b) "What has he done that scares you and makes you feel so uneasy?"

_____   c) "If you're not sure, then you've got the only answer you need. Under no circumstances should you say yes unless you feel absolutely certain."

_____   d) "It sounds like you might be afraid to say _yes_ and just as fearful to say _no_."

4.   You come home from work to see your son in a bad mood. When you ask him how his day went he replies; "I had an awful day. The teacher yelled at me in front of the whole class for no reason. Then later we were playing soccer in gym class and I accidentally scored on my own goal."

_____   a) "Wow, that's a tough day, but you've got to just shrug it off and forget about it. I've had a few days like that. I remember one time ..."

_____   b) "That's some day. You must be feeling like the whole world's out to get you."

_____   c) "Come on son, you were obviously doing something wrong. The teacher isn't going to yell at you for no reason. As for scoring on your own net, that's got to be one of your bigger screw-ups don't you think?"

_____   d) "That's a rough day. What got your teacher so excited that she yelled at you?"

5.   A fellow employee enters your office and says: "Since you know my boss pretty well, I'm wondering if you wouldn't mind listening to my problem. He's always taking on every new assignment asked of him so he can look good to senior management. The problem is, he's always dumping everything on my desk and I can't keep up. Whenever I don't get my work completed he insinuates that I'm incompetent."

_____   a) "Have you talked to him about your work-load and how you might handle it in the future?"

Week One: Commitment and Awareness ~ 123

_____ b) "Perhaps you're not being as efficient as you could be. After all, he should know how much work you can handle."

_____ c) "Don't worry about it. Just do the best you can. If you don't finish an assignment because he's overloading you, it's his fault."

_____ d) "You must feel like your in a no-win situation?"

6. Your son was one of the city's top little league football players the previous year. It seems like every boy, except your son, sprouted up over the past year. Your son will now be the smallest player on the team and he's clearly worried. It's the last day to sign up and he says: "Dad, I don't think I'm going to play this year. I think I'm too small and besides, I'm not that interested in football anymore."

_____ a) "Son, you've got to face your fears. You can't run and hide from them. I was a couple of years behind the guys when I was your age. I caught up, and so will you. Sign up, son. When you catch up to the others in size, you'll be glad you didn't quit playing."

_____ b) "Son, you haven't lost interest in football, you're just scared. You can't go through life being afraid. If you do, you'll regret it."

_____ c) "You must be feeling like you can't compete on the same level as you did last year."

_____ d) "Why do you think you're too small? Do you think you might want to try another position? Would you like to try playing another sport?"

7. Your father calls you on the phone and says there's something on his mind. He tells you that shortly after your mother died he met another woman. He's considering asking her to marry him but he's just not sure how the rest of the family will take it. He loves this woman but he doesn't want anyone to be upset.

_____ a) "You can't be serious. Mom only died eight months ago. You shouldn't be so selfish. You've got to wait a while."

_____ b) "Why don't you let everyone know that you met another woman. That will soften the blow. Then in a few months time you can propose to her and the 'fall-out' ... if there's any at all, won't be nearly as bad."

_____ c) "You must be feeling a whirlwind of emotions and uncertainty."

_____ d) "So who is she? How did you meet her? What's she like? What does her family think?"

8. Your wife comes home from the office in a strange mood. She excitedly tells you that she was chosen to give the key sales presentation in Hong Kong later in the year. Just as you begin to join her in celebration she turns all melancholy and says she's not so sure that she's up to the task.

_____ a) "It seems like you're feeling a little overwhelmed with this new responsibility."

_____ b) "You're always selling yourself short."

_____ c) "What makes you feel unsure about your ability?"

_____ d) "You should be proud of yourself. The company wouldn't have picked you if you weren't up to the task. Don't worry, you'll be fine."

9. Your daughter has just finished her third year of a four-year BA program. She's still not sure what she wants to do. She tells you that she feels going to school for another year is a waste of time and money.

_____ a) "If you don't go back to school do you know what you want to do?"

_____ b) "It's only one more year. You've gone this far. If you don't finish it's like wasting three years. Get your degree and then see what you want to do."

_____ c) 'You must be feeling a little lost and uncertain."

_____ d) "You can't go through life starting and stopping things. If you commit to something stick to it and finish it off. You're just not applying yourself enough."

10. A colleague at work storms into your office and says; "Can you believe it? They just replaced my boss with a woman from another firm. I thought it was company policy to hire from within. The president as much as told me that job was mine if it ever opened up. I don't know what I'm going to do yet, but I'm going to do something!"

_____ a) "I'm sure there's a perfectly good reason you didn't get the job. It probably opened up early than expected and the president knew you weren't ready for the responsibility just yet."

_✓_ b) "You must be feeling really let down, especially since you were practically promised the job."

_____ c) "I wouldn't take that. You should go and talk to the president and clear the air. After all, the least he owes you is an explanation."

_____ d) "Your boss left suddenly? What do you know about this new person? Do you think her assignment might just be temporary until they can get you properly trained?"

At the end of each question/scenario, you were given four answer choices. Please check the listening/answer choices you selected.

Questioning Response: You seek additional information before committing to a response. If you ask too many questions it could be construed as being grilled.

1 - c, 2 - d, 3 - b, 4 - d, 5 - a, 6 - d, 7 - d, 8 - c, 9 - a, 10 - d **TOTAL** _____

Critical Response: This response tends to be judgmental and critical. It closes the door on continued discussion.

1 - b, 2 - b, 3 - a, 4 - c, 5 - b, 6 - b, 7 - a, 8 - b, 9 - d, 10 - a **TOTAL** _____

Empathic Response: This response is nonjudgmental. It encourages the other person to open up and to feel safe enough with you to explore their deeper feelings and to find their own solutions.

1 - d, 2 - a, 3 - d, 4 - b, 5 - d, 6 - c, 7 - c, 8 - a, 9 - c, 10 - b   **TOTAL** _____

Advice Response: This response suggests that the solution is rather obvious. It does not invite discussion or evaluation. It simply slams the door on further exploration.

1 - a, 2 - c, 3 - c, 4 - a, 5 - c, 6 - a, 7 - b, 8 - d, 9 - b, 10 - c   **TOTAL** _____

After you've circled your choices, notice which response is most dominant. Do you have a tendency to "Ask Questions," "Offer Criticism," "Feel Empathic," or "Give Advice"?

Remember, there are no right or wrong answers. This assessment however, is very important toward creating awareness about your present listening behavior.

STEP 1 - Today's goal is to begin to become acutely aware of listening. Try to observe people in conversation. Can you tell if someone is really listening? If so what are the physical signs that indicate they are? Notice yourself in conversation. Does your mind wander off if the speaker drones on? Do you make assumptions about what the speaker is going to say and therefore only half listen? Do you listen to your colleagues at work differently than you listen to your family and friends? Simple observation and awareness will make you a better listener almost instantly. This week is all about becoming aware of the many facets of listening ... and there are many. Try to be as observant and honest as you can. One other thing: Why do you want to acquire the skills of becoming a good listener and communicator? What will it do for you? How will it make you feel? In what way will this skill change your life? How will it affect your life at work, at home and socially? How will your life be enhanced?

There's nothing that you need to write at this point. Today you will begin to plant the seeds of your *listening* expectations – this is a very vital step.

Wisdom is the reward you get for a lifetime of listening
when you'd have preferred to talk.
~ Doug Larson

PROGRAM

DAY ONE – P.M. MESSAGE

Welcome back. Were you surprised with the results from your listening assessment or was it what you expected? I hope you were able to observe some conversations in action. What did you notice about other people's physical reactions while they were in conversation? Did you notice anything about yourself in conversation either as a speaker or listener?

Did You Know?

⋄ 85% of what we know is learned by listening.

⋄ Human resource professionals estimate that more than 80% of the people who fail at their job do so for one reason - they're unable to effectively communicate with their colleagues.

⋄ Less than 2% of the population have had any training in listening skills.

⋄ Recent research shows that even in highly technical jobs, human relations skills are the most important factor in determining success or failure.

⋄ More than 35% of business studies find that effective listening is the number one rated skill for business success.

Just before you go to sleep tonight, spend just a few moments thinking about why you want to acquire effective listening skills and what you think they will do for you.

> *A good listener is not only popular everywhere,*
> *but after a while he gets to know something.*
> *~ Wilson Mizner*

See you tomorrow.

... to becoming a great listener and communicator!

DAY TWO
Awareness Is Vital
To Fundamental Change

DAY TWO – A.M.

Welcome back. You're on your way to acquiring a new set of invaluable skills. In fact, you'll soon see that being a good listener is like having a fifth ace up your sleeve. You'll have an advantage over everyone else who isn't a good listener.

Most people consider themselves to be better listeners than they really are. The first step to becoming a better listener begins with awareness. In today's assessment questionnaire, please don't try and assess the most desirable or seemingly correct answer. In order to understand your present listening skills, habits and tendencies, answer the following questions as honestly as you can. The idea behind yesterday's and today's assessment is to uncover your present habits. Later this week you're going to see why it's so vitally important that you get an accurate assessment of your present listening habits. That is why your complete honesty is so important in responding to the following questions. Put a checkmark on the *one* answer that most aligns with your first response.

Remember: It is only through awareness that we can begin to grow.

How Well Do I Listen?

	Almost Always	Often	Occasionally	Almost Never
1. I will listen to someone speak to me even when I'm not interested in what they have to say.	___	___	___	___
2. I remind myself when listening that I can learn something from everyone.	___	___	___	___
3. While a speaker is talking, I like to think about what I want to say so I can respond intelligently.	___	___	___	___
4. I pretend to be listening even when I'm not so I don't hurt the speaker's feelings.	___	___	___	___
5. While someone is telling me their problems, I concentrate on what advice I can give them.	___	___	___	___
6. I don't mind interrupting the speaker if I have something important to say.	___	___	___	___
7. When people complain to me about their problems I don't argue I just listen and allow them to vent.	___	___	___	___

PROGRAM

	Almost Always	Often	Occasionally	Almost Never

8. While a speaker is talking I like to think of a similar experience that I can share with them.

    _____   _____   _____   _____

9. I try to listen well enough so I can give my opinion and advice as soon as the speaker is finished talking.

    _____   _____   _____   _____

10. When someone is finished speaking I try to ask questions that will encourage the speaker to elaborate further about what's on their mind.

    _____   _____   _____   _____

11. I will focus on what the speaker is meaning and feeling and not just on the words they use.

    _____   _____   _____   _____

12. I will encourage people to go on when they have stopped talking.

    _____   _____   _____   _____

13. I can anticipate what a speaker will say before they finish, which allows me the chance to think of something else without getting bored.

    _____   _____   _____   _____

PROGRAM

	Almost Always	Often	Occasionally	Almost Never

14. When I'm talking to someone on the phone, my listening skill is good enough that I can multi-task (check email, read short notes) while they're speaking.

    _____   _____   _____   _____

15. When someone is explaining how upset they are, I will attempt to soothe their feelings by telling them I know exactly how they feel and that everything will turn out alright.

    _____   _____   _____   _____

16. As soon as a speaker pauses, I will share similar experiences of my own rather than encourage the speaker to elaborate.

    _____   _____   _____   _____

17. If a speaker has something important to say and I'm not in the mood or the timing isn't right, I'll suggest that we schedule another time.

    _____   _____   _____   _____

18. I try to make people feel that I'm interested in them and in what they have to say.

    _____   _____   _____   _____

19. I try to acknowledge what the speaker said before I respond with my point of view.

    _____   _____   _____   _____

PROGRAM

	Almost Always	Often	Occasionally	Almost Never
20. I focus on what the speaker is trying to communicate not just on the words they're using.	_____	_____	_____	_____
21. I wait until the speaker is completely finished speaking before forming my opinion.	_____	_____	_____	_____
22. I will often paraphrase what the speaker said so I know I've understood the message.	_____	_____	_____	_____
23. Whenever it's appropriate, and I need to remember certain points, I will take notes while the speaker is talking.	_____	_____	_____	_____
24. I can accept criticism without getting defensive.	_____	_____	_____	_____
25. When people tell me their problems I give them my helpful opinions and advice.	_____	_____	_____	_____
26. I consider good listening to be more instinctive than a skill that requires effort.	_____	_____	_____	_____

PROGRAM

	Almost Always	Often	Occasionally	Almost Never

27. If a speaker is interrupted and then asks me a short time later "where he left off," I can tell him where he left off.

    _____ _____ _____ _____

28. I can tell in the first few seconds if someone is worth listening to.

    _____ _____ _____ _____

29. While listening, I use body language (nodding my head, eye contact) to encourage the speaker to continue.

    _____ _____ _____ _____

30. If a speaker gets a little lost in finding the right word or words to express how they feel, I will jump in with the right words to help them out.

    _____ _____ _____ _____

Please circle the answer you chose in the numerical list that follows. For example; if you chose *Occasionally* for question number 1, then you would circle number 2 under *Occasionally* in that column. When you have finished circling all 30 answers add the totals in each column.

PROGRAM

	Almost Always	Often	Occasionally	Almost Never
1.	4	3	2	1
2.	4	3	2	1
3.	1	2	3	4
4.	1	2	3	4
5.	1	2	3	4
6.	1	2	3	4
7.	4	3	2	1
8.	1	2	3	4
9.	1	2	3	4
10.	4	3	2	1
11.	4	3	2	1
12.	4	3	2	1
13.	1	2	3	4
14.	1	2	3	4
15.	1	2	3	4
16.	1	2	3	4
17.	4	3	2	1
18.	4	3	2	1
19.	4	3	2	1
20.	4	3	2	1
21.	4	3	2	1
22.	4	3	2	1
23.	4	3	2	1
24.	4	3	2	1
25.	1	2	3	4
26.	1	2	3	4
27.	4	3	2	1
28.	1	2	3	4
29.	4	3	2	1
30.	1	2	3	4
TOTALS				

PROGRAM

Almost Always	=	_____
Often	=	_____
Occasionally	=	_____
Almost Never	=	_____
GRAND TOTAL	=	_____

What's your Grand Total?

Score/Ranking

- 100–120   Great
- 90–99   Very Good
- 75–89   Good
- 65–74   Fair
- Less than 65   You have a great deal to be excited about. You're going to experience massive change!

The higher the number the better your listening skills. If you didn't score a high number don't worry, that's why you're taking this program. If you happen to score a high number that means you're already a good listener but bear in mind, this is a life long skill that can never be fully mastered – there's always room for improvement.

STEP 2 – Today's step is a continuation of step one. Yesterday you began to notice both yourself and other people in conversation. When it comes to you, did you catch yourself thinking of something else during a conversation, or perhaps pre-judging where a conversation was going? While observing other people in conversation you may have begun to notice the myriad of physical signs that a "listener" will reveal to indicate either interest or boredom.

Try to observe (subtly of course) people in conversation and see how many nonverbal/physical signs you can begin to notice (on the part of the listener), that indicate their level of interest in the conversation. This is a vitally important communication skill that you will develop naturally over the next few weeks.

Here are just some of the physical signs ... I'll bet you'll have little trouble spotting which are positive and which are not!

PROGRAM

- Folding arms across chest
- relaxed open manner
- tilting the head
- drumming fingers
- smiling
- bouncing a leg
- nodding
- sitting forward in the chair
- sighing
- frowning
- looking away from the speaker
- remaining silent
- raising an eyebrow
- closed body posture
- open body posture
- sitting perfectly still
- glazed eyes
- forced or frozen smile
- eye contact
- fidgeting
- attending to distractions: cell phone, email
- wandering eyes, etc.

DAY TWO – P.M. MESSAGE

Give yourself a pat on the back for taking the time to assess your listening skills.

The Power of Visualization

A final thought – There are two times of the day that your subconscious mind is most receptive – when you first wake up and when you're just about to fall asleep. When you first wake, think about the many opportunities you have throughout your day to communicate with the most important people in your life. Think about the powerful influence you can have on your spouse, your kids, and your friends when you can listen empathically, and make them feel deeply understood.

Remember, in order to listen empathically and nonjudgmentally, and to see the world as the speaker sees it, is truly one of the greatest gifts you can give to another person. To do this requires skill and effort. We will examine this in depth later in the program, but for now, picture yourself exercising empathic listening, and imagine how much it will mean to the most important people in your life. How much will it affect your business relations? Picturing a desirable outcome for even ten or twenty seconds will have a powerful effect after a short period of time.

Since this is the last message for today, try to remember visualizing the way you would like to see yourself just as you are about to drift off to sleep. This will begin to set up active and magnetic forces unlike anything you can believe. Remember, the last thing you think of before you go to sleep is what your subconscious mind has to work with all night long. Whatever your subconscious mind consistently has to work with, you will consistently move toward.

Since you're always thinking about something just before you go to sleep, you might just as well train yourself to think of something you desire!

Whatever the mind of man can conceive and believe, it can achieve.
~ Napoleon Hill

See you tomorrow!

DAY THREE
Awareness Is Vital
To Fundamental Change

DAY THREE - A.M.

Welcome back to *29 DAYS ... to becoming a great listener and communicator!*

> *I remind myself every morning:*
> *Nothing I say this day will teach me anything.*
> *So if I'm going to learn, I must do it by listening.*
> *~ Larry King*

If listening is so important, why are we generally so poor at it?

Effective listening requires some effort, lots of awareness, but even more than that, it's vitally important to eradicate some faulty assumptions. Our formal education, from grades one through eight, is geared toward reading and writing. I'm willing to bet that the extent of your listening training went something like this:

- "Pay attention!"
- "Would you just shut up and listen?"
- "Why don't you ever listen to me?!?!"
- "You're too young to understand!"
- "Children should be seen and not heard."

Does that sound about right?

A number of years ago educational researcher Dr. Paul Rankin conducted a pioneer study on listening which has since been confirmed many times. These studies show that seventy percent of our waking hours involve some form of verbal communication.

PROGRAM

The four forms of communication are reading, writing, speaking and listening. Just as a quick exercise, see if you can put the four types of communication in the order in which we use them from *most* to *least*.

In the space to the right put a 1 beside the *most used skill* down to a 4 to the *least used skill*.

1. Reading   _____
2. Writing   _____
3. Listening   _____
4. Speaking   _____

Great. Now that you have ranked the four forms of communication, according to their daily use, let's do one more. This time rank them according to how much time is spent teaching us the four forms. Think back to the first eight years (grades one through eight) of your formal education. Proportionately, how much time was given to teaching us to effectively use these four communication skills?

In the space to the right put a number 'one' beside the communication skill that was taught the most, down to a number 'four' next to the communication skill that was taught the least.

1. Reading   _____
2. Writing   _____
3. Listening   _____
4. Speaking   _____

Now let's look at the actual results that studies have found. The ways in which we communicate throughout our typical day breakdown as follows: 9% of our time is spent on writing; 16% reading; 30% talking; and a whopping 45% listening!

We spend a total of forty-five percent of our verbal communication as listeners, and yet it's highly unlikely you received a single minute of *listening instruction* throughout your entire formal education! In fact, the order in which we use each skill is *inversely* proportional to the amount of time educational courses devote to teaching it.

Speaking can be taught but it will generally be relegated to an elective course that a student may or may not choose, and reading is generally taught only up to grade six. Writing, the least used skill of all, is given the most attention in formal English courses.

I believe the reason for this lack of training is simply this: as a society we take listening for granted.

We begin our formal education in grade one with the *basic ability* to "speak" and "listen" but as yet, we haven't acquired *any* skills in reading or writing. Therefore the given assumption is that speaking and listening are natural skills. It's further assumed that one's listening ability is based largely on intelligence. Smart students will naturally listen well and poor students will naturally listen poorly. It's all pre-determined like the color of our eyes. These assumptions are gravely mistaken. Listening effectively is as much a technical skill as is reading. In other words, it can be learned.

Learning to listen well is not necessarily based on I.Q. or intelligence. A poor listener is not necessarily an unintelligent person. A poor listener is generally someone who has never been taught the art and skill of *effective* listening. The typical student graduates from school with an "acceptable" level of reading skills, and an "unacceptable" level of listening skills that is neither graded nor considered. These students then enter the workforce where their listening skills will be required about three times as much as their reading skills, which makes it easy to see why the *effective listener* has such a distinct advantage over the poor listener.

How often do you listen to a speaker on a podium, or even when you're in conversation with a close friend, and you catch yourself half-listening and half-thinking of a completely unrelated subject? We may often write this off as simple boredom – which technically may be true – but the reason is that our conscious mind *is* actually bored if we don't train ourselves to listen effectively.

Unless you're an auctioneer, most of us speak at about 125 words per minute. Our conscious minds however can easily process and understand more than 400 words per minute. If we're not skilled listeners, we use the difference between "speaking speed" and "thought speed" to allow our minds to wander off to other "more interesting" matters. As you'll see later on, learning to keep your attention on the speaker is what separates good listeners from poor listeners.

There have been numerous studies and tests on our general efficiency as listeners. As I just said, we have the capacity to absorb much more information than the rate at which a speaker delivers it, but how good are we at retaining that which is delivered? Would you believe awful?

Quick question: When you tell someone a story, or give them instructions, how much of what you said do you think that person will usually remember? Go ahead, give this a moment's thought and come up with a guess.

PROGRAM

Week One: Commitment and Awareness ~ 141

I hope you *did* come up with a guess so that next time you're either thinking to yourself "Why don't people ever listen?" or, if you catch yourself saying directly to someone, "I just finished telling you ... what's the matter with you, can't you listen?!" then you'll know that the correct, and honest answer from most people would be, "Yes I can listen, but I only listen at a twenty-five percent rate of efficiency!" That's right, twenty-five percent! Our untrained listening ears will rapidly forget seventy-five percent of what was said.

There is however one exception to this rule, it happens every time we either commit a slip-of-the-tongue or we put-our-foot-in-our mouth, in those "rare" circumstances, you can count on the listener to accurately remember one-hundred percent of what we said. I think it has something to do with Murphy's Law!

Numerous studies have shown that immediately after listening to a ten-minute oral presentation, the *typical* listener has heard, understood and retained, only fifty percent of what was said no matter how hard they try to retain more. That wouldn't be too bad if it only stopped there, but it gets worse. Within eight hours, the retention rate drops off a further fifty percent for a net total of twenty-five percent retention. It's not a bad idea to be aware of that statistic the next time you're doling out large quantities of information ... especially if you consider that what you have to say is vitally important.

STEP 3 - Today's step is to continue to generate greater awareness of the art of listening. Try to be aware of your own self-dialogue. Try to catch your "self-talk" when your mind is wandering. (We will look into this much deeper over the next several days). Try to become acutely aware of your *present* ability to really listen to what other people are saying to you.

Notice how other people speak and listen to each other. You can have so much fun with this. If you keep a keen eye and ear open you'll probably have to keep from laughing at some of the pretend listening games you'll notice all around you.

JOURNAL ENTRY

Awareness Is Vital To Fundamental Change

Please answer the following questions as thoroughly as you can. You need an acute feeling of where you are presently, and where you want to be in the days, weeks and months ahead.

Without strong motives it may be very difficult to change. If you can begin to see the incredible power and joy that strong listening skills will give you, then you'll find the whole process to be fun and enriching.

Why do I want to acquire good listening skills?

_____

_____

_____

_____

_____

What will keen listening and communication skills do for my relationships at work?

_____

_____

_____

_____

_____

How will good listening and communication skills affect my relationships with my spouse, partner, family and friends? (Give this some serious consideration.)

_____

_____

_____

_____

_____

To become a truly gifted listener is a rare quality. When I become a good listener and communicator my life will be enriched in the following ways ...

_____

_____

_____

_____

PROGRAM

Week One: Commitment and Awareness ~ 143

Everything has been said before,
but since nobody listens
we have to keep going back and beginning all over again.
~ Andre Gide

DAY THREE – P.M. MESSAGE

Congratulations, you've completed three full days!

Did You Know?
There is an International Listening Association (ILA). Their website is;

http://www.listen.org

The ILA is an organization dedicated to the study, development and teaching of effective listening. They define effective listening as:

The process of receiving, constructing meaning from,
and responding to spoken and/or non-verbal messages.

They stress that this definition clearly includes non-verbal messages as well. In other words, if you're talking to someone and their head continually falls forward in a sleeping mode, it shouldn't be necessary for them to verbalize that they're bored!

When you go to bed this evening, and just before you go to sleep, visualize yourself immersed in effective communication. Picture successful results with your spouse, your kids, your business associates. Picture yourself being thanked or congratulated for making the time and effort to sincerely listen to someone else.

Remember, the last thing you think of before you go to sleep is what your subconscious mind has to work with all night long.

Patience and perseverance have a magical effect before which
difficulties disappear and obstacles vanish.
~ John Quincy Adams

See you tomorrow!

29 DAYS . . . to becoming a great listener and communicator!

DAY FOUR
Awareness Is Vital
To Fundamental Change

DAY FOUR - A.M.

Welcome back. It's day four. When it comes to effective communication, most of us tend to think that the words we use and how we string them together is the most crucial part of effective communication. In some cases it may be so, but in many cases it *may not* be nearly as important as we may think ... even in sales! Many sales people think that if they can only get their pitch down perfectly, they'll connect with the buyer and make the sale. Not necessarily so.

Several years ago, motivational speaker and basketball coach extraordinaire, Rick Pitino, wrote a wonderful motivational book titled, *Success is a Choice: Ten Steps to Overachieving in Business and in Life.* In that book he shared a most interesting story about the value of listening.

At the time Rick made this personal communication discovery, he was head basketball coach at the University of Kentucky. Part of his duties as head coach were to help recruit the best talent from the nation's high school ranks. To say that a top prospect would be heavily courted would be an understatement. A top high school athlete will be "sold" and cajoled from all the top schools and agents. He will see some very well-thought-out proposals, that outline in great detail, the advantages for choosing University X over University Y.

The normal procedure for recruitment would be to send the prospective player some promotional material that would immediately be followed up by a University representative. Following that, the assistant coaches would become involved and when the prospect is finally wide-eyed with wonder, in comes the head coach to close the deal.

PROGRAM

The problem lies in the fact that there's a whole bunch of schools all doing the same thing so the eventual winning school is going to have to do something unique to stand out from the others.

As Rick described it, his job on recruiting assignments was to try and *convince* both the player and his family that Kentucky was the best choice.

Please note: I put the word "convince" in italics.

Rick said he had his routine down cold. Along with a couple of assistants, who had already "softened" the prospect up, he would visit with the player and his family at their home, and talk at great length about the numerous advantages of the Kentucky program. He would rattle off how the player would get to play in front of twenty-three thousand fans, how Kentucky played a national schedule, their TV exposure, the weight-training facilities, the academic programs, the support programs and on and on. Along with all the enthusiasm, passion, charm, and persuasive powers he could muster, Rick used every possible nuance he could think of in his effort to *convince* the young player and his family that Kentucky was their "only choice."

When Rick and his coaches had finally finished their presentation and were driving away, Rick would throw out the inevitable question: "Well what do you think? How did we do? Do you think the young man's going to choose Kentucky?"

Invariably the answers Rick heard from the others was; "Coach, you were fantastic! You covered everything. How couldn't he accept? If we're not accepted, we'll be the second choice for sure."

Then Rick relayed that all too frequently they would follow-up with the player and his family in the next day or two, only to learn that they weren't even among the top five choices! Rick started to give this unexpected result a lot of thought and introspection. He began to ask himself what had he done wrong? What had he missed saying?

Rick would meet with the coaches and begin to question if he was lacking in enthusiasm ... after all, selling is mostly a transference of feeling. Or perhaps he hadn't stressed the academic part enough. Or maybe he hadn't articulated the overall program as well as he could have. The more Rick raised these concerns the more certain he became that they weren't the cause of his failure to get through to these young men and their families. His enthusiasm and performance were not the problem.

Rick's gut instinct told him he needed a radically different approach. From that point on, when Rick went to a new recruit's home he kept the laundry list of Kentucky's advantages in the bag. Instead, he went into the home with the attitude of learning about the player and what was most important to him. He began to ask what the player and the family were looking for from both an academic program and a basketball program. After asking the probing questions Rick then did the most powerful thing of all ... he *stopped talking* and began to *listen*. Rick was keen to let the player and his family do most of the talking.

When these *listening* meetings were over, and Rick and his coaches were driving away, once again the inevitable questions and impressions were discussed. "How do you guys think it went?" Rick would ask. "Well Coach, I'm not too sure about it. I have a feeling it wasn't your best effort. I think we're going to miss out on this one. You failed to mention a lot of the benefits that Kentucky has to offer."

The next day when they would do the follow-up call after a "listening" meeting, they would invariably find that they were either the first or second choice!

What had happened? Was it a case of the recruit not caring about all the wonderful facilities, the programs and the national exposure? Not at all. Those things are obviously important. But even as attractive as those perks may be, they simply don't rank when it comes to someone feeling like they've been listened to and understood. Rick realized that effective listening and communication was crucial to building a relationship of trust. Somehow next to the feeling of being genuinely listened to, a stellar presentation and slick performance carried little significance.

Rick Patino summed up the valuable lesson as this; *"It's not always what we say; often it's what we allow the other person to say. By listening, we gain trust and make other people feel more comfortable with us."*

Rick said that if he had to give a listening/speaking ratio, he would suggest that you strive to listen four times more than you speak.

Rick asks and answers the question: What is communication all about? "It's all about winning!" he says, but he doesn't stop there, he goes on to qualify what he means by winning. "We all know people who think that they can only win when someone else loses. We all know people who feel they must win every discussion and every argument. They're constantly bulldozing their way through life completely oblivious to the anger, hurt and disgust they leave in their wake. Besides being obnoxious and irritating they broadcast to the world that they don't care about anyone else's opinion."

If your goal in a discussion is to win, rather than to arrive at a meeting of the minds, you are simply *incapable* of being a good listener or communicator. Real winning is having the courage, the grace, and the fortitude, to find common ground. To seek solutions that literally benefit both parties. There are *always* win/win solutions available, but to find them requires desire and *courage*.

STEP 4 - Today's step is to continue to generate greater awareness of the art of listening. Can you recall any instances where you were in a sales mode in which you expressed greater concern for your delivery than you did to the prospect's needs and desires?

JOURNAL ENTRY

Awareness Is Vital To Fundamental Change

Can you recall a time when you know your focus was on what you were saying, and now looking back, you're certain the outcome could have been so much better if you had focused your energy and attention on listening.

I recall the time ...

_____

_____

_____

_____

Courage is what it takes to stand up and speak;
courage is also what it takes to sit down and listen.
~ Winston Churchill

PROGRAM

DAY FOUR – P.M. MESSAGE

Welcome back.

If A equals success, then the formula is A equals X plus Y and Z,
with X being work, Y play, and Z keeping your mouth shut.
~ Albert Einstein

One of the most important lessons in being a good listener and communicator is knowing when to "shut-up!"

In 1984, Mark McCormack, the founder of IMG (International Management Group), wrote an international bestseller titled *What They Don't Teach You at Harvard Business School*. It was a great title and an even better read. In the book he shared many stories, anecdotes and lessons he learned in his many years of business - the very things you *don't* learn in school.

One such story he shared was the value of silence ... especially in sales.

Mark was in London with one of his key executives who had just finished giving an outstanding IMG presentation to a group of business men. When the executive had finished there was a natural moment of silence as everyone took a moment to gather their thoughts and absorb the full implication of the proposal. As they glanced at each other to see who would be first to respond, the executive, who had made the presentation, leapt back into his presentation with a further summary of the positive aspects of the proposal.

Once again when he finished there was another natural moment of silence. Again, unable to allow the silence or to contain himself, the executive dove back in with yet another summation, never once allowing anyone a chance to speak. He actually did this a number of times until Mark McCormack had to laugh out loud, cut the executive off and suggest he allow someone else a chance to talk.

As Mark pointed out, there comes a point in any sales presentation when no one should be talking. Silence has so many different selling applications. In order to learn what the client wants the seller must listen. Silence can keep you from saying more than you need to and often more than you should.

A number of years ago, when I was in my late teens or very early twenties, (that's my excuse) I sold stereo equipment as a commissioned salesman. I'll never forget the time I talked myself right out of a sale. To this day it rankles as one of my life's most embarrassing moments.

A young man had just purchased a new home and his father's housewarming gift to his son was going to be a complete stereo system. I saw the two gentlemen browsing through the store and I approached them to see if I could be of any assistance. They told me roughly what they had in mind. I responded with the usual probing questions such as; What had they seen so far? What did they like, dislike? Did they have any preferences? And so on. The father mentioned that several years ago he purchased a complete "XYZ" system that he was happy with, but his son wanted something a little different.

After fully "qualifying" the son's needs and wants, I showed them a variety of amps, tuners, reel-to-reel tape players, speakers and on and on. Eventually the son settled on the items he wanted, which naturally brought us to the final question; "Would you prefer to take the equipment home today, or shall we arrange delivery?"

The father said that they would take it with them so I began to write it up. It was a rather substantial purchase and it took a number of minutes to fill in the serial numbers and all the other requisite warranty details. Then, as I was near the end of the paperwork, the father mentioned again that he had purchased his stereo package from us several years earlier and he and his wife had really enjoyed it. The father then asked me to give him my "honest" opinion of what I thought of his sound system.

To this day I shudder at what I said. I told him that I thought that particular unit was a little overpriced for what it was, and that there were a number of similar systems on the market that had better sound and were actually priced a little less. I told him that it was highly likely the salesman sold him that unit only because it payed out the highest commission. Can you imagine, in all your days anyone saying anything so utterly stupid, insensitive and purposeless as what I had just said?

As I was completing the last details of the bill of sale, while pontificating about how he should have really purchased "ABC" or "KYP" the father interrupted me just long enough to say he and his son wanted to think things over, but he would be sure to get back to me. The nice man was saying this as he and his son were walking toward the door.

PROGRAM

If I live to be the age of *Methuselah* I will never be able to explain what possessed me to say what I said. To this day I can't think about that incident without feeling queasy.

I share this embarrassing story for one reason; with any luck at all, it may serve as an extreme reminder of the value of silence.

Although anyone would be hard-pressed to come up with an example of someone saying anything as dumb as I did, I believe that a number of sales are lost *after* the sale is "all but made," because the salesperson just can't manage to shut-up. The salesperson too often has just one more thing to say, or worse, they begin to tell the customer how clever they are and what a great deal they just made. Nothing makes a customer more suspicious than a salesperson telling them they practically stole the goods at the price they paid.

If you do have to talk *after* the close, change the subject to something neutral, perhaps the weather.

> *One of the lessons of history is that nothing is often a good thing to do*
> *and always a clever thing to say.*
> *~ Ariel Durant*

Congratulations on another successful day.

See you tomorrow.

DAY FIVE
Awareness Is Vital
To Fundamental Change

DAY FIVE - A.M.

Hey, welcome back. We're on day five and you're still hanging in. Congratulations! By now you're noticing some of your own listening habits as well as the habits of other people in your life. Being aware of your thoughts and recognizing your unique patterns represents huge progress toward positive change. As I said earlier, before your goal can be accomplished you need both the desire and commitment. Commitment is crucial to carry you over, under, around and through the times when you find it "more convenient" to fall back into your old habits. You might also be surprised at what you're discovering, the most valuable communication skill we have, *listening*, is seldom practiced with any degree of awareness.

The Three Levels of Listening

It's only natural that we listen at different levels of interest throughout the day. If you're sitting at an airport and reading a novel while waiting for your flight to depart, it's highly unlikely you're listening to the extraneous surroundings at a very intense or active level. If you're in a job interview and the interviewer is relaying some details about the position, odds are that you're listening at a fairly intense/active level.

We are going to reference listening levels as *one, two* and *three*. Level *one* being highly focused, active listening, and level *three* being low intensity listening. These references will help you understand the different types of listening that we consciously or unconsciously employ, and when it's appropriate or desirable, to actively use each of them.

Naturally it's not practical, or necessary to listen at a highly focused level in many circumstances. In fact, if we tried we would be mentally exhausted before the day was half over. Some

PROGRAM

of us *may* find, for example, that at work we're highly-focused listeners but at home we're only partial listeners. Or perhaps the opposite is true.

Each level of listening requires a degree of concentration and sensitivity. The important thing is to be aware of our listening levels and intensity, and when to use the appropriate level.

Level-Three Listening

The characteristics of level-three listening are the trademark of *inactive* listening. Sometimes this is the appropriate or "acceptable" level of listening, and other times it's reflective of just plain bad listening habits.

Level-three listening is characterized by tuning in and out, passive listening, thinking of unrelated matters, forming rebuttals or advice, and highly selective listening. Like our airport example earlier, when you sense your flight information is being announced you quickly tune-in, your listening intensity goes to high alert. The moment the information is received your listening attention quickly returns to tune-out mode.

Another example of level-three listening is quiet, passive listening. You might be in a tour group and the guide is explaining the history behind an artifact in which you have little interest. In this situation you comfortably tune the speaker out to a level of a drone since you're confident no one will single you out to ask your opinion on the matter.

Other characteristics of level-three listening encompass the area of bad listening habits. "Fake" listening is the most likely scenario. In this situation you're supposed to be listening but you're clearly not. You've either fallen into a dumb, blank stare and perma-grin, or you're cherry-picking a few key words just to get the general drift but no more. Your only connection to the speaker's words are your physical responses such as nodding, or vocal sounds such as "uh-huh" "yeah right." Your main purpose is to give the impression of attentive listening while your mind considers other more interesting matters. If the conversation is of interest – but only in the realm of what *you're going to say* – then you'll focus only on your response, and at the first available opening – usually when the speaker stops for a millisecond to catch a breath - you leap in with your dialogue.

There are times when level-three listening is perfectly appropriate, but when it's not, it's the hallmark of poor listening habits.

Level-Two Listening

At level-two the "listener" is hearing the words but is listening perfunctorily. Ironically enough, the "listener" may even be capable of reciting back – verbatim – every word that was spoken, and still not qualify as having really "listened."

In most cases, listening at this level is surface listening – that is, the words are heard and registered, but the deeper meaning and intent is not heard. In other words, the listener hears what the speaker is saying but does not make any attempt to understand if the speaker is implying a deeper meaning. At this level a speaker is more concerned with content rather than feeling.

In many cases this level of listening can be perfectly adequate. In fact, it's a perfectly suitable form of listening for many occasions; however, in other situations it can become dangerous.

Suppose someone is telling you about their drive into work that morning. They describe the severe thunderstorms and high winds they experienced, and how they had to convert to the rules of a four-way-stop sign when they came to a traffic light that was knocked out, and so on. In this case the speaker is relating an incident that you might find interesting at a certain level, but you can be comfortable that there's not a deeper meaning or an underlying message. It's a simple story without any deeper implication. In this case the speaker doesn't expect us to hang on every word and only a certain level of listening activity is required.

In other instances level-two and level-three listening can become both critical and dangerous, as is the case when the speaker is relaying something of vital importance and we're going through the ritual of pretending to listen. When this happens in the case of important instructions, the problem is compounded. Not only has the message not been received, but the speaker is under the impression that it *was* received, and he/she will usually expect some kind of action or result from the "listener." If the speaker *knew* that the message wasn't received, or understood, then some action to correct the miscommunication could be taken. Since the speaker is unaware of the communication breakdown, some type of problem will invariably follow.

A third instance of level-two listening is in *interactive communication.* This is one of the most common causes of poor relationships at home or at work. This can often be classified as selective listening, where the "listener" is only interested in speaking – not listening. The listener is doing just enough to hear the words in order to support the point they want to make. This type of listening can be noted by one person interrupting the other to express his opinion, which obviously takes precedence over what the speaker is attempting to say. This type of listener is operating from his own agenda.

PROGRAM

Other tactics the level-two listener may employ is to fall into polite silence, maintain eye contact and even encourage the speaker to continue, but the listening level fails to penetrate any deeper than analytical listening, which is clearly detached from any form of empathy or understanding.

Level-One Listening

This is the highest level of listening. Level-one listening requires energy, maturity, skill and most of all, courage.

Within the realm of level-one listening we can include: *reflective listening* – summarizing our understanding of what the speaker said, *active listening* – which requires an injection of energy, both physical and mental, on the part of the listener to fully understanding the speaker's message.

Beyond *reflective* and *active* listening, there's an even greater form of listening that is called *empathic listening*. This is the area of skilled listening that requires the listener to put himself into the speaker's skin in an attempt to see the world through the speaker's eyes. It requires that the listener not only hear the words, but to also feel what the speaker is saying. The *empathic listener* is looking to find the deeper meaning of the words expressed. This means clueing into the speaker's total message: body language, tonality, language patterns, meaning and feeling.

Empathic listening is the only *acceptable* level of listening when someone is attempting to pour out their feelings or is talking about something that is personal, emotional or vitally important.

In all forms of level-one listening, the listener refrains from judging the speaker, interrupting, or attempting to share his/her view or give advice. The listener makes every attempt to suspend his own thoughts and feelings. The listener's goal is to see the world from the speaker's perspective.

It is vitally important that the speaker is able to sense *non-judgment* from the listener. The listener can aid the speaker by paraphrasing what the speaker has said, so that even if the listener wasn't correct in their initial understanding, it conveys a willingness to understand.

To fully listen at a level-one requires more than just active listening. It calls for full immersion into the perspective of the speaker. It means becoming fully aware of the speaker's feelings, emotions, values and beliefs. To achieve this requires acceptance of the person, not just acceptance of what they are saying.

STEP 5 - Today's step is to begin to become aware of the three levels of listening. Try to notice any patterns you may have to automatically listen at level two or three. Can you catch yourself listening at a level that isn't appropriate for the occasion? Can you notice other people listening at levels that aren't appropriate for the occasion?

If you're giving someone instructions or telling them something that you feel is important, what can you do to make sure that you've been understood?

JOURNAL ENTRY

Awareness Is Vital To Fundamental Change

Level-one listening requires energy, action, maturity and most of all courage. Without courage it is unlikely that we will risk our vulnerable feelings and opinions. When we listen to understand another person, we may find that our opinions of certain matters are susceptible to change. That is a high-risk venture that only a courageous person will attempt.

Can you recall a time in your life when you really listened (empathically) at level one? If so can you recall how it made you feel? Can you recall how it made the speaker feel?

_____

_____

_____

_____

_____

_____

Can you recall a time when you failed to listen at level one, (perhaps you were unaware of how to listen at this level) but in retrospect you wish you would have?

_____

_____

_____

_____

The need to listen empathically may not be a common everyday occurrence in your life. Usually because of fear, we all have a natural resistance to listen empathically. In the future, when empathic listening may be required, what may hold you back from doing so? Try to uncover the obstacles you might face when confronted by this situation. If you can't think of anything at this stage that's okay, we still have lots of ground to cover. If you can identify some obvious resistance areas to empathic listening jot them down.

_____

_____

_____

_____

_____

Listening is a powerful thing, a creative force.
The people who listen to us attract us.
When we are listened to, it creates us.
As if by magic it makes us unfold, expand and reach.

DAY FIVE – P.M. MESSAGE

Welcome back.

Since this *first week* is about commitment and awareness, you will also need to be aware of every trick your inner-self (amygdala) has in store for you, in its attempt to combat change. If you're aware of your amygdala's tricks, you won't be ambushed into failure. You have decided that you want to become a good (great) listener and communicator. Wonderful. Ask yourself, are there any negative consequences to this goal?

Your first reaction might be, "What, are you kidding? How could there be any negatives to becoming a good listener?" Think deeper. There are in fact a number of issues that your amygdala will drag out ... and implanting fear will be its ace card.

Many of us sidestep empathic listening because if we put ourselves into the speaker's shoes we might begin to see the world from another point of view and that may mean changing the way we think. In fact, it might mean that we need to alter our "safe, secure" views of the world. To take a deep interest in someone else means leaving our protective shell and suspending our own interests. This can be nothing short of terrifying for most people. It suggests abandoning - even temporarily - our most cherished beliefs and dogmas, our certainty that our view of the world is the one true version that's most inline with truth.

To listen empathically we must further suspend judgment, and our overriding desire to either criticize or dole out advice. For a parent to listen deeply, to really try and see the world through their child's eyes, and to suspend giving advice, can be one of the biggest challenges they face.

To become a good listener it is wise to consider what it really means. The dividends will be huge, but make no mistake, it requires courage and conviction.

For the next week or so you might want to give this a good deal of consideration. You might want to ask yourself if you will commit to this new challenge. The fact that you've chosen to take this program speaks volumes about your desire to become an effective listener and communicator. You can and you will become a highly skilled listener and communicator - provided you're really committed to change. Many people may think that the attainment of this skill simply requires that they commit a little more attention and focus on the speaker's words. This may be true for level-two and level-three listening, but if you want to become an effective level-one listener, you will need a deep desire. You will need resolve, and you will need courage.

I am telling you this now because it's vital that you begin to tell your inner-self that becoming a good listener and communicator is something you deeply desire. When you plant the desire with strong emotion, the inner forces at your disposal will magically come to your aid.

By being aware of these "hidden fears" now, you will be well prepared when they pop up ... and they will. That's your amygdala. Let it know who's in control. When the inevitable negative thoughts arrive you can readily dismiss them.

PROGRAM

Congratulations on another successful day.

When you go to bed this evening try to focus for a few seconds on how effective level-one listening might influence the most important people in your life. Imagine that deep connection with your spouse or child that would result from seeing the world from their perspective.

Any time you can strongly visualize, you are programming your future because your mind *will* move in that direction automatically.

Remember, the last thing you think of before you go to sleep is what your subconscious mind has to work with all night long.

> *"When people talk, listen completely.*
> *Most people never listen."*
> *~ Ernest Hemingway*

See you tomorrow.

PROGRAM

DAY SIX
Awareness Is Vital
To Fundamental Change

DAY SIX - A.M.

Welcome back, we're on day six.

Now that you're aware of the three levels of listening, take a deeper look at your listening habits throughout the day. See if you can catch yourself listening at a level-three when you should be at a level-two or even vice versa. Do you have a tendency to begin to listen to a conversation at a level-two or even a level-one and then quickly drop your attention to a lower level? This may be perfectly valid if you find a conversation doesn't warrant as much attention as you first thought. If you remind yourself to listen intently at the beginning of a conversation can you remain focused for the entire conversation? Do you take notes when it's appropriate? Does your mood or the time of day affect your ability to focus on what you're listening to?

Remember: The more important your goal is to you, the more your inner-self will try to keep you from going after it. Your inner-self sees an important goal as frightening, difficult, and potential for failure. It would prefer that you not attempt anything new, especially going out on a limb as "dangerous" as temporarily abandoning your "cherished, unshakable" view of the world. Your amygdala wants no part of change and no risk of failure!

Enjoying your life as a great listener and communicator will bring bountiful returns in your most valued relationships. The payoffs will be beyond what you can imagine right now. Be aware however, that your amygdala will try to paint a portrait of an empathic listener as being soft, easily manipulated, wishy-washy and someone without conviction. In fact, nothing can be further from reality. To become a great listener and communicator requires fortitude and courage. It's truly one of the most noble traits you can obtain.

PROGRAM

In the spirit of slow, gentle, daily progress, you *will* become a good listener in a surprisingly short period of time if you practice the first rule of lifelong change ... patience and perseverance. The best part is that once you begin to apply your new listening and communication skills, you're going to find this pursuit both fun and exhilarating.

This next statement may not be news to you but the fact is ...

You Are Surprisingly Similar to Your Parents!
(or early childhood caregivers)

Don't you just love it when someone says to you, "You're just like your mother or your father."

Whether you like it or not, and in many more ways than you may care to admit, you are!

I'll bet you're thinking: "That might be true for other people but there's absolutely no way it could apply to me." Whatever your present listening and communication skills may be, unless you've had specific training, your skills and habits will very closely mirror those of your parents. As I've said, being acutely aware of your present listening habits is vital to change, but equally important, is to be able to ascertain how you came to acquire your present habits and patterns.

The following informational piece is a little longer than the standard morning's information, so we're going to break it up into two parts. Today you will read part one and tomorrow morning you'll be given the second part.

PART ONE – Are We Really Clones of Our Parents? ... 'Fraid So!

Whether you realize it or admit it, in many ways you are a carbon copy of your parents, and the truth of the matter is, you genuinely don't realize it. Let's look at how this "insidious" thing happens.

In *29 DAYS ... to a habit you want!* we talked about the four states of mind: *beta, alpha, theta* and *delta*. To briefly recap – these states-of-mind indicate brain activity. When you're awake and totally active, you're in a beta state, which means your brain waves oscillate between 14 and 35 cycles per second (cps). That means you're conscious, active and aware. When you daydream or you're focusing on watching a movie for example, you're in an expanded state of awareness which is the alpha state. Your brain activity in alpha operates between 8 and 13 cps, which means that your "conscious intensity level" is turned down and you're much more receptive to incoming influence.

When you relax even further you enter the theta state where brain activity slows to 4 to 7 cps, which is often equivalent to a hypnotic state. Beta is associated with focus and awareness of the environment and the outside world, whereas the alpha and theta states are more internally focused and self-reflective. The fourth state is delta which registers 1 to 3 cps. When you're in the delta state you're in a completely non-conscious deep sleep.

The interesting thing to note for our discussion is this: adult humans spend most of their day in the beta state of awareness. Children six and under have not yet developed a beta state.

From the time you were a developing fetus up until you were about six years old, your entire life was spent in theta. When you were in theta, you were incapable of filtering, evaluating or screening incoming information. You simply downloaded everything as verbatim. The first six years of your life was all input. It equates to massive download and lots of programming. Once your impressions and experiences are programmed, unless deliberately changed, they become your character traits, habits and behaviors. They become the programs that run your subconscious mind. You weren't responsible for this early programming; in fact, you weren't even aware of the installation, but nonetheless, there it is. That's why we're so much like our parents. We are the direct result of our early environment and the nonconscious acceptance of suggestions and influence from our parents.

"That's NOT acceptable. I want to change my programming!"

The good news is you can. In fact, that's what this *29 DAYS* program is all about. You are going to change your pre-wired listening and communication habits to new, more desirable ones of your choosing. The bad news is that this involves a little more than simple positive thinking. As you may know by now, it's a case of getting both the conscious and the subconscious minds to begin pulling on the same end of the rope of your new desire.

Your conscious mind is the creative mind that you use to make "conscious" choices. It's with this mind that you create your personal identity. Your subconscious mind on the other hand is the vast "super recorder," an information processor that takes charge of every necessity in your life that the conscious mind either cannot or chooses not to focus on.

On the pure ability to process information, your subconscious mind is a million times more powerful than your conscious mind. A million times more powerful! Your subconscious mind is capable of performing billions of calculations per second in order to tend to your biological needs. Your subconscious thoughts run about ninety to ninety-five percent of your affairs. While your conscious mind is grappling with the weighty matters of deciding between "ham and cheese" or "turkey on rye" your subconscious is orchestrating the entire show.

PROGRAM

Remember what we said previously about our early years (up to six-years-old) when we lived in the magical world of theta? At that time we lacked screens or filters. We were *incapable* of deciding what made logical sense and what should be dismissed as irrelevant or subjective opinion. Everything was taken at face value and logged. If our parents said we were "wonderful" or if they suggested we were "selfish and lazy," our subconscious would store this information without qualification.

So what we have is this vast, super-powerful recorder-processor with a whole lot of programs … some good and some not so good. The good programs are the ones that make us confident and willing to take on challenges. The bad programs are the ones that suggest "I'm shy, I'm not artistic, I'm not athletic, I can't concentrate, I'm not very good at listening, I'm clumsy … and on and on.

These negative programs are our "kryptonite."

"How do I combat these negative programs?"

We hear over and over that the key to overcoming these negative programs is to just think positive thoughts. The problem with that oversimplified suggestion is that positive thinking takes place in the conscious mind. Stacking the conscious mind against the subconscious mind is like pitting the proverbial ninety-five pound weakling against the 800-pound gorilla. The conscious mind says, "I can achieve anything I set my mind to," while the subconscious mind says, "I don't think so. I've got an old program here from your early years where your father said you'd never amount to anything."

This represents two opposing thoughts pulling on opposite ends of a rope. Unfortunately, the subconscious isn't about to lose this tug-of-war.

Here's the further problem. While you might try to consciously flood your mind with positive thoughts, you can't continue to do so indefinitely. At some point you have to think about your job, getting dressed and what's for dinner. As soon as your conscious mind focuses on other matters, the subconscious takes over and starts up the old programs, which means that for ninety-five percent of the time you're running on pre-programs, ergo, reciting a few positive thoughts here and there when you remember to do so, will have limited effect on your daily life and long-term results.

"Are the conscious and subconscious minds locked in a never ending battle of our conscious desires? Always playing second fiddle to our old established progams?"

Until we can align the two minds to the same purpose … the answer is generally *yes*.

Our conscious mind is continually handing over duties and responsibilities to the subconscious. Imagine yourself as an overworked boss who is desperately understaffed. Then one glorious day your problems are over when in walks the employee of your dreams. He is capable of handling every single task given to him with absolute perfection. In fact, not only can he do the work of ten employees perfectly, he can handle *your job* as well. Before long, you realize you don't even have to show up for work. Your super employee can easily take care of all the tasks and you can spend the day at the beach.

Essentially that is what happens between the conscious and the subconscious minds. When you first learn to get dressed, ride a bicycle, drive a car, or shave, you have to be very conscious of every movement. Within a very short period of time you can do these tasks effortlessly and without thought. The very moment you perform a task without thought, is the very moment you've delegated the task to your subconscious. In other words, it becomes a program that your subconscious can run without effort and that means you can go to the beach!

Now herein lies the problem. While you're at the beach, you've left your super employee (subconscious mind) looking after all the functions at work. Everything is going swimmingly well until you get the uneasy feeling that says; "If my super employee can handle all the tasks with total aplomb, and still have time and energy left over, what else is he doing while I'm not there?"

In essence that is the exact scenario that happens throughout your life. While your conscious mind is thinking about A,B and C, your subconscious is taking care of D through Z and you're (the conscious mind) not privy or aware to what's going on. If your conscious mind decides to focus on X,Y and Z then the subconscious automatically takes over all the matters from A through W.

Remember that I said earlier that we're just like our parents no matter how much we wish to deny it ... in fact, we're probably not even aware of it? The reason we're not aware of it is because every time we're reacting, without consciously thinking about it, we're automatically running on previously installed programs, often ones that were installed in our early years ... the years when our parents where the overwhelmingly dominating influencers of our lives. So the next time someone says to you; "You're just like your mother/father," you can bet that you did something or said something in a way that you were completely unaware of, because you were *consciously* thinking of one thing while you were *subconsciously* running on an old program and habit. Naturally you'll vehemently deny it because this behavior can only happen when you're not aware. After all, *consciously* you weren't even there!

PROGRAM

Here's what's so interesting. Whenever you're on your "best behavior," you're aware and functioning from your conscious mind. Imagine yourself in a job interview. You don't mind relegating things like digestion, body temperature and respiration to your subconscious mind during the interview, but you'll be damned if you allow your subconscious to decide how you're going to sit, what you're going to say, or how you're going to act. You're going to be absolutely certain that you're fully aware of everything that presents the "real" you!

So What Is the Real You?

It's both your conscious awareness and the programs that you got from your parents and other influential people in your early years. You're probably screaming … "THAT'S NOT FAIR!" and perhaps you're right, it's not fair, but there it is.

The more important question is: What are you capable of doing about it, and what *are* you going to do about it?

Obviously the behavior we really want resides in our conscious mind. You consciously say to yourself, "I want to be more assertive, understanding, empathic, confident, courageous and … aware."

The first step – which you have begun to take – is to become aware. If you want better health, a more fulfilling relationship, or a fat bank account, and your positive thinking has so far failed to deliver, you know that blaming the outside world, or God, or even your parents, won't change or accomplish a single thing.

If you're thinking you can cast the blame at the feet of your subconscious you're wrong again. Your subconscious is a completely neutral entity. It simply responds to its programs. If you absolutely insist on casting blame, then you could blame the programs because in essence that's what's determining most of your results. You're running programs that are sabotaging your life with a lot of "unapproved" behavior. The importance of understanding this is to consciously put your focus and attention on the root cause – your own internal programs – not your boss, your spouse, your parents or the neighbor's dog. You cannot play a victim of outside forces and expect positive and permanent change.

End of PART ONE

Tomorrow we'll look at how you can "Change Your Thoughts, and Change Your Life."

STEP 6 – Think back as far as you can. What was your childhood like? Did you feel listened to? Were you told, "Children should be seen and not heard"? How did your parents listen to

each other, to their friends, to your sisters or brothers?
Can you recall having heart-to-heart talks with the most important people in your life throughout childhood? Did you keep your thoughts and feelings to yourself?

The more you can recall, the clearer you'll be able to see your present tendencies and habits. This awareness is vital to help you make positive changes.

Continue to be aware of the three levels of listening and note your natural tendencies.

> *You've got to say, I think that if I keep working at this and want it*
> *badly enough I can have it. It's called perseverance.*
> *~ Lee Iacocca*

Have a great day!

DAY SIX – P.M. MESSAGE

Congratulations on sticking with the program. You are well on your way to becoming one of the rare jewels in our modern society ... someone who knows the art of effective listening.

You are making great headway. Before long you will look back at the twenty-nine day span from a very different perspective. You will have drastically changed how you think ... permanently. You're going to cover a lot of ground in the next three weeks.

Please remember, slow gentle, effortless steps doesn't mean that your progress will mirror that. Slow, gentle, effortless steps will produce enormous results. Patience and perseverance is the key. Patience and perseverance.

> *Children have never been good at listening to their elders,*
> *but they have never failed to imitate them.*
> *~ James Baldwin*

See you tomorrow.

... to becoming a great listener and communicator!

PROGRAM

DAY SEVEN
Awareness Is Vital
To Fundamental Change

DAY SEVEN - A.M.

Guess what? We're twenty-five percent of the way there and today you've earned a reward! It's important to keep this reward *small*. Small rewards have a magical way of stimulating your internal motivation.

If you're feeling any doubt or resistance to granting yourself a reward for your efforts thus far … perish the thought, it's just your inner-self marshalling its negative forces. Your inner-voice might suggest, "You don't deserve a reward for something you should be doing anyway," or "I don't feel I should give myself a reward, I haven't done anything yet," or "It doesn't feel right," and so on.

You *have* earned a reward. You've completed six days of a *Listening and Communication* program that you didn't have to do, so there's no earthly reason that you shouldn't reward yourself. Research shows that tangible rewards provide psychological motivation. Rewards are the easiest, most effective psychological motivators known.

When thinking of a reward, think small. Small rewards are a form of recognition rather than becoming an end in themselves.

Your reward should have the following two qualities:
✓   It should be appropriate to your goal.
✓   It should be free or inexpensive.

PROGRAM

What's an Appropriate Reward?

One that supports your goal. If your goal was to quit drinking alcohol, then clearly a celebration reward with a bottle of champagne would be somewhat counter-productive.

What Reward Could You Give Yourself that Would be Free or Inexpensive?

Inexpensive is certainly a relative term. After all, if you're a Saudi Sheik taking this program you may consider a small reward as going for an afternoon cruise on your yacht! However, for the rest of us "poor schleps," here are a few suggestions: go see a movie, rent a movie, buy a paperback, call a friend, enjoy some TV time, listen to a great piece of music, go for a walk, buy a magazine, etc. Think of something that you may not normally do and "DO IT!" It's important to do something you really enjoy doing.

STEP 7 – Think of a reward and make sure you enjoy it ... today! Enjoy!

> **Possible Ideas for a Reward:**
> - **Give yourself a manicure**
> - **Go see a movie**
> - **Read a book**
> - **Go for a walk**
> - **Watch a movie or TV**
> - **Buy a Magazine**
> - **Play a round of golf or a game of tennis**
> - **Think of something you seldom take time to do and "DO IT!" It's important to do something you really enjoy doing.**

We finished yesterday's Part One with a promise that Part Two would show you how to change your thoughts in order to change your life. (Please go back and read the last portion of yesterday's A.M. message if you need to refresh your memory).

PART TWO

Change your thoughts, change your programming, and you change your life. But how?

First, understand that your subconscious is not an entity that's out to sabotage you. It's simply an immensely powerful processor waiting to do your bidding. In fact, it has been doing your bidding all along. Don't forget, your subconscious mind doesn't make judgment calls. It simply reacts, flawlessly, to the programs it's given. I've caught myself yelling at my "stupid" computer more times than I care to admit, and every time I was absolutely certain that it was the computer that "screwed up," time would inevitably reveal that I was the culprit. Invariably I was giving it bad instructions.

Many people attempt to change their lives through the therapy route. You can lie on a couch for ten years while you bemoan your problems, dredge up past deeds, and blame your parents for all your faults, but when it's all said and done it won't change your programming by a single bit or a single byte.

The key to change is to learn how to install brand new programming. Programming that is "YOU APPROVED."

The first step is to tune into your present thoughts and self-talk. What kind of thoughts flow from your subconscious mind? Very often when we become aware of our self-talk we're shocked and appalled at the negativity. Science has learned through research studies that eighty percent of our self-talk is negative. Habitual negative dialogue can become so crippling it leaves us stressed out and powerless. By developing the ability to accept ourselves and understand our old self-defeating behaviors, we can listen to ourselves nonjudgmentally – we can become our very own therapist rather than our worst enemy. (We will examine self-talk at a deeper level later on).

Helping you to change and reprogram your dominant thoughts is one of the key purposes of this program. By conscious awareness of your thoughts – changing them from negative to positive – incorporating affirmations, visualizations, focus, and twenty-nine days of commitment, you will lay new neuron tracks (read "programs") that lead to new thoughts and behaviors of *your* choosing. You will literally re-write your subconscious beliefs and no longer run the old listening and communication programs.

Picture this. You're walking down a well-worn path one day and you come to a distinct fork in the road. You can bear left or you can bear right. You can't help but feel that you want to go left for two reasons: one reason is that's the path you always take, and the second reason is that the right path has a fair bit of growth on it. There are a lot of weeds and overhanging branches you'll have to deal with if you go to the right, so perhaps it's just easier to go left; after all, the path is well worn and quite smooth.

PROGRAM

Herein lies the problem. You already know what lies ahead on the left path and if you're totally honest with yourself you don't really like that particular journey any more. However, the right path would certainly be more interesting and, who knows, it could lead to bigger and better things. You decide to hell with it, you want to try something new; so you get out your machete and your determination and you set off down the right path. To your amazement it really is unique and more fun and interesting than the old left path. Each day when you come to this fork in the road you begin to resist your natural tendency to go left and you make a *conscious* effort of going to the right.

Then one day, after a few weeks of traversing the right path a funny thing happens, you no longer feel any pull or desire to take the left path. In fact, you now notice that the two paths have completely reversed their terrain. The left path is now becoming overgrown with weeds and overhanging branches while the right path, the preferable path, is smooth and easy to travel. That is exactly what happens to your thoughts, habits and behaviors. If you can make a conscious effort to change them, within a surprisingly short period of time, the new thoughts and habits of your choosing will be the programs that your subconscious mind will run, even when you're not there. You can go back to the beach and top up your tan, secure in the knowledge that your super employee is doing exactly as you instructed.

In *29 DAYS*, when we ask you to visualize and affirm your desires just as you go to sleep or wake up, and to think about the goals you wish to accomplish throughout your day, you are opening your mind to the same susceptible programming that you were subject to in your earliest years. With your newly installed programs you will begin to see things happen in your life without your conscious effort. You can be at the beach all day and know that your super employee (subconscious mind) is bringing all the necessary forces into your life in response to your new desires and programs.

That is the secret to the power of new beliefs and new programs – to harness and direct the limitless power of the subconscious mind.

STEP 7 – Think of a reward and make sure you enjoy it … today! So … enjoy!

Now that you know how you *unconsciously* acquired a sizeable portion of your listening and communication habits, try and think back to your childhood days and see if you can recall the type of listening environment in which you were raised. For example, as a child were you encouraged to express your opinion? Did you feel understood and listened to? How did your parents communicate with each other? If your parents had a tendency to talk *at* each other, rather than communicate, this might shed some light on your present tendencies even if you're not aware of them. Did your parents communicate judgmental attitudes through a certain posture or facial expression?

Please note: If your childhood experiences and recollections were not the most pleasant, please understand that the purpose of this exercise is NOT to dredge up old hurts, blame or accusations. Very few of us were fortunate enough to be raised by parents who understood early childhood development. In most cases our parents simply passed on the same ineffective communication skills that they were taught. They were merely acting in response to the best they knew. Keep in mind that the prevailing knowledge of twenty, thirty or forty years ago were based on clichés such as, "Spare the rod and spoil the child," or "Children should be seen and not heard," or "Children should never interrupt an adult."

The purpose of this exercise is simply to create nonjudgmental awareness. With awareness you can begin the process of lasting change. Years of entrenched listening habits will take focus and commitment to change. It's very difficult, if not impossible to change an undesirable habit if you're not even aware of its existence. So take a few moments and see if you can answer the following questions. As soon as you become fully aware of some habitually dysfunctional habits you may have acquired, you will become that much more motivated to change them. Once you witness the results that effective listening quickly reveals, you will be energized and highly motivated for continued improvement.

JOURNAL ENTRY
Awareness Is Vital To Fundamental Change

As a child, did you feel like your parents genuinely listed to you in a non-judgmental manner?

_____

_____

_____

_____

Did you feel that they had a tendency to dismiss your thoughts as irrelevant or unimportant because you were "just a child"?

_____

_____

Did they interrupt your speech or cut you off in an effort to give you their opinion and advice?

_____

_____

_____

_____

Was your attempt at communication turned into a barrage of questions that made you feel like you were in an inquisition?

_____

_____

_____

While expressing your thoughts, feelings or opinions did the response often feel like a long series of disinterested "Uh-huhs, hmms, and oh yeahs?"

_____

_____

_____

Whether you felt listened to or not, how did you respond to the reaction you received?

_____

_____

_____

_____

Did it help you to open up? Did it arouse feelings of anger? Hurt? Did you withdraw and keep your thoughts and feelings to yourself?

_____

_____

_____

_____

_____

Did you look forward to sharing your thoughts and feelings? Did you develop confidence or self-consciousness?

_____

_____

_____

Please be sure to take a few moments to answer these questions as deeply and honestly as you can. In many cases they will exactly mirror your present listening habits and skills.

For my reward I gave myself:

_____

DAY SEVEN – P.M. MESSAGE

The first week is complete.

Week one was all about awareness and commitment: I know I'm committed to becoming a great listener and communicator.

"By directing my attention and awareness toward my daily communication habits, I learned some interesting things about myself. I learned ..."

_____

_____

_____

_____

I hope you had a great day and that you took the time to enjoy your reward. You have successfully finished twenty-five percent of the program. That's great. You really did earn your reward, you know.

Awareness of who we are, and what we are, is one of the joys of being human. It is *awareness* that makes us distinct from other life forms. It is awareness of our existence that makes us human.

Everything in the universe is composed of energy, of vibrating matter. It is a scientifically proven fact, that the only thing that separates one form of matter from another is its vibratory nature. Since that is so, what separates humankind from a rock or from an amoeba? It's vibration and awareness. We have the ability to know that we exist. More importantly, we have the unique power to shape and create our existence. While living in the moment we can remember our past, and by the same token we can plan our future.

> *The present moment is highly overrated.*
> *From an evolutionary perspective,*
> *the past and the future are where it's at.*
> *Any aardvark, antelope, cat, or cockroach can effortlessly reside in the*
> *present moment. Only human beings can engage deeply with the past*
> *and consciously co-create the future. By doing so,*
> *by looking outward with aims of bettering our world,*
> *big or small, we also walk a path that leads to inner fulfillment.*
> *~ Michael Dowd*

To enjoy the human experience is to enjoy the process of creation. To know our past, to plan for our future, and then to know that we can determine our future, is the most exhilarating feeling of our humanness.

Although our past is unchangeable, our view and interpretation of it is not. Where once we held blame, scorn, and anger, we can transcend those lower feelings to acceptance, understanding, forgiveness and gratitude for what we were able to discern from our past.

Accept the past. Perhaps you can even consciously alter your perception of your past, but more importantly plan for and embrace the future. You can and will create your future you know. Deliberately or not. Decide to make it just as you desire it. With awareness comes change. Make the skill and talent of listening and communicating an integral part of your future.

Tomorrow you will consider setting some communication goals.

You are now officially one quarter of the way there!

See you tomorrow.

 . . . to becoming a great listener and communicator!

— WEEK TWO —

www.29daysto.com

PREPARATION FOR ACTION

DAY EIGHT
I'm the best reason in the world to change ... so I'll change!

DAY EIGHT - A.M.

Welcome to week two, you're doing great! In the first week you accomplished two key things in building a foundation toward a lifetime of being a great listener and communicator. You established awareness of your listening habits, and you confirmed your commitment to becoming a great listener and communicator.

Week two is PREPARATION WEEK. This is the week that will get you fully prepared for action in week three. You will continue to build your awareness and understanding of listening and communication, and you will begin to ask yourself simple but vital questions on how to make minor, but permanent, changes to your habits and behaviors.

As you can well imagine, it's rather impossible to arrive at a destination if we don't have one. Without a destination or goal, we're simply wandering aimlessly about. Today we're going to look at goal setting and then ask you to write out two goals. The first goal will be what you wish to accomplish by the end of this program. The second goal will be your lifetime goal, or better still, a lifestyle by which you wish to live.

Remember, we want small changes. They may even seem too trivial to matter, but over time they will produce significant results. The daily reminders, your visualizations, affirmations and simple rewards are already forming powerful new neuron tracks. These new thought patterns are beginning to produce deep-seated changes.

Written goals and affirmations have a magical way of unlocking your subconscious mind, which will begin to release ideas and energy for your goal attainment. Clearly written and well-thought-out goals will increase your self-confidence and enhance your levels of motivation. By

PROGRAM

simply deciding exactly what you want, you will begin to move unerringly toward your goal, and your goal will start to move unerringly toward you.

In *29 DAYS ... to a habit you want!* we talked about goal setting and how to do it. Today is a recap of the correct way to write, set, and achieve your goals.

Recap to Goal Setting

There are two ways to think about goals. You can write a goal for your conscious mind, and you can also create a goal for your subconscious mind. There is a difference.

Conscious Mind – Goals

Your conscious mind thinks in terms of time: past, present and future. If your goal is to become a good listener and to build a strong rapport with your spouse and kids for example, then a clearly written, conscious goal might be written like this:

By X date, I will have managed to listen deeply and empathically to my wife/husband/child.

This is a goal that is written in a positive tense with a specific time.

Subconscious Mind – Goals

Your subconscious mind has no concept of time. It only functions in the present. Therefore when you communicate with your subconscious mind you will do so in the form of an affirmation. A goal for your conscious mind written as:

"By x date, I will have managed to listen deeply and empathically to my wife/husband/child,"

... would become an affirmation to your subconscious mind that you would repeat as:

"I listen deeply and empathically to my wife/husband/child."

The only difference is that you don't put a date on it. You relay this desire to your subconscious mind and it will find the shortest route to your goal.

You put the date on it for your *conscious* mind so that it becomes a believable goal for you. For example, if were trying to lose weight and you said that you will lose thirty pounds in ten days your conscious mind would refuse to buy into it or believe it. If you put a reasonable date to it, such as, "I will lose thirty pounds in the next five months," then your conscious mind would say, "Okay, we can do this." This aligns the believability your conscious mind needs to the positive, emotional feeling that fuels your subconscious mind.

As noted earlier, our subconscious mind is vital to our success. Unfortunately, most of us were never taught how to use it effectively. If you wish to eliminate a bad habit it is imperative to write your goal in a positive/positive way.

Your goals must have the following characteristics:

Written Goals for Your Conscious Mind

1. It must be something that you really want – since you're still with the program, this one can definitely be checked off.
2. It must be clear and specific with a definite date on it.

Written Goals/Affirmations for Your Subconscious Mind

1. Your affirmation goals must be positive because your subconscious mind cannot process a negative command. It is only receptive to a positive, present tense statement. In this case, you wouldn't write, *"I don't want to be an ineffective listener,"* or even *"I don't want my mind to wander when I'm listening."* but rather *"I listen to others with an open heart and mind"* or *"When listening I see the world from the speaker's perspective."*

2. When communicating with your subconscious mind, you should always state and write your goals in a positive, present and personal way. So by positive we mean that you don't write what you don't want. Example: *"I don't want to be a poor listener."* Positive means, *"I am an effective listener"* or *"I listen empathically to my family and friends."* These are positive statements. Present statements mean that your goal is written in the present tense. Again you wouldn't write: *"I will become an effective listener,"* but rather, *"I am an effective listener."*

    Writing "I will become ..." keeps it in the future, and writing "I want ..." keeps you longing and never having. All *wanting* affirms the *not having* – to your subconscious mind.

    Finally your goal must be both measurable and quantifiable. To meet this requirement you merely need to fill in some specifics. So instead of saying "I want to become an effective listener," you would write your goal and the time period in which it will happen.

PROGRAM

3. It must be believable and achievable. People will often say: "Hey, I thought you said that anybody can achieve anything that 'the mind can conceive and believe'?" That's true to a point. If, for example, you say; "I will live forever," your subconscious mind won't buy into it, which means you're wasting your time.

Shaquille O'Neal is a 7' 1", 325-pound world-famous basketball player who happens to have many interests. One of his interests is law enforcement. Now if Shaq decided he wants to become an undercover cop when he retires from basketball, or if he wants to become a thoroughbred racehorse jockey, it doesn't matter how badly he wants it, it's not happening! We have to make sure that what we're setting our hearts on is within the accepted realms of what our conscious and subconscious mind will buy into. If our subconscious mind won't buy into it, it won't offer the required support.

Your goal must be positive because your subconscious mind cannot process a negative command. It is only receptive to a positive, present tense statement.

STEP 8 – According to the above guidelines, write down a goal that you know you can achieve by the end of this program, and a second goal (or lifestyle) that you would like to achieve at some future point following the conclusion of this program.

That's your step for day eight.

JOURNAL ENTRY

I'm the best reason in the world to change ... so I'll change!

Keys to Setting My Goals:
1. It must be something I desire
2. It must be clear, specific, positive and present tense
3. It must be believable and achievable

Things you might want to think about or consider while making your goals:

- Is there a person you would like to emulate? i.e. Do you happen to know a really good listener? What makes that person such a good listener? Can you clearly define those qualities into a desirable goal?
- Would you like to be able to communicate your inner thoughts and feelings to your loved ones?

- Would you like to become a natural listener who can easily listen at *any* of the three levels of listening?
- Can you think of a definite achievement that you would acquire by becoming a good listener?

Most important to goal setting – "What do I want to accomplish and how will I know when I have?"

EXAMPLES OF SOME POSSIBLE PROGRAM GOALS:

By day twenty-nine I will have:
- Listened empathically to someone I love.
- Listened to someone criticize me without getting angry or emotional.
- Ask open-ended questions to encourage a speaker to continue.
- I will listen openly without prejudgment.
- I will listen to someone without giving my advice or opinion.
- I will listen to someone vent or complain without interruption or judgment.
- When communicating I will be sensitive to the listener and read their response.

My listening and communication goal(s) for this 29 DAYS program is:

_____

My affirmation for my subconscious mind is:

_____

EXAMPLES OF SOME POSSIBLE LIFETIME GOALS

- I listen empathically when someone needs to be heard.
- I put my feelings aside when I want to see the world through another's eyes.
- I communicate my true feelings openly and honestly when I need to be heard.
- I always listen intently with "understanding" as my true desire.
- I look to understand "before" I try to be heard.

Remember: "What do I want to accomplish and how will I know when I have done so?"

_____

_____

My lifetime Listening and Communication goal for the way I will strive to live my life is:

A "successful life" is nothing more than a sum total of
many "successful years."
A successful year is the compilation of a dozen successful months.

PROGRAM

A successful month is the result of four successful weeks,
which in turn, are seven successful days.
If you can make today a successful day,
then a wonderfully successful life will be yours
one day at a time.

DAY EIGHT – P.M. MESSAGE

Give yourself a hearty congratulations. Writing down your goal is a huge step toward its attainment.

Remember: Everyone has an image of himself. See yourself connecting positively with all of the important people in your life. Can you recall how you felt the last time somebody really listened to you empathically? Picture yourself doing that for somebody else and see the effect it will have on both you and them.

⋄ What does it feel like to really listen to someone else?
⋄ What does it feel like when someone really listens to you?

Visualize yourself communicating effectively with other people and imagine the results of your new skill. See yourself as you really want to be. Empathic listening is really one of the greatest gifts you can give another person. It may take some desire and practice, but the results will be worth any effort you expend.

You're making great headway. See you tomorrow!

 ... to becoming a great listener and communicator!

DAY NINE
I'm the best reason in the world to change ... so I'll change!

DAY NINE – A.M.

Nobody plans to fail, but many people fail because they failed to plan.

This week is about planning for action.

Yesterday you set your goals. Today you will begin to think of small questions that you could ask yourself that will help you achieve your listening and communication goals. When you ask your brain small questions, you engage it. It *will* give you answers. Be patient. Asking small questions will also not disturb your amygdala. We don't want to bother waking up that part of your brain. Let's let sleeping dogs lie!

In *29 Days ... to a habit you want!* we talked about your *Reticular Activating System* or your RAS. Every single impulse, whether derived from thought, touch, taste, smell, seeing or hearing, first passes through your RAS. The RAS then sends signals to the proper area of your brain for interpretation. When something important is on your RAS, it sends a signal to the conscious level for your immediate attention.

If you ask the same question over and over, your brain (RAS) will begin paying attention and subsequently it will begin to create answers.

Begin to ask yourself some questions that could help you toward achieving your communication goals. In order to really listen to another person you have to put your own feelings, prejudices and thoughts aside. You need to think and feel from the perspective of the speaker. This is probably one of the most difficult tasks for anyone to master. In following the *29*

PROGRAM

DAYS philosophy, you're not going to set unrealistic tasks, instead you're going to ask yourself what small thing you could do today to help you to see the world through the speaker's eyes.

How can you begin to learn to get inside another's shoes and see the world from *their* perspective?

Over the course of the next several days we're going to examine the world of social psychology and how it affects our ability to listen and communicate.

In 1964, Dr. Eric Berne wrote a landmark book on social psychology titled, *Games People Play.* This groundbreaking work was the basis of *Transactional Analysis,* which explains how our feelings, thoughts, and behaviors affect the way that we communicate to ourselves and each other. Today there is an *International Transactional Analysis Association* with more than 10,000 people who define themselves as transactional analysts.

A general awareness of Transactional Analysis (TA) will give you valuable insight into your behaviors, habits and subconscious programming, and more importantly, will explain what you can do to change the behaviors and habits that you find undesirable.

Human beings are social creatures. Without stimulation from another human all of us would die in infancy. To quote Berne; *"What has been said so far may be summarized by the colloquialism: 'If you are not stroked, your spinal cord will shrivel up.'"*

What are strokes?
According to Berne, *"'Stroking' may be used as a general term for intimate physical contact ..."* he further summarizes, *"By an extension of meaning, 'stroking' may be employed colloquially to denote any act implying recognition of another's presence. Hence a stroke may be used as the fundamental unit of social action. An exchange of strokes constitutes a transaction, which is the unit of social intercourse. As far as the theory of games is concerned, the principle which emerges here is that any social intercourse whatever has a biological advantage over no intercourse at all."*

Okay, that's a little dry. Basically a stroke is any form of recognition or attention one person gives to another. By definition, a stroke can be either positive or negative. A frown, a slap, a smile and a hug are all strokes. In short, people need strokes to survive and thrive.

In fact, we will willingly accept negative strokes to no strokes at all! Even negative human contact, is preferable to no contact at all. This is a key factor in understanding human interaction. It's why solitary confinement in our prison system is considered an unusually cruel form of punishment and torture. In fact, solitary confinement for an extended period will impact a prisoner's mental state and often lead to mental illnesses such as depression and even death.

Strokes are as vital to our state of health as the food we eat, and like food, strokes come in a wide selection. To use a food analogy, it can be as light as a snack, such as a nod, all the way to a three-course dinner such as empathic listening and a hug.

In *Games People Play,* Berne gives examples of how we naturally incorporate strokes into our daily rituals. When I go for a morning run I often see many of the same people walking their dogs. An example of a typical two-stroke greeting while I'm running would be a quick hello or a nod. Today was the first real warm day after a long winter. I had just finished my run and I was now walking to cool down. Because of the weather, my walking, and the dog owner standing still while his dog soaked a nearby tree, our two stroke (Hello-Hello) ritual required just a little more effort:

> *Me: "How's it going?" (Good morning.)*
> *Neighbor: "Good and you?" (Good morning.)*
> *Me: "Looks like spring's finally here?" (How are you?)*
> *Neighbor: "Yes indeed, it's about time." (Fine. How are you?)*
> *Me: "Speaking of time, looks like it's time to get the clubs out." (Okay.)*
> *Neighbor: "I'll be out on the weekend."*
> *Me: "Have a good one."*
> *Neighbor: "Thanks, you too."*

This typical scenario is played out billions of times each day. It's the type of interaction between two people who see each other in passing, or at a bus stop or subway. They know each other by sight and location but that's as far as it goes. Neither party wants to get involved any further than the simple daily greeting. Berne calls this daily greeting an eight-stroke ritual in which he asserts that each has contributed to the other's well being in preventing the shriveling of the other's spinal cord.

I had no sooner finished the above encounter and had turned the corner when I was somewhat startled to see a mid-sized dog charging at me. My first reaction was to brace myself for an attack but then a moment later this adorable canine locked all four legs and literally came to a skidding stop at my feet. His tail was wagging vigorously as he positioned his head within easy reach of my hand. This happy guy had put in a good deal of effort to greet me (I'd say about eight to ten strokes' worth), and as far as he was concerned I owed him a few strokes in return. I gladly patted his head, stroked his back and gave him a number of "that's a good boy," affirmations. He still didn't move, which meant only one thing: *he* would decide when our stroke account was square. He continued to allow me to pet him and tell him how wonderful he was and, within a short time and clearly by his calculations, we were at last even on the stroke-exchange and he happily trotted away.

So with that brief incident on my radar I guess I should make a slight modification to the initial definition of strokes. A stroke is any form of recognition or attention one *being* gives to another.

Although it's only a little anecdote it's vitally important to be aware of the concept of strokes. Strokes are key to fulfilling our social needs whether that be a casual nod from a stranger to a hug from a loved one. But let's continue with the above example just a bit further. The two acquaintances, A & B, have concluded (by general social upbringing) that they owe each other four strokes each morning they meet. Should they chance to see each other later the same day, they will likely reduce their greeting to a single stroke each with a quick nod of recognition.

In another example C and D carry on a daily (Hi – Hi) one-stroke ritual. Then C goes away for several weeks. When C returns, if D picked-up from his last one-stroke routine, C would feel a slight twinge in his spinal cord. Mr. C clearly expects something more from D than a measly single stroke. In fact, he expects a full thirty-stroke ritual. In the following example taken from *Games People Play,* Berne states that each unit of "intensity" or "interest" is equal to one stroke. If D is to play by the rules of ritual he owes C some requisite strokes as follows;

1D: "Hi!" *(1 unit.)*
2D: "Haven't seen you around lately." *(2 units.)*
3D: "Oh, have you! Where did you go?" *(5 units.)*
4D: "Say, that's interesting. How was it?" *(7 units.)*
5D: "Well, you're sure looking fine." *(4 units.)*
6D: "Did your family go along?" *(4 units.)*
7D: "Well, glad to see you back." *(4 units)*
8D: "So long." *(1 unit.)*

This gives Mr. C a total of 28 units. Both he and Mr. D know that he will make up the missing units the following day, so the account is now, for all practical purposes, squared. Two days later they will be back to their two-stroke exchange, Hi-Hi. But now they "know each other better," i.e. each knows the other is reliable, and this may be useful if they should meet "socially."

Our first reaction may be to smile at this simple illustration as a trite example of something that's not too serious one way or the other, but in the realm of listening and communication, it's very important in maintaining social connections.

Let's look at the above example of C and D and suppose that when C returned from his absence D would have ignored his absence and resumed the usual one stroke ritual. This would have undoubtedly had an effect on C. It may have caused C to wonder what he did or said to deserve such a reaction from D; after all, he felt that he was clearly owed something more. In the currency of strokes, D clearly had a debt and a moral obligation to fork over a number of strokes to C.

Now let's take that a step further. Your child comes home from a bad day at school and in her cry for *strokes* and *attention*, she slams the cupboard door only to have you give her some strokes – but not of the positive kind! How does that affect the strokes bank account? If your response is frequently negative, the stroke-account will register in the "red" which results in a negative relationship. When a parent laments, "My children just don't open up to me," you can bet that the stroke-account is all but empty.

As we discussed on days six and seven, our early programming, and the way we were *stroked* as children, plays a major role in our habits, beliefs and listening behaviors. Empathic listening is the gold standard of strokes. One session of nonjudgmental, level-one listening, will top up the stroke-bank-account with a loved one faster than almost anything else you can do.

STEP 9 — For the rest of today try to be aware of the phenomenon called strokes. Notice the interchange of strokes from the person who serves you your morning coffee to the way you greet your spouse, your kids and your associates at work.

JOURNAL ENTRY

I'm the best reason in the world to change ... so I'll change!

Social strokes are given and received by all of us on both a conscious and subconscious level throughout our day. Can you think of any examples that happened today that would fit into the following definition:

One-stroke interchange:

PROGRAM

_____

_____

Five- to ten-stroke interchange:

_____

_____

Using intensity and level of interest to add up a quantity of strokes, can you think of any examples where you may have short-changed someone who could have needed more strokes (attention, empathy, etc.) from you than you had either time or inclination to give?

_____

_____

_____

_____

At this stage there's nothing more to do than to try and be aware of the little nuances of communication that we often overlook.

If you go to a teller at a bank and merely say, "Hi, I wish to pay this bill," you may register a single stroke because you managed to mumble the most basic greeting. Suppose you were to approach that same teller with a smile, eye contact, and a clear friendly greeting? That single stroke from the first greeting would suddenly balloon to a value of ten or more. Not much extra effort on your part, but a huge social and psychological return for both you and the teller. Each of you would have just a little better day because of your willingness to ante up a few extra strokes.

DAY NINE – P.M. MESSAGE

You're doing great! Give yourself a pat on the back for the effort you put into becoming aware of our daily rituals and how they relate to strokes.

Perhaps the term *strokes* may seem a little archaic, but rest assured the need is not. You may have never given much thought when you nodded a greeting to a stranger or you extended a simple compliment or courtesy to a person at a check-out counter, but trying going through your day without extending the courtesy of strokes. Better yet, try going through your day and see where you can turn a single stroke encounter into a multiple sroke encounter. In some cases a single stroke may be all that's needed or even desired. In other cases perhaps we've been unduly stingy with sharing from our bottomless well of strokes.

You are making great headway. Stay the course!

When you go to bed this evening, and just before you go to sleep think about the currency of strokes and how they can positively affect your ability to communicate to all the people in your world. You have an unlimited supply, you know. Why not imagine yourself passing a few extra srokes around and picture their magical effect on the recipients.

See you tomorrow!

 . . . to becoming a great listener and communicator!

PROGRAM

DAY TEN
I'm the best reason in the world to change ... so I'll change!

DAY TEN – A.M.

Welcome to day ten.

Yesterday we talked about asking your brain to supply you with some small, easy-to-accomplish ideas that would help you to become a better listener and communicator. If you ask a question often enough, your brain will turn it over and come up with some surprisingly interesting answers.

Remember: Always ask positive questions. Never, never, never, ask a negative question such as "Why can't I do this?" or "Why can't I stop doing that?" Asking small positive questions can be a powerful habit within a habit. We want suggestions that will be so small they may seem too trivial to matter. We know better. Trivial is good. Small, continuous steps over a short period of time can produce miraculous results. Asking questions will throw your brain into creativity. Your brain will have fun with this ... like solving a crossword puzzle or a riddle.

Today is a continuation of yesterday's introduction into Transactional Analysis. Yesterday you were introduced to the concept of *strokes*. We said that a stroke is any form of recognition or attention one person, or being, gives to another. We then concluded that by definition, a stroke can be either positive or negative. A frown, a slap, a smile and a hug are all strokes. We also concluded the day with saying that each of us has an unlimited supply of strokes which we can freely pass out. If we think of strokes as social currency, we can see the wisdom and the exponential return in spreading the wealth ... uh, that would be the good strokes!

I'm Okay, You're OK … or Maybe NOT!

Taking off from the Transactional Analysis (TA) theory first introduced by Dr. Berne, Dr. Thomas Harris wrote an international best seller titled, *I'm OK–You're OK*. In his book Dr. Harris posits that there are four "life positions" that we can adopt in relation to ourselves and others:

1. I'm OK – You're OK
2. I'm Not OK, You're OK
3. I'm OK, You're Not OK
4. I'm Not OK, You're Not OK.

The particular "OK" belief we have about ourselves will have a strong bearing on our attitudes toward life and on our ability to listen, communicate and interact with others. Harris asserts that the most common position is *"I'm Not OK, You're OK." As children we see that adults are large, strong and competent and that we are little, weak and often make mistakes, so we often conclude "I'm Not OK, You're OK."*

I'm Not OK, You're OK

Susan was raised in a home that was governed by the creed, "Children should be seen and not heard." As a child Susan learned that her opinion and feelings were secondary to the opinions and feelings of adults. Consequently she held the "I'm Not OK–You're OK" attitude. Susan had low self-esteem and often assumed the inferior position to others. She was desperate to please but often failed because her focus was on avoiding mistakes rather than on accomplishment. She wouldn't dream of voicing her opinion at work because she "knew" it wasn't important. Her listening and communication skills were poor resulting in an inability to follow instructions well. This lead to reprimands at work which exacerbated her problems.

General Character Trait – A need to please others
- Overriding desire to make others happy in a desperate attempt to receive praise and approval.
- Sense of self-worth can only come from other people's approval.
- An overriding need to apologize when things go wrong even if they weren't at fault.
- Will say yes even when they want to say no.
- Often worried, easily bullied.
- Any criticism is viewed as catastrophic.

I'm OK, You're Not OK

Oscar was raised by a domineering, egotistical father who felt that there was only one opinion that mattered … his. In this case the apple didn't fall far from the tree. Oscar acquired the listening habits of his father through an attitude of "I'm OK, You're Not OK." Oscar was a brilliant mechanical engineer, and following *The Peter Principle* (the theory that all members in a hierarchy rise to their own level of incompetence), he was promoted to supervisor. From that point on Oscar's poor communication skills became a serious problem. During staff meetings he would either dictate the way things would be or he would run roughshod over anyone else's ideas. Whenever he did take the time to listen it was often from a position to find fault with his staff's ideas and suggestions.

Oscar's listening skills were never better than a level two. He was convinced that his opinions were the best so there was little point in listening to anyone else. He prejudged other people's comments, which meant he couldn't hear any more than his personal barriers and filters would allow. His management style quickly had his department frustrated, angry and performing poorly.

General Character Trait – Assumes a Superior Attitude, Desperately Tries to Be Perfect

- Feels he's superior to others who are inferior and not OK.
- Quick to overlook their own "nonexistent" mistakes.
- Finding fault with others comes easily and naturally.
- Desperate need to gather accolades.
- Difficult to please.
- Expect everyone to share their attitude of perfection.

I'm Not OK, You're Not OK

Okay then! This one is the most rife with problems. Fortunately it's also the most rare. When a person sees the world from this vantage point they have little hope of communicating effectively with either themselves or anyone else. The person in this position may bounce between "I'm OK, You're Not OK," and "I'm Not OK, You're OK," but they cannot communicate effectively and they seldom listen above a level three. Because they view themselves and others as "Not OK," they have no compelling reason to care about effective communication. People stuck in this position are characteristically negative and pessimistic. Their general view is "What's the use? Everything always turns out crappy anyway." The person who lives in this position is easy to recognize because they're understandably alone. The rest of us may catch ourselves slipping into this attitude on occasion, but the stay is only temporary.

PROGRAM

General Character Trait – Withdrawn, Introverted, Pessimistic and Negative

- Feels that neither he nor anyone else is worth listening to.
- Not interested in new things or other people.
- Often depressed on almost always depressing to be around.
- Because they don't listen and communicate, they will seldom solve problems or deal with issues.

I'm OK, You're OK

The person who can see the world from this position fails to see anyone as inferior or superior. This is the mark of the well-balanced person who is an highly effective listener and communicator. They are happy, confident, and comfortable with who they are. They will typically be nonjudgmental, understanding, logical and empathic.

General Character Trait – Balanced, optimistic, see value in themselves and other people

- Ability to listen intently to other people.
- Strong sense of their uniqueness and self-worth.
- They see value in all people.
- Open to new ideas and enjoy discussing and learning.
- They are empathetic and nonjudgmental.

Although using the term OK does sound rather mundane and pedestrian, in the realm of "I'm OK, You're OK," and living one's life from this viewpoint, it's a monumental achievement. Seeing yourself and others from this viewpoint is venturing into the realm of unconditional love, a rarified atmosphere indeed. Certainly the great spiritual leaders saw the world through this lens. Could you view the Queen of England, the President of the United States and a beggar on the street in the same light? Very few humans can. People like Ghandi and Mother Teresa are modern examples of people who see people for what they are (spiritual beings) not for the worldly images and labels they wear. To see the world from a position of "I'm OK, You're OK" is a great accomplishment indeed. Most of us will never achieve it to the degree that some of the great spiritual leaders have, but nonetheless, it shouldn't stop us from striving toward such a goal.

Each of us will see the world from any one of the four positions from time to time. When we're frustrated and angry we may very well see the world through the lens of "I'm Not OK, You're Not OK," and at other times when we're feeling smug and superior, we may pass a homeless person on the street and feel a sense of "I'm OK, You're Not OK."

PROGRAM

STEP 10 – Throughout the day, try and be aware of the four OK views that each of us can harbor. As you can well imagine, it would be pretty difficult to listen to someone empathically if we're harboring a view of "I'm OK, You're Not OK." Conversely, it would be rather difficult to genuinely express ourselves with a an attitude of "I'm Not OK, You're OK." None of us, accept the enlightened avatars, can continually dwell in the realm of "I'm OK, You're OK" toward all people, but that should *not* stop us from trying. As you know by now, awareness is the first step toward lasting change. Try your best to be aware of these thoughts.

JOURNAL ENTRY

I'm the best reason in the world to change ... so I'll change!

Can you catch yourself throughout your day unconsciously assuming the various OK positions depending on the person or situation you may find yourself in?

_____

_____

_____

_____

I realized I was assuming an 'I'm OK, You're Not OK" position when ...

_____

_____

_____

_____

I realized I was assuming an "I'm Not OK, You're OK" position when ...

PROGRAM

_____
_____
_____
_____

I realized I was assuming an "I'm Not OK, You're Not OK" position when ...

_____
_____
_____
_____

I realized I was assuming an "I'm OK, You're OK" position when ...

_____
_____
_____
_____

Although you may not have felt each of the four positions today, try to be aware of the OK attitudes you assume. You may find this exercise to be very enlightening.

DAY TEN – P.M. MESSAGE

Congratulations for another day of focus and being aware of your internal OK positions. Something else you may want to keep in mind when communicating with other people is that they have their own particular OK position. Can you readily detect it?

PROGRAM

The more often you can put yourself into an "I'm OK, You're OK" position the better your life will become. It has to. You will become aware of consciously choosing how you will interact with other people. Seeing yourself and others as equal beings is infinitely better than seeing either yourself or others as being inferior or superior. Your relationships with everyone will improve in surprising ways.

Promise yourself that you will consciously try to operate from an "I'm OK, You're OK" position. If we really think about, how naive and cruel is it to really think we are inferior or superior to anyone else? By what right? By what criteria?

If you catch yourself taking an inferior or superior position to another person (we all do and will continue to do so from time to time ... short of enlightenment), ask yourself questions such as: Is this really true? Where did this notion come from? What is the evidence for this feeling or conclusion? Does it really apply in this case?

I'm betting that any position outside of "I'm OK, You're OK" will rapidly crumble under serious evaluation when using any of the above questions.

Congratulations on another great day.

See you tomorrow!

DAY ELEVEN
I'm the best reason in the world to change ... so I'll change!

DAY ELEVEN – A.M.

Welcome back, it's day eleven!

This week's goal is to get mentally prepared to take action starting next week. For the next three days we will continue to examine your inner thoughts, which can inhibit you from becoming a great listener and communicator.

My concern is that today is day eleven and it's possible, just possible, that your inner-self (amygdala) is working overtime to plant seeds of doubt in your mind. It might be making suggestions such as: "This program won't work," or "It's been eleven days and I still haven't noticed any dramatic changes in my listening skills and relationships," or, "Maybe I'm not such a bad listener after all. Besides, no one seems to be very good at it!"

Remember all of the reasons and advantages you'll enjoy by investing the time and making the effort to become a great listener. If this nagging self doubt is setting in, it shouldn't come as any surprise. We knew right from the outset that this would happen. Your amygdala does not want you to enter the action stage next week, and your inner-self is terrified of failure. The surest way to avoid failure is to avoid change of any kind.

Change is always frightening, but without change we cannot grow. Through this program you are asserting yourself; you are taking control of your thoughts and actions. Growth doesn't have to be frightening. It can be both fun and very rewarding. Remember, we're going to go slowly and steadily so that the change you make will be permanent. As you move further into this program you will begin to feel your inner growth. You will begin to realize that your new

PROGRAM

listening and communication lifestyle will become a habit that you can very comfortably live with. One success will build upon another. The changes are small, the results are magnificent!

The last two days we've been reviewing the most basic fundamentals of *Transactional Analysis* by looking at the currency of human interaction known as *strokes*, and the four "life positions" categorized as:

1. I'm Not OK, You're OK,
2. I'm Okay, You're Not OK
3. I'm Not OK, You're Not OK, and
4. I'm Ok, You're OK.

Digging one layer further into the theory of Transactional Analysis is the aspect of *The Drama Triangle*, first introduced by Dr. Stephen Karpman. He posits that whenever we are acting from the "Not OK" position, we are assuming one of the three triangular positions; *persecutor, rescuer* or *victim* – and we will often rotate around the triangle (assuming different positions in mere minutes or even seconds), depending on the situation.

The drama triangle shows the dramatic roles that people act out in their daily life. These roles are fraught with instability, misery, and emotional dependency on the given drama of the moment. The switching that occurs between persecutor, rescuer and victim is what generates the drama and the predictable painful feelings.

Note: All drama triangle players have a preferred entry point, i.e., they will usually enter the triangle as either a persecutor, rescuer or victim, but the end result will always be that of *victim*.

The three *Drama Positions* of *Rescuer, Persecutor* and *Victim* can be described as follows.

Rescuers – People who enter the triangle as *rescuers* see their role as helpers. In order for the rescuer to feel that his life has value and meaning he must find someone to rescue. The rescuer cannot objectively see himself as filling a victim role, after all, they're the rescuer with all the pat answers.

Persecutors – People who enter the triangle as persecutors see themselves as victims. They simply cannot see themselves for the blaming, argumentative and relentless fault-finding natures they exemplify. In fact, the persecutor sees himself against an evil world. Any criticism of a persecutor will be repelled by a full frontal attack, which will be justified as self-protection.

Victims – People who enter the triangle as victims believe they are inadequate and incapable of dealing with life. They will naturally seek out rescuers by suggesting they need assistance. Children who were coddled by their parents will assume the role of victim and seek out the rescuer in adult life. Should a rescuer either quit the role or fail to meet the victim's needs, the victim can quickly adopt a persecutor's persona and blame both the rescuer and the rest of the world for abandonment.

Note: The rescuer and persecutor assume a superior position over other people. They view themselves as stronger, smarter, and more capable. The victim accepts his lowly position but only for just so long. While in victimhood, they will stew and brew like a boiling volcano. Eventually the victim will erupt and become the persecutor, which means if either the rescuer or persecutor are in range, they will be forced to temporarily assume the victim position.

Example: A senior manager of a shipping firm walks into one of the junior manager's offices to hear her tearing into her assistant for failing to complete an assignment on time. The senior manager (playing rescuer to the assistant), interjects to suggest that perhaps the assistant was overloaded with duties.

Here comes the drama: The junior manager can assume the momentary role of victim and then lash out at her boss for interfering, which immediately repositions the junior manager from victim to persecutor and the senior manager from rescuer to victim.

The other possibility is that the assistant realizes she has to work with the junior manager all day long so she decides to move from being victim (to her immediate boss), to rescuer by suggesting to the senior manager that the junior manager is right and that she wasn't applying herself as well as she should. With that said, the senior boss feels rather awkward for playing the rescuer so he assumes the persecutor role and begins to reprimand both employees for their disagreement and inability to work efficiently. And on and on it goes. This game is played out in the home, the office or wherever two or more people can assemble.

At this point you might be thinking that this is just a lot of nonsensical labeling, after all, can't someone reprimand someone else without being accused of playing the drama triangle? Of course!

PROGRAM

There is a difference between an interactive exchange between people, heated or otherwise, and someone who happens to be entrenched in the roles of persecutor, rescuer or victim. As we get into this a little further you will see that in most cases these are *not* one-off or once-in-a-blue-moon positions. These drama triangle positions are where many people spend their entire lives.

The Persecutor

The persecutor functions from the "I'm OK, You're Not OK" mode. The persecutor can be summed up by their favorite accusation: "It's all your fault." Whether the persecutor is a critical parent or a domineering manager, people operating from this behavior are both dangerous and ruthless. They play a mean game of, "I'm out to get you and I will if it's the last thing I do." You can easily identify the type. They are critical, oppressive, and they'll make a point to set unnecessary restrictions. They function from a place of anger. When things are going well and everything is done to satisfaction they're virtually invisible. The moment anything goes awry, which inevitably happens, the persecutor will magically appear to unleash his wrath. The persecutor deals in the currency of "negative strokes." When it's all said and done, the persecutor can justify his behavior because as he truly believes he's only defending himself from a world of incompetent people whose sole purpose is to make his life miserable … thus he really is a victim after all.

I once had an office manager who was either groveling (victim) at his boss's feet or tearing at the throats (persecutor) of his employees. During an office move from a smaller to a larger office he made certain he commandeered the corner office with the large windows and view. In fact, the new premises were so much larger than the previous space, there were actually three more offices than there were employees. A little matter like that however would never dissuade a persecutor who has to constantly assert his position of authority. He insisted on cramming two employees and their desks into a single, one-desk-sized office, while four offices across the hall sat completely empty!

The Rescuer

The Rescuer will often play the martyr by taking on tasks they really don't wish to take on. They can be spotted as the pushover parent or the inept manager. They are quick to assume other people's responsibilities and their mission in life is to rescue the world whether it wants to be rescued or not. The rescuer can't help himself, it's his nature. Rescuing fuels a need. Like persecutors, they operate from the "I'm OK, You're Not OK" attitude. The rescuer is needy for praise and approval. Because a rescuer will take on any and all tasks, they will agree to far more than they're capable of handling, which inevitably leads to failed tasks. Whether it's the over-bearing parent or the inept manager, they will interfere in other people's affairs. They simply cannot allow other people the freedom and independence to make mistakes and learn to solve their own problems. The rescuer likes to be the indispensable fireman who races about saving the day. When people are talking, the rescuer is already thinking of advice. They tend to diagnose a solution to a problem they neither heard nor understood.

In Stephen Covey's phenomenal best seller, *The Seven Habits of Highly Effective People*, he relayed one of the most powerful examples of the debilitating effects of rescuing, and the transformational power of breaking free from the drama triangle cycle.

Stephen's son was facing some academic challenges at school. His reading and comprehension were well below standard. To compound the problem he was socially awkward, small, skinny and uncoordinated. When it came to competing at sports with other kids his age, he was woefully inadequate. The other kids would often laugh at him because of his inability to hit a baseball well or compete at the "perceived" level.

A parent's natural instinct is to help, to try and rescue their child from both himself and a hostile world. In the Coveys' attempt to help, they tried an uplifting approach toward their son. They did their best to encourage him, to psych him up using a positive mental attitude. When they saw a glimmer of improvement they would praise him and encourage him. When other kids laughed at him they would reprimand the kids to protect their son from ridicule. But it was all for naught. Their son would cry, feel inferior and insist that he didn't like sports anyway.

Everything they tried in an attempt to prop-him-up seemed to fail. Eventually they had the wisdom to throw in the towel and walk away from their role as rescuers. They began to realize that their attempts to help their son were not in harmony with the way they saw him. When they examined their deepest feelings they realized that their perception of their son was that he was *inadequate*, that he was somehow *behind*. They saw him from the lenses of, "I'm OK, You're Not OK." They were unconsciously communicating that he wasn't capable, that he needed to be protected. Stephen and his wife decided to focus on themselves by changing their perception of their son.

Instead of trying to change their son to the "acceptable" social image, they began to see him for his own uniqueness and his underlying potential. They dropped the role of rescuer and adopted the role of "I'm OK, You're OK." They saw their natural role as being able to affirm and accept him for who he was. No attempt to change him. They simply began to enjoy their son instead of comparing him or judging him. Since they began to truly see him as being perfectly capable, they stopped all pretenses at trying to protect him from other kids and from life. As their attitude and actions changed their son experienced withdrawal pains. Their unspoken and implied message back was, "You're OK. You don't need us to protect you." Then a miracle happened. As the weeks and months passed he began to accept himself and magically, both his confidence and capabilities began to soar.

Before long he was at the very top academically, socially and athletically. As he matured he was elected to several student body leadership positions, he developed into an all-state athlete and brought home straight-A report cards.

I love that story on so many levels. For one thing it shows that we *can* get off the drama triangle if we:
1. Recognize we're on it.
2. We desire to get off.

It also perfectly demonstrates the effectiveness of looking after our own behaviors rather than focusing on how to change someone else. Another thing that it so beautifully demonstrates is that we cannot change the world, but we *can* change ourselves. If we change ourselves, our world will change.

The Victim

People in the victim mode operate from, "I'm Not OK, You're Ok" attitude. Their *modus operandi* results in large and frequent helpings of negative strokes. They feel victimized, hopeless, ashamed, and oppressed. They will often look for a rescuer that will support their feelings of helplessness. They're inevitably poor communicators and inept listeners. As a result they will fail to comprehend instructions and subsequently fail to carry them out correctly. Naturally enough this will lead to further negative strokes, which serve to compound the feelings of inadequacy.

I once had a salesman working for my company who was the exclusive representative to many of the company's key clients. Unbeknownst to me, he experienced some personal problems and before long I couldn't help but notice that our clients were not receiving their usual level of service. Our company tried repeatedly to reach out to this missing-in-action salesman, in an attempt to discuss the problem and hopefully find a solution. Since our company was under contract with him, despite the growing urgency of the situation, we had to abide by certain procedures and protocol. Finally, after several weeks of messages and unreturned phone calls, the mysterious salesman returned to our "solar system" and called in. When I began to urgently question him about his absence and my concern for his whereabouts, he said that he had really tried his best to return our calls but it simply wasn't possible. He further insisted that he was not responsible for his actions since life had recently decided to throw so many problems his way. As he phrased it; "I make a daily list of the most important people to call. I began each day with you on my list but then more important calls continued to crop up, which meant you were continually bumped off my list. It wasn't my fault," he pleaded, "I really couldn't get back to you until today."

Well, if nothing else, at least he was honest! When we told him that his services were no longer required, he screamed bloody murder. He insisted that he had a binding contract and that he would see us in court!

What does all this mean?

As long as we play victim and blame the world for our troubles, we render ourselves helpless. We neutralize ourselves. We hand over our power to outside, random forces. From time-to-time we all have assumed the roles of persecutor, victim, and rescuer. The key is to recognize this debilitating game and then to stop playing it. It's a no-win game with predictable results … all players always end up as powerless victims.

Learn to quickly recognize the three roles, in others, ourselves and most importantly in our self-talk.

Rescuer

A rescuer rushes out to help other people whether they need it or not. At some point the rescuer wants to be paid back for their effort. They seldom are. Their natural thought is; "After all I've done for you this is how I'm rewarded?"

- The inevitable result – the rescuer is a victim of an ungrateful world.

Solution – Use your rescuing talents to rescue *yourself*. Forget rescuing others. The greatest benefit to yourself and the world is to become a self-determining individual. That means accepting one-hundred percent responsibility for your life.

Persecutor

Just like the rescuer needs someone to fix, the persecutor needs someone to blame. The persecutor is generally the recipient of childhood abuse – mental, physical or both. They will hide their anger and shame behind wrath and uncaring detachment. Their method of survival in a cruel world is to adopt the aggressive behaviors that caused their misery. Since they rule as iron-fisted dictators, they will bully, preach, threat, lecture and blame. They will always be right. The persecutor, like the Rescuer, unconsciously requires a victim.

PROGRAM

- In spite of all appearances, persecutors are not bad people. They are frightened, wounded individuals who see the world as a constant enemy that must be relentlessly fought.

Solution – Recognize the futility and fault of the underlying assumption – that the world is out to get you. There is no conspiracy. Listen to your self-talk and inner dialogue. You'll be both mystified and amazed at the unfounded and unsubstantiated negativity.

Victim

From time to time all of us need help. To think otherwise would be foolish. The victim however is convinced they need help for all things at all times. They see themselves as powerless, helpless victims of a cruel world who need rescuing. At some point a victim will temporarily rise above the victim role, which is caused by exploding resentment. Through their need to be "equal" they will strive to *get even* with a rescuer through passive-aggressive behavior. They will play the "Yes, but ..." card. The rescuer offers advice or help to the victim who replies with the classic; "Yes, but that won't work because of ..." All solutions and attempts by the rescuer will be rejected in the attempt to prove their problem cannot be solved.

- Although victims feel they must have a rescuer, they despise the rescuer because it fuels their feelings of inadequacy.

Solution – Listen to your inner negative thoughts and begin to reject them. Take slow gentle steps toward achieving just one small success. Success breeds success. With confidence beginning to build you will see the fallacy of all other negative assumptions. With just a little self-confidence you will begin to restore your belief in yourself and your innate abilities.

Getting Off the Drama Triangle

There is only one way to get off the dreaded drama triangle ... take total responsibility for your feelings, thoughts and actions. Any time you're casting blame, criticizing, or meddling you can be rest assured you're on the triangle. Living on the triangle means a life of reaction. Rather than living a self-determined life, we succumb to the whims and ways of outside forces and our unconscious negative beliefs.

To embrace a life of "I'm OK, You're OK" requires a willingness to get off the triangle and to extend both care and understanding to those still trapped in their drama. Strive to change what you can change. That means yourself, not someone else. If you get off the triangle, like the Coveys did, everyone's world will take a dramatic shift into self determination and joy. Over the next three days we are going to take a much deeper look at this insidious trap and how to escape its clutches.

STEP 11 – Throughout the day try and be aware of the three positions (rescuer, persecutor, victim), that anchor the drama triangle. Can you identify anyone in your life who might major in one of these three positions? All of us have been on the triangle from time to time and quite likely we'll all visit it again. The key is to recognize the symptoms and diagnose a cure as quickly as possible.

How do we know if we're on it? Simple. Any time you catch yourself casting blame, criticizing, or meddling you can be rest assured you're on it.

JOURNAL ENTRY

I'm the best reason in the world to change ... so I'll change!

Can you recall a time in your life when you were behaving as rescuer, persecutor or victim?

_____

_____

_____

_____

If so, can you also remember getting off?

_____

_____

_____

If you got off, can you recall what you did to get off?

PROGRAM

_____

_____

_____

_____

Can you see anyone in your world who seems to be a captive of one of the three roles? If so, what do they do that makes you think this?

_____

_____

_____

_____

Remember at this juncture we are only trying to create awareness of listening and our interpretation of the world around us. There's nothing more that you need do just yet.

DAY ELEVEN – P.M. MESSAGE

You are doing fantastic. Let's keep going!

Affirmations are one of the most effective ways of laying down thoughts.

Affirmations that you use over a period of time program your subconscious brain to help you make positive changes – especially the ones you are finding hard to do. Affirmations create DSP connections in the brain that change the beliefs and attitudes that lead to changes in your behavior.

Remember, your subconscious brain takes every statement you send as literally real. Every time you repeat an affirmation, your subconscious brain forms new DSP connections. If you repeat them over a long enough period of time – say twenty-nine days – it will change your beliefs and subsequently your behavior.

Write out one very simple affirmation that you feel completely comfortable repeating. For example:

◊ "I am a great listener."
◊ "I can hear what people say far beyond their words."
◊ "I have the ability to see the world through another's eyes."
◊ "I'm OK, You're OK."
◊ "I can listen empathically to others."
◊ "I can listen to others without judgment"

My Affirmation:

_____

Out of this affirmation will come the results you seek. Loving and approving of yourself will give you an aura that will extend to the important people in your world. To listen to another person, really listen, is one of the greatest gifts you can give.

Whatever your affirmation, find something that resonates with you and it will come to be.

> *You will be a failure, until you impress the*
> *subconscious with the conviction you are a success.*
> *This is done by making an affirmation which "clicks."*
> *~ Florence Scovel Shinn*

Affirmations take a period of time to work, but when they do they are extremely powerful. Trust in the process, it's been proven to work.

Write out your new affirmation every now and again. If you are the type of person who occasionally doodles, try writing out your affirmation instead. Writing affirmations is a dynamic technique because the written word has so much more power over our minds. When we write self-messages down we are reading them as we write them, so it's creating a double hit of positive psychological support for our actions.

Congratulations on another great day.

See you tomorrow!

PROGRAM

... to becoming a great listener and communicator!

PROGRAM

DAY TWELVE
I'm the best reason in the world to change ... so I'll change!

DAY TWELVE – A.M.

Welcome back, it's day twelve already! You've shown all the qualities of patience, perseverance and the inner self-confidence that is so vital to permanent results. How do I know? You're here, that's all the proof necessary. If you stick with it, you *will* reach your goal of becoming a great listener and communicator and it will happen sooner than you may have thought possible.

Over the next three days we are going to take a deeper look at the three positions of the drama triangle. Understanding social psychology can be very useful toward your goal of becoming great listener and communicator?

If you're seeing the world from any of these three positions:
"I'm Not OK, You're OK"
"I'm OK, You're Not OK"
"I'm Not OK, You're Not OK"

then you cannot sincerely listen to another person. If you're stuck in any of these three positions your thinking will be clouded and judgmental.

You're also aware that the only way you can be on the drama triangle is if you're taking one of the three "negative" OK positions.

For these reasons we're going to take a closer look at each position over the next three days.

Today we're going to examine the role of persecutor.

PROGRAM

LEARNING TO LISTEN TO YOURSELF: PART ONE

No one can really change *the* world, but we *can* change ourselves. If we change ourselves, *we can* change *our* world.

We cannot change ourselves until we become *aware* of ourselves – that means becoming aware of our self-talk and inner thoughts.

This program is designed to help you become a great listener and communicator. It's highly likely that most people never thought that the first step to becoming a good listener is to listen to *themselves*. That's right, who would think it's necessary to eavesdrop on one's very own self-talk? After all, we know what we say and what we think … don't we? Probably not!

As we said on day seven, when we become aware of our self-talk we're very often shocked and appalled at our self-generating negativity. Most of us wouldn't dream of talking to other people in the manner in which we regularly talk to ourselves.

Science has learned through research studies that eighty percent of our self-talk is negative. Habitual negative dialogue can become so crippling it leaves us stressed out and powerless. By becoming aware of the flow of our debilitating thoughts we become aware of the source of our self-defeating behaviors. This simple awareness can quickly help us to become our very own therapist rather than our very own worst enemy.

Over the next three days you're going to administer a self-examination. You're going to see if you subconsciously consider yourself a victim. Feelings of victimhood can usurp your power and leave you feeling guilty, angry, and taken advantage of by others. Establishing clear self-awareness of your internal thought process will have a dramatic effect on your life.

At one time or another, all of us have spent some time on the drama triangle. Some people choose to stay on it for life. Some people get on and off on a regular basis. As you'll soon see, there's a foolproof way to know if you're on it. Once you know you're on it … you can *consciously get off it.* Doing so – taking the proactive steps to get off the drama triangle – will dramatically change your life and the lives of those around you.

Wiretap Your Subconscious Thoughts

The easiest way to begin the process of introspection is to "listen-in" on your self-talk. This self-talk is nothing other than the life-long programs that your subconscious mind runs in an endless loop. That means your conscious mind is going to be the hunter and the old subconscious programs are your prey.

Suppose you're driving home from work and you're stuck in traffic. You're consciously thinking about approaching your boss for a well-deserved raise, but you also begin to listen-in on some competing thoughts that are rolling around in your mind such as:

- "He's not going to give me a raise; I know he'll turn me down."
- "After I do something really positive, I always do something negative and screw things up."
- "Maybe I should just accept where I am and leave it at that."
- "Why should I get a raise? There are probably other people in the department more deserving than I."

Whatever your internal dialogue may be, it is vital that you wiretap these thoughts because they are the true source of your beliefs, feelings and behaviors. If you have a sense that your life is determined by other people and outside forces, you can be certain that you're riding the drama triangle. As long as you're on this *drama ride* you will see yourself as a victim. As long as you see yourself as a victim, you've rendered yourself powerless to change. If, however, you can tap into your inner thoughts and understand how they sabotage your life, then you have stepped off the drama triangle and you're no longer subject to living your life in frustration, helplessness and victimhood.

Today we will look at the role of persecutor.

The Drama Triangle – Persecutor, Example #1

Martha, a senior supervisor for an overnight delivery service, oversees a staff of several hundred people. Martha takes her job very seriously and will do anything in her power to make sure her department runs smoothly. She often works late into the evening and on weekends. She's a perfectionist and expects her employees to follow her work ethic and perform their work without error. Martha has created a world of unachievable demands and expectations.

Martha fails to see that she often projects an angry aura. She is often upset with her staff because "they refuse to take their work seriously." In fact, hardly a day goes by that somebody doesn't make an unnecessary mistake. Martha believes her employees are deliberately careless in their duties in order to make *her* look bad. As far as she is concerned, if they want to be that way, two can play at this game! Is it any wonder that Martha has more ulcers than she has friends?

When Martha started to eavesdrop on her inner dialogue, she was surprised at the extent of her self-generating negativity:

- "They want to get me fired so they can slack off like they did before I came onboard."
- "The only thing they care about is their paycheck. Nobody cares a wit about job performance."
- "I'll have the best department in the company, even though my staff are out to sabotage me."
- "I have to carry the entire department on my back!"

Martha's superiors liked her personal work ethic, her attention to details, and her many other abilities, but they were also concerned with the general morale of her department. When one of Martha's superiors spoke to her about the staff morale, Martha immediately began to consider which of her employees were responsible for the breach. She would see that they lived to regret it!

Something Must Give to End This Cycle

Problem – Martha lives most of her life as a persecutor. She has a deep-seated belief that the world is a hostile place and that she must attack to survive.

Typical Thought Process
"The people in my department don't care about the work they do. If I don't use the whip they'll get nothing done and I'll be out on the street. It's either me or them."

Resulting Action from Her Typical Thoughts
Martha's demanding and intolerant. She fails to recognize good work, but never overlooks a fault. She's usually irritable because her life is one crisis after another.

Breaking Free of the Drama Triangle
When Martha got angry with her employees she was a persecutor with a mission. When her superiors spoke to her about the poor staff morale, she instantly became the victim. The staff was out to get her. She had to fight back. They totally deserved her wrath. When Martha finally stopped long enough to realize the never-ending drama her hostile thoughts were creating, she began to ease up on her staff. She began to realize that mistakes are made. There wasn't any grand conspiracy against her.

When Martha began to examine her inner thoughts, she was surprised at the anger and intolerance that she had been subjecting upon herself and those around her. When she began to change her internal thoughts from, "It's a dog-eat-dog world," to "The world will mirror back my thoughts and actions," she began to change her thoughts and behavior. Almost as if by magic her world changed right along with her. She quickly realized that she was not a helpless victim of a hostile world. There was no grand conspiracy against her. If hostile thoughts could create a hostile world, then cooperative thoughts could create a cooperative world.

Freedom from the Drama Triangle – persecutor > rescuer > victim
As soon as Martha changed her thinking she broke free from the persecutor, rescuer, victim cycle.

Real-World Situation
Martha's department gets overloaded with packages following a long weekend. A key corporate customer lodges a complaint about a delay in shipments. Martha is confronted by her superior about the problem. Martha no longer plays the victim to her boss or the persecutor to her staff.

Resulting Action
Martha calls a staff meeting and asks her employees for their views on the problem and what they might do in the future to avoid a similar experience.

New Thought Process
"We're all in this together. Problems are part of life. If we work as a team we can find solutions and our department will function as a cohesive unit."

Future Behavior
Martha changes her internal thoughts and no longer plays the victim/drama game. She deals with problems as they come up. She no longer sees problems and mishaps as personal attacks. By wiretapping her subconscious thoughts, she could consciously change those irrational negative thoughts to conscious thoughts that she could begin to believe in. Both her job and her world quickly become an enjoyable place to be.

The Drama Triangle – Persecutor, Example #2
Bill was a natural, all-around athlete who had gone to university on a football scholarship. When he finished school he joined the city police force and quickly rose through the ranks to senior detective. His passion for sports never left him. As soon as his son Mark was old enough to play little league baseball, Bill had him enrolled and took over as the team's coach.

Although Mark was a good player, he lacked the natural athletic talent that had always made Bill the stand-out star. Bill was convinced that Mark wasn't applying himself. It seemed to Bill that the more he urged Mark to push himself to get better, the more Mark would deliberately rebel. Bill began to take Mark's cavalier attitude as a personal attack. Bill (assuming the persecutor role), decided to give Mark after-school batting lessons and to make him practice throwing and fielding several extra hours each week.

Naturally Mark started to push back to the point where he told Bill that he hated playing baseball. In fact, Mark insisted he hated playing all sports. He preferred playing video games to running around outside in the grass and mud. Bill didn't know how or why, but he was convinced that Mark was deliberately turning his back on sports to make him look bad. Bill began to feel like a victim. "What would everyone think if the coach's own son quit playing? He would look like a fool," thought Bill. Bill told Mark in no uncertain terms that if he didn't play baseball he could forget about playing video games or watching TV.

Something Must Give to End This Cycle
Problem
Bill sees Mark's disinterest in baseball as a deliberate attempt to undermine him. For some "unknown" reason Mark's rejecting to play for the very team Bill's coaching. Bill feels victimized.

Typical Thought Process
Bill sees himself going out of his way to help his son become a great ball player. Instead of gratitude, Mark throws it right back in his face. As far as Bill sees it, if Mark's going to deliberately make him look foolish then he deserves to be punished in return. Mark will have to learn how the game of life is played.

Resulting Action from Bill's Typical Thought Process
Bill sees himself as the victim. Instead of letting his son enjoy playing baseball at his own level, or even choose not to play at all, Bill pressures his son into playing, and when Mark fails to live up to Bill's expectations, he takes it as a personal attack. The more Bill persecutes, the more Mark lashes back leaving Bill to play the innocent victim card.

Breaking Free of the Drama Triangle
When Bill finally slowed down long enough to listen to his inner thoughts he was stunned to hear how he was aggressively attacking his son and then playing the victim when his son lashed back.

Freedom from the Drama Triangle
When Bill began to realize his duties as a father, and as a coach, he quickly dropped the role

PROGRAM

of victim. He could see that the more he tried to manipulate his son into playing ball, along with the added pressure to perform at Bill's expected level, the greater the likelihood that Mark would either curl up as a victim or strike back as a persecutor.

Real World Situation

By examining his negative thoughts, Bill quickly came to the realization that his job as little league coach was to return to his personal love of sports and to enjoy coaching the kids on the team, whether that included Mark or not. Bill owed it to himself and his players to be the best coach he could be. If Mark lost interest in baseball, he was entitled to that choice. Bill owed Mark his love and guidance as a father.

Resulting Action

As soon as Bill withdrew his persecution of Mark to play and perform at Bill's ideal level, he immediately eliminated the pressure on Mark. It wasn't long before Mark willingly re-joined the team and began to show a natural talent that surprised even Bill.

New Thought Process

Each of us are responsible for our own happiness. It comes from within.

Future Behavior

Bill escaped the drama triangle by examining his inner thoughts and then changing what and who he had the power to change ... himself. He realized his old patterned thoughts were wildly untrue. It wasn't his son Mark who had created the problem. The sole source of Bill's anger and frustration were his false assumptions about the world. There wasn't any conspiracy and people weren't acting to spite him. These were self-created delusions and incorrect programs that were written and installed many years ago.

Freedom from the Drama Triangle

As soon as Bill tuned into his inner thoughts, analyzed and examined them, he changed his thinking and quickly broke free from the deadly cycle of prosecutor/victim.

STEP 12 – Consider the phenomenon of the persecutor role. I'm sure all of us can associate playing the role at one time or another. Many of us may know of people in our lives who are clearly entrenched in the role of persecutor. Our goal at this stage is to achieve awareness. To avoid branding, labeling or categorizing ourselves or anyone else.

PROGRAM

JOURNAL ENTRY

I'm the best reason in the world to change ... so I'll change!

I remember the last time I played the role of persecutor. In the future if I catch myself slipping into the role of blaming other people I will do the following to stop myself from playing this destructive role.

I will –

_____

_____

_____

_____

A man can fail many times, but he isn't a failure
until he begins to blame somebody else.
~ John Burroughs

DAY TWELVE – P.M. MESSAGE

I hope you gave some thought to the drama triangle and to the role of persecutor. You may very well know someone who is presently trapped in this role. Perhaps if you do, and you have the unfortunate experience of crossing paths, you might now be better equipped to understand and cope with the experience. If you catch yourself in this role, think of something to snap yourself out of it. Perhaps it's an affirmation, or perhaps it may mean some meditation or deeper introspection. Maybe it's just a simple matter of wiretapping your subconscious thoughts and being aware of some old faulty programs.

Congratulations on another great day.

A good leader takes a little more than his share of the blame,
a little less than his share of the credit.
~ Arnold H. Glasgow

See you tomorrow!

29 DAYS . . . to becoming a great listener and communicator!

DAY THIRTEEN
I'm the best reason in the world to change ... so I'll change!

DAY THIRTEEN – A.M.

Hey, welcome back. You have been with us now for thirteen days, and rest assured, you have traveled far.

LEARNING TO LISTEN TO YOURSELF: PART TWO

No one can really change the world, but we can change ourselves. If we change ourselves, we can change our world. In order to change ourselves we need to become aware of ourselves – that means becoming aware of our self-talk and inner thoughts.

Today we are going to examine the second position on the drama triangle. Remember, everyone on the triangle will assume each of the three roles as they swing from corner to corner, sometimes changing roles within hours, minutes or even seconds. Everyone on the triangle will eventually end up a victim, but all players have a preferential entry point, i.e. persecutor, rescuer or victim.

Today is day two of your self-administered examination. Establishing clear self-awareness of your internal thought process will have a dramatic effect on your life. At one time or another, all of us have spent some time on the drama triangle. Some people choose to stay on it for life. Some people get on and off on a regular basis. As you'll soon see, there's a foolproof way to know if you're on it. Once you know you're on it ... you can consciously get off it, and that response will dramatically change your life and the lives of those around you.

Rescuer | Persecutor

Victim

Yesterday we examined the entry point of the person who favors the persecutor position. Today we will look at the person who favors the rescuer position.

Wiretap Your Subconscious Thoughts

The easiest way to begin the process of introspection is to "listen-in" on your self-talk. Whatever your internal dialogue may be, it is vital that you wiretap these thoughts because they are the "true" source of your beliefs, feelings and behaviors.

The Drama Triangle – Rescuer, Example #1

A core belief to remember about a rescuer is their overriding thought process, which basically states, "My needs are not important ... I am only valued for what I can do for others."

Six months earlier Gary was promoted to project manager for a large architectural firm. Gary had shown himself to be a hardworking, conscientious, dedicated employee. In spite of his many qualities, Gary is beginning to experience a number of work-related problems that are affecting his job, his family and his health.

Gary didn't realize that he was trapped on the drama triangle and that his favored position was playing the role of rescuer. He felt that as project manager he had to personally make sure every task was finished on time and that everyone was happy with his performance. If a project fell behind schedule, Gary would take on the assignment himself to make sure the deadlines were met. In his effort to please his associates and superiors, Gary accepted every project that was given to him despite the fact that he and his staff were already overwhelmed with their current tasks. It didn't take long before the cracks started to appear. Gary went from working late each day to working full weekends. Communication between Gary and his staff started to break-down. Timelines were missed occasionally, at first, and then gradually grew in extension and frequency. Before long Gary grew irritable and his health began to deteriorate. His department and the projects they worked on were in disarray. Gary had gone from being a valued, conscientious employee, to a manager who was viewed as incompetent. Senior members of the firm began to openly complain about missed timelines and the poor execution of many projects.

As the pressure mounted Gary began to take sick days, which only compounded matters.

One day, while lying in bed with a terrible cold, Gary began to ponder what had gone so terribly wrong in such a short time.

After all he had done for everyone, taking on extra assignments and working weekends, nobody seemed to appreciate him. While thinking things through it began to dawn on him

PROGRAM

that he had created the entire mess because he had failed to listen and understand the thoughts that had created the situation. In his desire to please everyone, he had managed just the opposite. Gary suddenly had an "aha" moment, when he saw that his rescuer mentality was completely responsible for the entire messy affair. Gary saw himself as a victim. Everyone had turned on him. His associates were upset, his superiors were upset, even his own body was letting him down. It seemed like the whole world was out to get him and all he had tried to do was help!

When Gary listened-in to his self-talk, he heard himself say that as project manager he had to manage every project given to him *and* he had to make sure everything was done to perfection. As project manager he had to keep both his associates and superiors happy with his performance. Gary saw that by accepting every project presented to him he had set himself and his department up for certain failure.

Something Must Give To End This Cycle
Problem
Gary was desperate to please everyone and incapable of saying no.

Typical Thought Process
"As project manager I am responsible for seeing that all projects are accepted and completed. I must be certain that no one is displeased with me or my department."

Resulting Action from His Typical Thoughts
Gary took on far too many assignments. He set himself and his department up for certain failure.

Breaking Free of the Drama Triangle
Gary had to realize his limitations. He had to learn to properly evaluate what was being requested. Gary learned that saying *no* to his superiors was part of his job as project manager. He realized that his job was to manage his department. No one expected him to play the role of super rescuer who could do all things.

Freedom from the Drama Triangle
When Gary tapped into his inner thoughts, he instantly saw how destructive they were. He realized that he had every right to say *no*. He realized that his rescuer thoughts and expectations were totally unrealistic.

Real-World Situation

When Gary returned to work he found that there were several new project requests on his desk in addition to the overloaded assignments his department was currently addressing.

Resulting Action

Gary called a staff meeting and explained how his thinking had led to the present situation. Gary then met with his superiors and told them what he had just realized about his management style and how he would change things in the future.

New Thought Process

Gary suggested to his staff that they would begin to review assignments as a group. As a team, they would determine tasks and completion dates. Everyone would be responsible for their share of the work.

Future Behavior

Gary stopped playing the role of rescuer. He began to manage his staff and the projects they could complete. When Gary and his department accepted assignments, Gary made sure that each staff member carried their load. He realized it wasn't his duty to pick up the slack for anyone else. Everyone had a job to do and each person was responsible to see its completion. Most importantly Gary learned to say *no* to his superiors when he and his department had more work than they could responsibly handle. The results were almost instantaneous. Projects were completed on time without confusion, stress and errors. Morale returned and work was fun and productive.

The Drama Triangle – Rescuer - Example #2

Kathy was a highly over-protective mother. She was a rescuer. Kathy had grown up in a home where she was largely ignored. Her mother was a busy socialite and her father was usually away on business. Kathy had an overwhelming unconscious desire to be needed and valued. As a single, divorced mother, Kathy unwittingly became an overprotective mother to her daughter, Sandy.

When Sandy was young, Kathy would interfere if Sandy had a childhood disagreement with a playmate. If a teacher or family member said anything even mildly reproachful about Sandy, Kathy would defend her daughter with a vengeance. If Sandy misbehaved at school, Kathy would find an excuse for the behavior. Kathy tried hard to remove any form of negativity from Sandy's life and as a result, she unwittingly robbed Sandy of the experience of making her own decisions and learning how to handle the consequences of those decisions.

As Sandy grew into her early teens Kathy continued to assume complete responsibility for her rebelling daughter. Sandy was caught shoplifting and Kathy blew it off as a foolish mistake that many young girls make. When Sandy began skipping school in her early high school years, Kathy said that Sandy was just too bright and consequently bored with the curriculum. Sandy's next unconscious "cry for help" was when the police picked her up at a local shopping mall for disorderly conduct, public intoxication and under-age drinking. When Kathy went to the police station to pick Sandy up, she found herself trying to justify Sandy's behavior. When she finally realized what she was doing, her justification quickly switched to anger and the victim's cry of, "How could she do this to me? After all I've done for her this is the thanks I get!"

Something Must Give To End This Cycle
Problem
Kathy is a rescuer who desperately needs someone to rescue. Since Sandy was a little girl, Kathy tried to be everything that her parents weren't. There's nothing wrong with a mother showering her child with attention, but Kathy was so overprotective that she removed the lessons of life that every child has to learn on their own. Kathy was unconsciously fulfilling her own needs to rescue and be needed, and consequently she robbed Sandy of the chance to experience life and to find her own way.

Typical Thought Process
Kathy saw herself trying to be the parent that she never had. She would always be there for her daughter no matter what. She would make certain that Sandy never felt alone, unloved or abandoned as she had when she was growing up.

Resulting Action from Kathy's Typical Thought Process
When Sandy was picked up by the police and Kathy found herself trying to make excuses for Sandy's inexcusable behavior, she finally began to see her role in Sandy's desperate situation. When Kathy began to listen to her self-talk she started to realize that she alone had created this problem.

Breaking Free of the Drama Triangle
As Kathy began to wiretap her inner thoughts and she caught herself actually trying to justify Sandy's public intoxication as "part-of-growing-up," she had an instant awakening. She finally admitted to herself that she was looking after her own interests when she continued to over-protect and cover for Sandy's poor behavioral choices.

Freedom from the Drama Triangle

As soon as Kathy realized her thought process and what her over-protection was doing to Sandy's life, she forced herself to step back.

Real-World Situation

Kathy also had to learn to drop the rescuer role. She began to understand that Sandy had to learn to make her own decisions and deal with the resulting consequences. Kathy had to let Sandy know she was there for her and that she loved her, but that didn't mean she would always have to protect her and bail her out from making egregious choices.

Resulting Action

Kathy forced herself not to interfere in Sandy's latest predicament with the police. After all, Sandy had made the decision to behave the way she did, she would have to learn that those behaviors had consequences. Kathy made sure that Sandy knew she was there to listen and support her, but she would no longer interfere or try to protect her from the consequences of poor decisions.

New Thought Process

Kathy realized that she had been subconsciously fulfilling her own needs by playing the role of Rescuer. When Kathy stepped back and let Sandy make her own decisions, and realize that she would have to live with the consequences, both good and bad, Sandy quickly grew up and began making responsible decisions.

Future Behavior

Kathy escaped the drama triangle by examining her inner thoughts and then changing what, and who she had the power to change … herself. Sandy realized that being overprotective and justifying Sandy's behavior was damaging her life and Sandy's as well. Kathy had to pull back from assuming the rescuer role and learn to let the people in her life live their own lives and make their own decisions.

Freedom from the Drama Triangle

As soon as Kathy caught on to her old thinking and habits, she identified the problem and changed her way of thinking. Within a short time Sandy had learned to become a responsible student, and Kathy learned to become a mother who showered her daughter with love rather than protection and interference.

STEP 13 – Consider the phenomenon of the rescuer's role. I'm sure all of us can associate with playing this role at one time or another. Many of us may know of people in our lives who are clearly entrenched in the role of rescuer. It's very easy to be pulled into this role especially as a manager or concerned parent. Any form of rescue will only be a temporary solution. Inevitably it will lead to much greater long-term pain. Our goal at this stage is to achieve awareness. It's not to brand, label or categorize ourselves or anyone else.

JOURNAL ENTRY

I'm the best reason in the world to change ... so I'll change!

I remember the last time I played the role of rescuer. In the future if I catch myself slipping into the role of rescuer or meddling in other people's affairs for personal gain, I will do the following to stop myself from playing this destructive role.

I will –

_____

_____

_____

Rescue someone unwilling to look after himself,
and he will cling to you like a dangerous illness.
~ Mason Cooley

Remember, it's never a good idea to act as a rescuer and take care of other people's affairs. if we haven't been asked explicitly, and even if we have been asked, we might still wisely and respectfully decline.

DAY THIRTEEN – P.M. MESSAGE

Today we looked at the second role of the drama triangle, the role of rescuer. Since we're on the topic of rescuing, I think the following story so perfectly illustrates the danger of following our natural inclination to rescue our children, spouses and anyone who *appears* to need help.

PROGRAM

I don't mean to suggest that everyone who tries to rescue another is guilty of being a rescuer on the drama triangle. Far from it. I'm also not about to imply that we shouldn't offer our aid to people who may require it. Enough said, read this story and I think you'll see what I mean by being aware of the act of rescuing and its myriad ramifications ... both to ourselves and the person in distress.

A number of years ago Earl Nightingale shared a story that he attributed to Henry Miller, an author, about a little boy in India who went up to a guru who was sitting and looking at something in his hand. When the little boy approached the guru he was puzzled by what he saw the guru holding. "What is that?" asked the boy.

"It's a cocoon," answered the guru, "You see son, inside the cocoon is a butterfly. Very soon the cocoon is going to split, and the butterfly will come out and fly away."

"Could I have it?" asked the little boy.

"Yes," said the guru, "but if I give it to you, you must promise me that when the cocoon splits and the butterfly starts to come out and it begins to beat its wings to get out of the cocoon, you won't help it. It's very important not to help the butterfly by breaking the cocoon apart. It must do it all on its own."

Well the little boy promised not to help the butterfly as he took the cocoon and went home with it. He then sat and watched it. Not too long after he saw the cocoon begin to vibrate and move and quiver, and finally it split in half. Inside was a beautiful damp butterfly, frantically beating its wings against the cocoon, trying to get out but not seeming to be able to do so. The little boy desperately wanted to help. Finally, he gave in, and pushed the two halves of the cocoon apart. The butterfly sprang out and began to fly upwards, but as soon as it got a little ways into the air its wings stopped beating and it fell to the ground and died. The little boy picked up the dead butterfly and with tears in his eyes he went back to the guru and showed it to him.

The guru looked at the little boy and then at the dead butterfly and said, "You pushed open the cocoon, didn't you?"

"Yes," admitted the little boy, "I did."

The guru spoke to him gravely, "You didn't understand what you were doing when you tried to help the butterfly. When it first comes out of the cocoon, the only way it can strengthen its wings is by beating them against the cocoon. It beats against the cocoon so its muscles will grow strong. When you helped it, you prevented it from developing the muscles it would need to survive."

It's a story all of us should remember the next time we're inclined to rush in and rescue someone who appears to have a dilemma. Whether it requires us to wait patiently while a child or student tries to solve a problem, or we allow an employee to find a solution on his own, it's often the only way a person can grow. If we continually jump in with advice, solutions and aid, we may be committing the very mistake the little boy did with the butterfly. We are robbing the person in distress of the chance to experience life, to learn and to grow. This is known as "learned helplessness," and it's the result of never being given the chance to develop one's own resources and self-confidence.

When you wish to rush to someone's aid, check your motives. Are you being impatient? Do you find it too difficult not to dipense advice? Often, if you just sit and listen and maybe pose a question or two, the distressed person can figure out their own solution.

In most cases, what may appear to be harsh or cruel in nature, is, in actual fact, a vital process for survival and growth. It's something to think about the next time we instinctively want to rush to someone's aid.

Congratulations on another great day.

See you tomorrow!

DAY FOURTEEN
I'm the best reason in the world to change ... so I'll change!

DAY FOURTEEN – A.M.

Hey, welcome back. Huge congratulations, you're almost halfway there. You have come a long way. Today, is reward day. You have earned it and you deserve it. Let's recap what we said a week ago about rewards. Research shows that tangible rewards provide psychological motivation. Rewards are the easiest, most effective psychological motivators known.

When thinking of a reward, think small. Small rewards are a form of recognition rather than becoming an end in themselves. Your reward should have the following two qualities:

1. It should be appropriate to your goal.
2. It should be free or inexpensive.

What's an Appropriate Reward?

One that supports your goal.

What Small Reward Could You Give Yourself that Would Be Free or Inexpensive?

Possible Ideas for a Reward:
- Give yourself a manicure
- Go see a movie
- Read a book
- Go for a walk
- Watch a movie or TV
- Buy a Magazine
- Play a round of golf or a game of tennis

- Think of something you may not normally do and "DO IT!" It's important to do something you really enjoy doing.

LEARNING TO LISTEN TO YOURSELF: PART THREE

Today we are going to examine the third position on the drama triangle. Remember, everyone on the triangle will assume each of the three roles as they dance from corner to corner, sometimes changing roles within hours, minutes or even seconds. Everyone on the triangle will eventually end up a victim, but all players have a preferential entry point, i.e. persecutor, rescuer or victim.

Today is day three of your self-administered examination. Establishing clear self-awareness of your internal thought process will have a dramatic effect on your life. At one time or another, all of us have spent some time on the drama triangle. Some people choose to stay on it for life. Some people get on and off on a regular basis. As you know there's an easy way to know if you're on it. If you catch yourself on it, you can consciously get off it, and that will dramatically change your life and the lives of those around you.

Yesterday we examined the entry point of the person who favors the rescuer position. Today we will look at the person who favors the victim position.

The person who enters the drama triangle from the victim position will often incite others to use them as verbal, mental, emotional and physical punching bags. They see themselves at the mercy of outside forces and events. They don't accept responsibility for their actions, after all why should they when they have *no control* over events and situations? They are merely defenseless victims of a cruel world. The victim can easily be identified by their frequent complaining, and general incompetence.

Wiretap Your Subconscious Thoughts

The easiest way to begin the process of introspection is to "listen-in" on your self-talk. Whatever your internal dialogue may be, it is vital that you wiretap these thoughts because they are the "true" source of your beliefs, feelings and behaviors.

The Drama Triangle – Victim, Example #1

> *Definition of a victim: a person to whom life happens.*
> *~ Peter McWilliams*

PROGRAM

People entrenched in the victim mode view the world as "I'm Not OK, You're OK."

Jim was born the third child of four boys. His father, Jack, was a hard-driving entrepreneur who owned a large number of car dealerships. In fact, over the past thirty years Jack had systematically bought up just about every dealership in the city allowing him to enjoy a near monopoly.

Since the time Jack's sons were old enough to work, he had brought them into the business. After each had learned the automotive retail business, through various positions from washing cars to sales to management, they were each given their own dealership.

Three of the brothers managed to increase sales year after year. Jim was the exception. The first year Jim was in charge of his own dealership sales slipped for the first time. Jim blamed it on the economic downturn. The next year sales fell a little further and Jim suggested to his father that some of the sales managers he had inherited were at fault. Jim let a number of key people go and replaced them with some longtime friends whom he felt he could trust.

When Jack called an annual meeting to review each of his dealerships with his sons and the other supervisors, everyone had shown an increase in sales except Jim's dealership. When it came time for Jim to give his report and his plans for the future he flew into a rage and said that the slumping sales had nothing to do with him. The dealership he had was for high-end foreign cars and due to the economy and the price of fuel, what could anyone expect him to do? These sales results were beyond his control. If he had been given a "proper" dealership like everyone else, he would be showing a profit as well. What could anyone expect? How were the economy and fuel prices his fault, he demanded to know.

Before long Jim turned the blame onto his father for giving him the most difficult dealership to manage. Jim suggested that one of his brothers or someone who was running one of the other dealerships trade stores with him and see how they liked it. Besides, Jim wailed, he never asked for this responsibility in the first place.

Jack was desperate to see his son Jim succeed so he decided to give Jim the most lucrative dealership he had. When Jack told Jim the good news Jim was internally gripped with terror. He knew this store could practically run itself and if he screwed things up, which he feared he would, how would he deal with the shame?

Not long afterward Jim developed a stomach ulcer and had to take time off. He started to drink heavily, which only compounded matters. Before long, Jim was in hospital. It was a

PROGRAM

fortunate thing. Jim finally stopped the whirlwind of anger and blame and began to wiretap his subconscious thoughts. Jim could hardly believe the negativity, hate and anger that he was inflicting on himself.

Jim heard himself say once too often that nothing was his fault, that he should be looked after, that the world was out to "get him" and how he was just a helpless victim. When Jim started to analyze his life, honestly and openly, he quickly began to see his world from a different view. Jim realized that the excuses and negativity had no bearing in reality. He began to lash out at the persecuting programs he had so willingly played. He began to see that he had actually been given a great deal and that any failure he might have experienced could be attributed to his internal dialogue, thoughts and programs.

Jim had had an epiphany. No longer would he play the victim card. No longer would he allow the internal negative programs to play. Jim vowed to shut that part down and begin to focus on all that he had been given and the unlimited potential that he could exercise.

Something Must Give To End This Cycle

Problem
Jim sees himself as a victim. Everyone's capable but himself. He runs his life on negative self-defeating programs.

Typical Thought Process
"Things never seem to go well for me. In fact, I'm not cut out for a role of responsibility. Since I know things are going to go wrong, I need to identify the outside forces that are the cause of my failure. If I can find the cause of my downfall, then nobody will hold it against me. They'll see the problem and lend me a hand."

Resulting Action from His Typical Thoughts
Jim became his very own fortuneteller with an uncanny ability to predict the future. The fact that the world was pitted against him is an obvious fallacy; the world, as it were, has bigger fish to fry. To Jim's mind however, he saw the world "for what it really was." As long as he assumed the role of victim, his belief became his reality.

Breaking Free of the Drama Triangle
Jim had an "aha" moment. He began to see how he shaped his "truth." Jim suddenly realized how he had allowed his internal negativity to create his role as helpless victim. Jim's "aha" moment was the clarity that he indeed had powers, but he was using those very powers to destroy himself. Jim saw that his negative thoughts created a negative reality, and since he

PROGRAM

created his thoughts, he directly created his reality. In an instant Jim saw that he had the power to change his thoughts and that by doing so he could replace the negative world with a positive one. Jim was no longer a helpless victim of outside forces, he would shape his world as a result of directing his thoughts.

Freedom from the Drama Triangle

When Jim tapped into his inner thoughts, he instantly saw how destructive they were. He realized that his life was the result of destructive thoughts, and they were *his* thoughts. Jim finally understood that his self made and self manufactured negative thoughts kept him in the drama triangle dance of a perpetual victim.

Real-World Situation

Jim soon left his hospital bed and returned to work with an entirely different attitude. He no longer carried the doom and gloom of a victim. Jim began to manage his staff. Everyone had their duties and everyone had a job to fulfill. Everyone was responsible to carry their share and Jim saw himself as ultimately being responsible for his staff and the performance of his organization.

Resulting Action

Jim called his staff together and explained that they were a team with a mission. He was counting on them to help him fulfill their corporate goals, because as Jim put it, "We've got the number-one dealership in the state, and I'm going to see to it that we have the number-one dealership in the country."

New Thought Process

Jim's thoughts, energy and focus went from negativity and excuses to channeling his focus to becoming pro-active and accepting responsibility.

Future Behavior

Jim dropped the role of victim. With his new attitude of accepting responsibility his staff responded in kind. Since Jim began to hold himself accountable, he could confidently request the same from his staff. The change in attitude permeated throughout the entire organization. The results were almost instantaneous and sales volumes began to rise.

STEP 14 – Consider the phenomenon of the victim's role. All of us can associate playing the role at one time or another. Since it's the end result of any of the three roles, by definition it's the most "popular" position. None of us can avoid embracing the role of victim from time-to-time, but the key is to quickly recognize when we're embracing the role and then

PROGRAM

immediately abandon it. To lay blame or claim helplessness can be as alluring as the "call of the sirens," but succumbing to *the call* is to give away one's power to live. By playing the role we become as helpless as a baby, dependent on others to carry us.

The drama triangle is so alluring because it gives us a ready excuse to blame and avoid responsibility. Although it would be nice, getting off the triangle forever is most unlikely. Now that you have awareness of the triangle and how it's played, your ability to recognize yourself and others on it will go a long, long way to ensuring you spend very little time blaming or scapegoating in the future.

JOURNAL ENTRY

I'm the best reason in the world to change ... so I'll change!

I remember the last time I played the role of victim. In future, the moment I catch myself playing the role of helpless victim or I begin to blame misfortune or others for any results in my life, I will do the following to immediately stop myself from playing this destructive role.

I will –

_____

_____

A strong, successful person is not the victim of his environment.
He creates favorable conditions. His own inherent force and energy
compel things to turn out as he desires.
~ Orison Swett Marden

Today is reward day. For my reward I gave myself –

_____

The second week is complete.

- Week one was about awareness and commitment. "I know I'm committed to becoming a great listener and communicator."

PROGRAM

- Week two was about further commitment and embedding those neurological tracks into a new, powerful way of thinking.

On day eight you wrote out two sets of listening and communication goals. Please take a moment and review those goals. Are they still in alignment with the way you feel today? Are there any changes you would like to make?

Please take some time to do the following assignment. Write out a short paragraph, or even a one-line affirmation, that will help you overcome any negative thoughts or doubts about your success. Your amygdala will challenge you but only for a short time. Once it knows you are serious and that you won't be dissuaded from your goal, it will work to support you. That is when you know, and you know that you know, that listening and communicating effectively is a life long commitment.

Whenever I am tempted to discard my new commitment to effective communication and listening, whenever I feel lazy and want to slide back to my old ineffective listening habits, I will recite the following statement to bring myself back to focusing on my new skill. Whenever I catch myself NOT listening effectively I will say:

_____

_____

DAY FOURTEEN – P.M. MESSAGE

Way to go. You've completed two full weeks. You must be primed and ready to get into action.

As you know, when most people set goals, they start off at the action stage. The high rate of failure, from New Year's resolutions to diets to spur-of-the-moment promises of change, are a testament to the problem of quick change and ignoring our self-image.

You are travelling a different path. You spent the first week building commitment and awareness. The second week you continued to build on your psychological commitment to listening and communicating and you began to prepare yourself to face the challenges of action.

You have laid the groundwork. You have prepared yourself mentally. Tomorrow we begin the action phase. You will begin to practice small steps toward your goal of becoming a great listener and communicator.

PROGRAM

The steps you take have nothing to do with willpower, these are simple changes that you will make. You're not looking for a quick-fix, but in a very short time, you will see enormous results.

Remember Julie and Tom from the book *29 DAYS ... to a habit you want!*, they achieved their goals in spectacular fashion, but they went about it like the tortoise from the wonderful fable of *The Tortoise and the Hare.* "Slow and easy does it every time."

Social Interaction

We have spent most of week two in an overview of the various forms of social interaction and social psychology and how they might relate to our behavior and ability to listen and communicate.

You can see the vital importance of listening to our own self-talk. It's the first step to change and it's the most important step. You've taken it. With your new awareness you have the ability to identify those feelings and behaviors of persecutor, victim or rescuer. You will notice the drama triangle being played all around you. This is not to imply that you should judge or assume a superior position, but rather it allows you to understand. Remember, listening to another person, really listening to another person from a position of understanding, is one of the greatest gifts you can give because it validates the other person, reinforcing to them their self-worth. If you doubt that for even a second, think of the opposite scenario. Think how you feel when someone doesn't listen to you or fakes interest. How does that make you feel?

Step one is to wiretap your old habitual thoughts. Notice how your old beliefs impact your life. Catch yourself thinking "I can't do this," or "I can't do that," or "If I do x,y and z, then I'll be liked and valued" or "They're deliberately trying to hurt me!"

By now you know that the way we see the world is not necessarily the way the world is. However, our beliefs will create our world. Suppose someone thinks that the world is an evil place and its sole purpose is to do them harm. Because they have this belief with all their heart, does that make it true? Is that the purpose of the world? Of course not! If, however, one does have thoughts like that, then he will see evidence and hard proof everywhere he goes. His "faulty" belief will be validated over and over.

Simple yet very profound.

PROGRAM

We have the power to create our world and what we we will see and experience. Understanding this is the beginning of consciousness, self determination and freedom from snares like the drama triangle.

Congratulations on reaching the halfway mark. Tomorrow we begin the action week toward becoming a great listener and communicator.

See you then!

 . . . to becoming a great listener and communicator!

— <u>WEEK THREE</u> —

TAKING ACTION

PROGRAM

DAY FIFTEEN
I'm on my way to permanent results!

DAY FIFTEEN – A.M.

Hey, welcome back. Today is the day we've been working toward since the beginning of this program. Up until now you've been tuning into the world of listening and by now you're acutely aware of many of the nuances that make for good and bad listening.

As we said in the *29 Days ... to a habit you want!*, when most people decide to take on a new challenge they immediately dive into the action stage, which often results in failure. Investing the last two weeks by creating awareness and getting emotionally and mentally ready for the challenge has you *so well prepared* that the next steps may be relatively easy.

You have demonstrated the two ingredients necessary for success:
1. Patience and perseverance – it's been two weeks and you're here with us every day.
2. Self-confidence – you took the task on and followed the daily steps. Without self-confidence we would all assume failure and not even bother to take on new challenges. With self-confidence we assume success.

We are going to begin action week by taking action on one of the most pervasive and insidious barriers to communication ... multi-tasking. The key to becoming a really great listener and communicator is to develop the skills of focus and to dispel any myth of our ability to focus on more than one task at a time.

Multi-Tasking – The Grand Illusion

Multi-tasking is the scourge of modern day society. It is the root cause of poor listening, poor communication, and sloppy execution of many day-to-day tasks.

PROGRAM

Slowly and assiduously we have adopted one communication device after another until they have evolved into the tail wagging the dog. Watch some harried person who is plugged into the complete system; that would mean instant messaging, Twitter, smartphone, internet, Facebook etc. The "plugged-in-person" will literally live their daily life in response to the never-ending flow of incoming information.

You might be thinking, "Yeah, so what's your point?"

The point is this, if one continually responds to the beeps and buzzes and onslaught of information, then clearly one is *not* in control of one's daily life. Put another way, would that person live their day differently if all the devices stopped their ringing, vibrating, chirping and chiming? Obviously they would.

The purpose of today's lesson is to create awareness to a serious problem that we've allowed to control our lives. Incredibly most of us are completely unaware of this growing problem – the ceaseless intrusion into our conscious thoughts. In fact, many of us have come to believe that orchestrating several different communication gadgets, while studying, watching TV, or keeping our social life moving forward is a sign of our adeptness, mental prowess and infallibility. In reality it demonstrates inefficiency and promotes an inability to focus.

Numerous studies have shown that the human brain is incapable of multi-tasking. Most people who attempt to multitask are under the delusion that they can perform several cognitive duties at the same time, in perfect harmony, and at a fraction of the amount of time than if they focused on one task, then another and another.

Before we explore our capability (or lack thereof), to multitask, the first step is to define what multitasking is. There are two definitions of multitasking:

1. From a computer perspective it's the concurrent operation by one central processing unit of two or more processes.
2. From a human perspective it's the carrying out of two or more tasks at the same time by one person.

Your subconscious mind is a master at multitasking. It can perform millions of calculations per second as it orchestrates your heart rate, body temperature, digestion and everything else required to keep you alive, and while it's doing all that, you can safely toss it the task of effortlessly steering your automobile down the highway while you concentrate on the station you're listening to.

Your *conscious* mind however, is not capable of multiple, simultaneous calculation. It is capable of doing a maximum of one thing at a time. Period. One thing at a time. That's it. If you're about to protest by giving examples of your ability to watch TV while writing a report then you have landed on the very point of this writing … it's an illusion.

By definition when you attempt to watch TV and write a report, what you are doing is very rapidly shifting your focus from watching TV to writing your report. You are not doing both at the same time. In fact this is where the inefficiency comes in, most of your mental power is burned up in high-speed travel as you switch focus from the television program to your report and back again.

Multitasking is the modern day version of the person who is incapable of concentration and focus. This is the person who is at work but is thinking of his family and what he wants to do when he gets home. When he gets home, he's at work thinking of all the things that need to be done at the office. Result: he's never really anywhere or truly present for anyone.

The above example is an ultra-slow version of the inefficiency of switching attention.

You might be thinking "That's different, when I multitask I'm getting both tasks accomplished with perfect aplomb so who cares if I'm actually shifting my attention back and forth?" That's just it. We fool ourselves into thinking that we're magically doing more than one thing at a time, but in reality we just switch from doing one thing inefficiently and then to another thing inefficiently. Studies have shown that people who multi-task are 50% more likely to make mistakes and 34% less productive because of the wasted time and effort when switching from one task to another.

> *People who are regularly bombarded with several streams of electronic information do not pay attention, control their memory or switch from one job to another as well as those who prefer to complete one task at a time, a group of Stanford researchers has found.*
>
> *High-tech jugglers are everywhere – keeping up several e-mail and instant message conversations at once, text messaging while watching television and jumping from one website to another while plowing through homework assignments.*
>
> *But after putting about 100 students through a series of three tests, the researchers realized those heavy media multitaskers are paying a big mental price.*

"They're suckers for irrelevancy," said communication Professor Clifford Nass, one of the researchers whose findings are published in the Aug. 24 edition of the Proceedings of the National Academy of Sciences. "Everything distracts them."

(http://news.stanford.edu/news/2009/august24/multitask-research-study-082409.html)

So the key point to remember is that the *conscious* mind can only do one thing at a time, it cannot do two things simultaneously. Do you remember when someone told you to try and pat the top of your head while at the same time you were to rub your stomach? It was impossible to do until you focused your attention on one task (rubbing your stomach), and then delegated that assignment to your *subconscious*, while your *conscious* mind focused on patting your head. Then if you were asked to try and reverse the process, pat your stomach and rub your head you had to once again focus on a task, assign it to your subconscious mind, and then your conscious mind could perform the remaining task.

How often do you drive down the highway deep in thought or conversation and perhaps realize that you've driven way past your exit? In situations like that who was driving? You were a million miles away. Your subconscious was driving of course. You delegated the duty. That was a form of multi-tasking, but notice that your conscious mind delegated that task because it decided to focus on another task ... one task at a time.

Still not convinced? Try this little exercise. Pick up a pen or pencil and hold it tightly in your outstretched hand. Now "will" yourself to drop it. The pencil fell, no problem, right? How did you manage to actually drop the pencil? Your conscious mind told your hand to release its hold and the pencil fell. Now I want you to hold the pencil in your outstretched hand again and while squeezing the pencil tightly I want you to say to yourself, "I can drop the pencil, I can drop the pencil ..." repeat this over and over. You will clearly see that if you focus on what you are saying you will be *incapable* of releasing the pencil. The only way you will be able to actually drop the pencil is stop your internal dialogue and change the focus of your conscious mind to your hand and then instruct it to open. In order to do that you had to stop your conscious mind from repeating, "I can drop the pencil." You see? As simple as this task is, you cannot consciously do two things at once. You cannot think, "I can drop the pencil," and at the same time say to your conscious mind "Now, I will drop the pencil."

So what does all this have to do with listening and communicating?

The point is to show you that you cannot consciously do two things at the same time, and that includes listening. In other words, if you're talking, you're not listening, and this *includes* the talking you're doing inside your head while *pretending* to listen. Anytime you catch your-

PROGRAM

self thinking of something else while someone is talking, do not fool yourself into thinking that you were doing two things at the same time. You may be switching back and forth, but you're not listening ... not *really* listening. You're listening at a level-three or a level-two at best.

Good listeners have always been appreciated and in today's society they are valued more than ever. Human needs have not changed, nor will they. As humans we will always need to be listened to and validated. It's been said of former president Bill Clinton, that when he was in conversation with you it felt like he saw you as the only person in the world. His focus and attention on you was complete. The same thing has been said of President Barack Obama. Experiencing a person's full attention is a rare gift to both give and receive.

In the April 2, 1960 edition of the *Saturday Evening Post*, Norman Rockwell talked about the time he spent with General Eisenhower while painting his portrait for the magazine. The thing that most impressed Rockwell was the quality of Eisenhower's attention. It was completely devoted to him. He said it felt as if the General didn't have a care in the world and that their conversation about painting and fishing was all that mattered.

Many years ago the high school I attended had the honor of being visited by Canada's Prime Minister, Pierre Trudeau. Several of us were chosen to be on a panel to ask the Prime Minister a number of questions. The entire session lasted about forty-five minutes and, like Norman Rockwell, I was absolutely stunned by Mr. Trudeau's ability to listen and focus. I was second in line to ask him a question, which he answered with his usual eloquence. He continued answering questions from a number of people for the next twenty-five minutes or so and then he said something that blew me away. While answering a query from one of the teachers he said something to the effect of: "What you're asking is along the same lines as Richard's question ..." What! My simple question was already some twenty-five minutes old. How could he remember not only my name, but the question I asked? He was an absolute master at listening and focusing on each moment.

The fact that these four men (Obama, Eisenhower, Trudeau and Clinton) shared the ability to be able to completely focus on the speaker and on the moment, is hardly a coincidence.

In an article titled *The Myth of Multitasking*, Christine Rosen writes in *The New Atlantis*:

> *For the younger generation of multitaskers, the great electronic din is an expected part of everyday life. And given what neuroscience and anecdotal evidence have shown us, this state of constant intentional self-distraction could well be of profound detriment to individual and cultural well-being. When*

people do their work only in the "interstices of their mind-wandering," with crumbs of attention rationed out among many competing tasks, their culture may gain in information, but it will surely weaken in wisdom.

(http://www.thenewatlantis.com/publications/the-myth-of-multitasking)

To become a good listener and communicator is to forever put aside the notion that you can listen to someone while doing something else. That doesn't mean to imply that we should spend our listening lives at the high intensity level of empathic listening. Heck, we would burnout by noon! There are many times when it's only necessary to pay mild attention such as when you want to catch tomorrow's weather so you "eavesdrop" on the evening news until you hear the part you're interested in and then you turn your full attention to what's being said.

Becoming a good listener is to understand that you're either *listening* or you're *not*. If someone is speaking to you, then it's just common courtesy (although it's getting rarer) to ignore your cell phone, and incoming email messages. If you're going to be with someone, then be with them. If you're not going to really listen to the other person then quit faking and do both yourself and the other person a favor.

Listening, really listening has unfortunately become a quaint notion from days gone by when life progressed at a gentler pace. Our modern communication devices have literally robbed us of our ability to communicate. From twittering tidbits of incoming information that demand our constant attention, to internet surveillance and responding to ringing cell phones while attempting to converse with someone, we are suffering from the worst kind of listening and communication counterfeiting.

In today's harried world the simple act of making eye contact is becoming increasingly rare. Just because so many people are adopting bad habits hardly makes it acceptable. Here is what can be so exciting. If you make it a point to be different, and to really become a good listener, you will be noticed, appreciated and rewarded beyond what you may think possible.

STEP 15 — Make yourself a simple promise that you will no longer succumb to the multi-tasking delusion. When you are writing a letter, you are going to write a letter to the exclusion of all else. When you are speaking on the phone, you will put aside all distractions,(even though you can't be seen by the person you're speaking with), and focus on your conversation. When you are speaking with someone you will give them all your attention and focus on that person with genuine interest. Try this and note the difference to your mental well being as well as your speed and efficiency in completing your tasks.

If someone wishes to speak with you, and all they have to communicate is a lot of gossip and drivel that holds no interest to you, there is nothing wrong with excusing yourself or cutting the conversation short. *The point to being a great listener and communicator is to either get into the conversation or get out.* Don't waste your, or the other person's, time and energy by standing in front of them with a forced smile as you nod out of sync and think of something else. That is simply what most people do. You are going down a different path. You are going to develop the assertive skills of effective listening and communication.

Tomorrow we're going to look at dealing with the wide gap between a person's slow speaking speed and our mind's super fast thinking speed.

JOURNAL ENTRY

I'm on my way to permanent results!

One step to becoming a good listener, is to stop being a poor listener, which means to forever drop the bad habit and delusion that the conscious mind can do more than one thing at a time ... which includes internal chatter while pretending to listen.

From now on I will be aware of my tendency to multi-task. Reading the daily paper while simultaneously watching TV does not qualify as a habit that requires urgent change. When I am doing something important, such as talking to another person, writing or studying, I will remind myself that I can only *effectively* perform one task at a time. When I am speaking with someone I will given them my full attention.

Today I was very aware of my natural tendency to multi-task. From now on when I am in conversation with someone I will practice the following good listening habits.

- "I will not answer the phone."
- "I will turn off my email."
- "I will focus on the other person."
- "I will maintain eye contact with the speaker."
- "I will focus on listening at level one when required (empathic listening)."

You cannot truly listen to anyone and do anything else at the same time.
~ M. Scott Peck

DAY FIFTEEN – P.M. MESSAGE

Congratulations on your first day of action toward becoming a great listener and communicator.

I hope you will always be aware of the insidious habit of multi-tasking and how it affects not only our ability to listen and communicate, but our very ability to perform important tasks. I'm certainly not implying that multi-tasking is never appropriate. If you're watching TV and surfing the net then you're multi-tasking and it's perfectly acceptable. What is not acceptable is when your full concentration is required on a task and you divide your conscious attention by attempting a second task.

The most difficult multi-tasking habit to eliminate is the one that is kept hidden, often from our own conscious awareness. You know the one: the wandering, random thoughts that creep in when we're bored. Because no one can see it, we tend to ignore it. The best listeners and communicators have developed the ability to restrict their mind from wandering away from their point of focus. This focus takes energy and commitment. It's why you feel so good when you talk to someone with this ability. They literally pull you into their high-energy space. When you feel like you connect or resonate with someone it's because your energy is aligned.

Just before you go to sleep this evening think about having a heart-to-heart conversation with someone, and you're totally focused on that person. Feel what it's like to completely be there for someone else. It's a very real, vibrant feeling.

See you tomorrow!

 **... to becoming a great listener and communicator!**

DAY SIXTEEN
I'm on my way to permanent results!

DAY SIXTEEN – A.M.

Welcome to day sixteen. You're making huge progress!

Yesterday we looked at the increasingly popular habit of multi-tasking and we saw that for the most part its effectiveness is a total illusion. The conscious mind cannot focus on two tasks at the same time, but rather, it quickly switches from task to task as we change our focus. We also saw that this was an extraordinarily inefficient formula toward completing necessary tasks because much of our time and energy is wasted through the process of switching back and forth between them.

Plodding Speech, Racing Thoughts – How to Fill in the Gap

The average rate of speech is 125 words per minute in regular conversation, and about 100 words per minute if someone is engaged in more formal speech such as speaking to an audience.

Our conscious brain can think at a rate of about 2,000 words per minute and can quite comfortably absorb listening at a rate of 400 to 500 words per minute. At first this might look like a great ratio since it appears to indicate that we can listen to and absorb every word the speaker is saying and still have thinking capacity to spare.

Unfortunately therein lies the very problem. When a person first begins to speak, we're usually completely focused and engaged on what is being said. Soon after however, several things inevitably happen that derail our ability to listen.

The first thing that often happens is that our filters kick in. Our filters are the way in which we interpret and actually see the world. The way we see the world does not mean that that is how the world actually is, it simply means that it is our *interpretation* of what the world actually is.

For example, if someone starts to speak in a clipped, formal style of speech, using complex words, we might immediately form an opinion and dismiss the speaker as pompous, arrogant and not worthy of attention. If a speaker has awkward mannerisms or their command of the language is poor, we might quickly ascertain that they are ignorant and not worthy of our attention. Both assumptions, and by definition our filters, could be completely wrong.

The second possibility, and the focus of today's topic is bridging the gap between our ability to listen and our ability to think. Suppose we don't engage any of our screening filters (read prejudice or pre-judgment) and we're really interested in the speaker and what is being said. Since the speaker will talk at 100 to 125 words per minute, and we're quite capable of absorbing 400 to 500 words per minute, we could conclude that we will hear and comprehend all that is said. Not so!

The actual dynamic that takes place between the speaker's "plodding" words and our conscious mind is very similar to the classic race between the *Tortoise and the Hare*. The speaker's words saunter along at a slow steady pace while the conscious mind circles the tortoise then leaps and bounds off to find something of greater interest, then races back to check on the tortoise's progress, then races off again for more interesting things to consider. Sometimes the hare will even decide to take a quick nap knowing full well it can catch up a little later.

We're all familiar with this result because any time we catch ourselves daydreaming or we find ourselves in the embarrassing moment when the speaker asks, "Where did I just leave off?" – and we weren't even aware that they had left – we've allowed our conscious mind to flee the scene. Just like the hare, we get lulled into a false sense of security because of our certainty that we can catch up to the speaker any time we choose by simply racing back, tune in for a few words to catch the gist, and then race off again to more interesting matters.

Most of us are far more interested in sharing our thoughts, opinions and feelings than we are in listening to someone else's. As you know by now, the most successful salespeople, managers, parents and friends are successful because they've sharpened their skills of listening.

A husband and wife were looking to replace their aging van. They went to several dealerships to gather information before they arrived at Susan's dealership. When Susan saw the young couple wandering through the showroom, she approached them, introduced herself and asked if she could be of any service.

The husband said that they were looking for a new SUV to replace their aging van and the wife quickly interjected that they were actually looking for a new van to replace their old one. Because Susan was listening, she noted the two opinions and began to ask some follow-up questions. A while later the husband casually mentioned that at some point he wanted to purchase a power boat, while the wife stressed the importance of having lots of room to drive the kids and all their luggage to hockey and soccer games.

Susan didn't get caught up in any of the differences in wants and needs between the husband and wife but rather listened carefully and noted their desires.

Within a short time Susan had taken the couple from looking at vans and SUVs to a new type of spacious, four-door pick-up truck that would be perfect for everyone's needs. This truck would not only seat six adults, but it would allow for the smelly sports gear to be packed in the back rather than in the passenger seating area. The truck was more than capable of pulling a five-ton boat and it seemed to appeal to the couple's every need.

Because Susan really listened objectively she was able to make the sale and meet all their needs rather than see them leave her showroom in a continued state of disagreement and uncertainty of their automobile purchase.

Whether we're listening to customers, our boss, our spouse, our kids or a speech, it's vital that we are able to focus on what we are hearing and not allow our minds to wander. We need to learn how to use all that extra horsepower for what is being said rather than allow it to race off to other non-relevant topics.

With awareness, focus and practice, we can use this extra energy and speed to read between the lines and evaluate the speaker's message as it unfolds. The key to allay boredom and keep our wandering mind on a shortleash is to turn the task of listening into a bit of a game.

There are three techniques we can use to keep our attention on the spoken words:
- Anticipation
- Basis
- Summary

Anticipation – Try to anticipate where the speaker is headed and what will be their point or message. For example, if your spouse comes up from the basement telling you that it's such a mess and then asks you if you have a couple of spare hours this coming Saturday, you might quickly ascertain that he or she is going to want your involvement in cleaning the basement.

That type of assessment might be rather easy.

Now suppose you're listening to your boss talk about his plans for the next quarter. In this case there could be a number of directions such as sales quotas, hiring, customer service, new projects, new purchases etc. The list could be endless. If you guess the general topic correctly then you might subdivide the topic into subtopics so that your mind is constantly engaged in the words at hand. If you keep all that mental energy on the speaker's possible direction, your rate of retention will rise dramatically as opposed to passively listening and allowing your mind to tune in and out while it considers where you might go for lunch.

Basis – While listening, try to understand the *basis* for the speaker's message. In the case of your spouse wanting to clean the basement, you can be fairly certain that their *desire* is all the basis you're going to get.

In the case of a speaker suggesting that our nation has to begin to pay greater attention to our automobile and industrial emissions because of their effect on global warming, you might turn your attention to the basis for the speaker's argument. You might focus on the supporting material the speaker used as the basis for his position.

Suppose you listen passively while the speaker talks about the impending global warming crisis. At the end of a thirty-minute speech you might be completely alarmed at their predictions of impending doom and crisis. If someone asked your opinion about the matter you might possibly even be a little panicky. On the other hand, if you were listening for supporting material as the basis for the speaker's conclusions, but never heard a shred of supporting evidence but rather a lot of unsubstantiated opinions, then you might come away from the speech with a radically different reaction about both the speaker and the subject matter.

Summation – The third technique toward harnessing the extra energy of the conscious mind is to periodically summarize what the speaker has said. When the speaker pauses to take a sip of water, jot a note or just takes a momentary pause, you can hone in on your notes by selecting a couple of key words that will summarize the speaker's message. If you manage to do this every three or four minutes you can dramatically increase your overall level of understanding and long-term recollection.

If you're involved in a heart-to-heart conversation, then you will use the excess energy to mentally summarize while trying to actually *see the world* from the speaker's perspective. If and when the time is appropriate, quickly and succinctly rephrase what you believe the speaker has just shared.

STEP 16 - For the rest of today, and maybe forever, try to be aware of *the gap*. The gap between the speed of our minds and the speed of the speaker's words. We've all been there many times, and we'll all be there again. With that said however, through conscious effort we can learn to limit those wandering excursions our conscious mind makes when we really know we should be focused and in the speaker's presence. The quicker you can catch yourself the better you'll become at reeling in that scampering hare (your conscious mind). Being aware of the extra speed and horsepower of your mind, as compared to the cumbersome plodding speed of speech, will help you to use the spare listening power to evaluate and use the techniques of *anticipation, basis,* and *summation.*

DAY SIXTEEN – P.M. MESSAGE

In the automotive industry ABS is an acronym for anti-locking brake system. We can use the ABS acronym as a useful reminder for the three keys of effective listening. Think of ABS (Anticipation, Basis, Summation) the next time you're about to listen to a speaker or you're going to be involved in a lengthy conversation. Think of putting the brakes on your racing conscious mind.

Just the very thought of saying ABS will help you to use one or all of the tools to harness your racing mind and to channel all that extra energy to focus on the the speaker's message and dramatically increase your retention.

JOURNAL ENTRY

I'm on my way to permanent results!

I had a number of conversations today in which I was acutely aware of the dynamics between speech and thought. I understand how I can use the extra energy of thought to increase my listening power and retention.

During a conversation today this is how I actively used the skill of *anticipation* to help me focus:

_____

PROGRAM

_____

_____

_____

During a conversation today this is how I actively used the skill of finding the speaker's *basis* to help me focus:

_____

_____

_____

_____

_____

During a conversation today this is how I actively used the skill of *summation* to help me understand the speaker's overall message:

_____

_____

_____

_____

_____

A good listener tries to understand what the other person is saying.
In the end he may disagree sharply but because he disagrees,
he wants to know exactly what it is he is disagreeing with.
~ Kenneth A. Wells

PROGRAM

Just before you go to sleep tonight, try to recall a conversation where you actively used ABS. If you cannot recall a conversation where you used it, can you think of a conversation where you could have used it?

Congratulations. Big changes to your listening and communication skills are beginning to happen.

See you tomorrow!

 . . . to becoming a great listener and communicator!

PROGRAM

DAY SEVENTEEN
I'm on my way to permanent results!

DAY SEVENTEEN – A.M.

Welcome to day seventeen. The third day of action week.

Although it's only been two days of *action*, I will guess that by actively thinking about listening and applying just a little effort and focus you're already noticing a positive change in your ability to listen and communicate. You're beginning to see the tremendous power of becoming a good listener and how it can transform your relationships and experiences.

Yesterday we talked about becoming aware of your conscious mind's tendency to become bored with "plodding" speed of speech, and how you can use that excess energy by applying it to the simple formula of ABS (*anticipation, basis* and *summation*). Just reminding yourself of ABS when you're involved in an important conversation will help you to focus and increase your retention.

Today we're going to look at one of the greatest barriers to objective listening and communicating ... filters. We all have them. We all use them. They make up a large part of *who* and *what* we are. Recognizing and understanding our filters is vital to becoming an *objective* listener.

Listening through Filters

Whether we're aware of it or not, we see, hear and experience our world through filters. Like our fingerprints, our filters are unique to us, no two sets of filters are alike. Many of our filters were first created through our childhood experiences and subconscious programming. Our filters are comprised of our beliefs, memories, prejudices, values, expectations, assumptions and attitudes.

If ten people are told that someone is rich, there will be ten different interpretations of what "rich" is. If we are told someone is a "nice" person, the child who was raised in a functional loving family would interpret "nice" differently from a child raised in an abusive dysfunctional family.

> *Meaning is not in the words. Meaning is in the minds of people*
> *and the interpretation they attach to the words.*

People with strong beliefs or a "fundamentalist" attitude tend to see the world as black and white. Their beliefs are strengthened by what they see happening around them. We tend to see the world in a way that reinforces our beliefs. People with so-called "narrow vision," are so heavily influenced and blinded by their self-made filters, they often cannot even conceive of their existence. Folks who are more in-tune and evolved, are fully aware of their filters and strive to dismantle their prejudices and assumptions in order to see the world as it *really* is.

Whenever we communicate, either as a speaker or an active listener, it is vitally important to be aware of filters and how drastically they can distort *effective* communication.

Picture a television audience watching the following thirty-second infomercial introduction.

> *Good evening ladies and gentlemen. Tonight I want to introduce to you a remarkable young man, who has made a fortune for both himself and hundreds of his students. His methods and techniques in real estate investment will show you just how easy it is for you to make a fortune as well. He will show you how to turn a small investment into hundreds of thousands of dollars in just a few years. And the best part, it requires little effort on your part.*

If we had a thousand listeners that singular message would result in a thousand different messages.

Let's look at how this occurs.

- John is a nineteen-year-old college student who wants to become an electrician. He comes from a hard working blue-collar family who believe in eight hours of work for eight hours of pay.

- Mary is a recently retired lawyer who worked for a prestigious law firm. She came from a wealthy family and inherited a large fortune when she was in her mid 30s.

- Bob is a forty-two-year-old entrepreneur. He earned his fortune through a medical invention he spent over fifteen years developing. He recently sold his company for millions of dollars.

John, Mary and Bob were each flipping channels one evening when they all happened to land on the above infomercial introduction. Same message for all three, but let's imagine how each may interpret the following snippets through their individual experience and filters.

Listener	Broadcast Comments	Listener's Interpretation
John	*"remarkable young man"*	Probably 20 to 25 years old
Mary	*"remarkable young man"*	Probably 40 to 45 years old
Bob	*"remarkable young man"*	Probably 25 to 30
John	*"made a fortune"*	Probably made a million dollars ...
Mary	*"made a fortune"*	Made it or swindled it?
Bob	*"made a fortune"*	The guy's probably one step ahead of the law.
John	*"his methods and techniques"*	Does he take possession, or just invest in real estate?
Mary	*"his methods and techniques"*	Makes his money from his students, not real estate.
Bob	*"his methods and techniques"*	...Are either illegal or impractical.
John	*"turn a small investment into"*	I could turn a couple of thousand into ...
Mary	*"turn a small investment into"*	He can take a half-million and churn it into nothing.
Bob	*"turn a small investment into"*	Another infomercial scam.

Although this is a simplified example, it's vitally important to be aware that everything we hear is analyzed, categorized and interpreted through *our* filters. The way we hear and interpret a message will be different, maybe only slightly, from what another person heard and interpreted. If you can remember this simple fact, it will help you to see the importance of summarizing and clarifying what you said or heard depending on whether you're the *speaker* or the *listener.*

Even as I was writing the above examples of John, Mary and Bob I realized that everything from the scenario, to the characters, to the characters' individual interpretations, were assembled using my own filters. In fact, it's almost impossible to completely remove them.

With that being said, filters are not necessarily bad, filters are merely our interpretation of what we see, feel and hear. They're our view of things and how we interpret our world.

Filters Have Different Settings

A man will listen through the filters of being a man. A woman will listen through the filters of being a woman. We all listen with the filters of our cultural, religious, and political heritage and experience. We may listen through the filter of someone being young, old, smart, slow, arrogant, humorous, rich, poor, disabled and so on. You can see just how quickly the filters can pile on.

People can have their filters set in a positive state or a negative state – and quite often do. People who have their filters set low tend to see the world clearer than a person who has their filters set at high. People who have their filters set too high tend to exaggerate minor issues into major catastrophes. They can create a wild rumor over the most innocuous event. I used to work at a factory where the common joke was: If you didn't hear a rumor by nine o'clock in the morning you should start one. And that was pretty much the way it was.

I had a business partner a number of years ago who had a very high setting on his filters. He could hear the most innocent comment and make it sound like his very life had been threatened. We could be in a sales meeting and a "potential" purchaser might say our product looked interesting and my partner would take that simple comment as a done-deal. This kind of filtering and exaggerated interpretation is the basis behind twisting words, meaning and scandalous gossip.

Learning to Listen through Our Filters

If our filters are set too high they can result in selective hearing which prevents us from listening actively and objectively. In order to limit your tendency to listen selectively you need to be aware of your particular filters and then concentrate on keeping them at bay while keeping an open mind.

PROGRAM

If you're in an important conversation with someone, the easiest way to check the validity of the message you heard is to reflect back or summarize in your own words, what you believe the speaker said. If you're wrong you can immediately be corrected. If you're listening to a speaker from a large audience, at the conclusion of the speech you can discuss what you heard with other members to check for filters.

Picture yourself as a lone Democrat sitting-in at a large Republican convention speech. Do you think you're going to hear the same message as the Republicans in the audience? Suppose you listen to the speech and you focus on dropping all your "Democrat" filters, would you hear the speech any differently? That is not to say that you drop *all* your filters and you listen to the speech as an innocent newborn baby, that would neither be practical nor desirable. In that case you would lack judgment and experience. You might actually *believe* that the budget will be balanced in the next four years and that there will be a chicken in every pot and a car in every garage!

Dropping our filters doesn't suggest innocent naivete, it *does* suggest that we try to see past our built-in prejudice and old programs that often distort reality. If we were listening to our Republican speaker in the above example for the first time, whether she is from the North or South, should have no bearing on the words we hear. Naturally we can form an opinion and some of these factors can be important. If the speaker is from the South, it's not unlikely that her interests will be more inclined to lean to the southern jurisdiction than they will to the north. That's natural and inevitable. On our part, did we draw any conclusions or assumptions before the speaker even began to speak? Not doing so is the key to becoming a keen, objective listener. Just the simple act of being aware of our filters is a HUGE step toward becoming a great listener and communicator.

Can you listen to your child without the filters of, "I've been there?" The hard facts are: you haven't been there! Your experiences as a child were uniquely yours. Your child's experiences are uniquely his/hers. Can you drop your filters and really see the world as your child sees it? If you can you will begin to relate and experience your son or daughter in a way you never have before ... and visa-versa.

STEP 17 – Today's step is to be cognizant of your filters. Do you have your filters set high? Perhaps your filters are actually low, except when a "hard-core" Democrat/Republican joins in the conversation, then your filters get ratcheted up a few notches! When we're not aware of how our beliefs influence our lives and how we view other people, it's difficult to really listen to others and accept their point of view or behavior.

Perhaps it's your work, or maybe your family, or that impossible teenager or those nosey neighbors. Really try to understand your filters, what arouses them and how they prevent you from seeing the world objectively.

Try to catch yourself, even just once throughout the day, when you're seeing or listening through high-set filters. What triggered that response? What was the outcome? Can you turn them lower, or even off, just by being aware of them? Think about your child or spouse who may want to share something of a personal or of an emotional nature. Can you step outside your filters for a moment and listen at level-one? Can you temporarily drop your filters and see the world as they see it? That's what it means to really control your filters.

JOURNAL ENTRY

I'm on my way to permanent results!

I will begin to pay closer attention to my filters. I will try to notice what type of people, events or situations hinder my ability to interpret the world through an objective lens.

Remember, filters are not necessarily bad. Without our filters and our ability to interpret our world, we would be as innocent, helpless and naive as a new-born child. Filters become harmful when they unduly cloud our vision and prevent us from seeing things as they really are.

I have a pretty good idea of some of my key filters. I think that my positive filters (tendencies, beliefs) are:

_____

_____

_____

I believe that some of my negative filters (tendencies, beliefs) are:

_____

PROGRAM

_____

_____

_____

I can recall a time when my filters were set high and they prevented me from listening and communicating objectively. I know I wasn't listening objectively because:

_____

_____

_____

_____

Remember, filters are a part of who we are, what we believe, and how we see the world. Filters are vital for our success and well-being. Our goal should be to see the world as it really is, not how we *wish* it to be, but as it truly is.

It's a formidable task that will never be *fully* accomplished, but that shouldn't dissuade you from striving toward improvement.

Do the best you can throughout the day to be aware of filters, yours and others.

DAY SEVENTEEN – P.M. MESSAGE

Welcome back. I hope you had an opportunity observe how filters, yours and everyone else's, can have such a powerful influence on our perceptions and on our ability to listen and communicate.

If we go back to the seventies and eighties, when the Cold War was raging, I had a hard time imagining how anyone could live in a communist country and feel love for it. As there have been many stories of people risking their lives to defect from communist countries, scaling the Berlin Wall (which wasn't built to keep people from getting in) being a good example, I always had a hard time believing anyone living under a dictatorship could say, "I love my country."

My filters are that I live in the greatest country and I just can't imagine everyone else in the world not thinking the exact same thing ... whether they live here or not.

Now that we've witnessed the great thaw in world politics, and many people can leave their country of birth much easier than ever before, we can see that there hasn't been a mass exodus from many of the eastern European countries. When watching the World Cup or the Olympics one can see the love and pride that both participants and spectators feel for their respective homelands.

When we think of the recent Middle East conflicts, it's so easy to pick a side and fall into the belief that everything said on "our side" is right, and everything said from the "other side" is wrong. In fact, everything we see and hear will only serve to reinforce our opinions, (whichever side we're on) even when both sides witness the identical event.

Attempting to see the situation through another's eyes doesn't mean we have to agree with their position, but if we don't make the attempt to see through their eyes, then understanding, communication and resolution is impossible.

Whether we're talking religion, politics, family squabbles or office politics, a willingness to drop our filters and attempt to understand the other person's view is the foundation and starting point of all *effective* listening and communication.

See you tomorrow!

... to becoming a great listener and communicator!

DAY EIGHTEEN
I'm on my way to permanent results!

DAY EIGHTEEN – A.M.

Welcome to day eighteen. Yesterday we looked at filters, which are comprised of our beliefs, memories, prejudices, values, expectations, assumptions and attitudes. Although our filters are a key part of who we are, they can also be responsible for clouding our judgment and hindering our ability to listen and communicate objectively.

Just your basic awareness of filters, yours and everyone else's, will go a long way in helping you to listen and communicate more effectively. At times you will literally want to disconnect your filters and really try to see the world through the speaker's eyes.

Up to this point we have given a great deal of attention to the *importance* of listening. Today we're going to look at the *power* of listening. One of the reasons most of us are poor listeners is because we don't equate it with power. Speaking is obviously powerful because it's active and often accompanies orders and directives. Real power however *always* begins with effective listening.

The Hidden Power of Listening

Throughout the ages, it's the notable speakers and orators who have charted the course of history; from Aristotle to Jesus Christ, down through Abraham Lincoln, Winston Churchill, Mahatma Gandhi and Martin Luther King, great speakers and their speeches have inspired, moved and motivated individuals, armies and nations. The memorable speeches and the people who delivered them are mileposts in mankind's progress. Is it any wonder that we tend to think of speakers and speech as being all powerful?

What about the listener? Are there any chapters in history dedicated to great listeners? Are there any monuments or statues erected in their honor?

Although the great orators and their words have historically received the accolades, an uncanny aptitude for listening had to precede their spoken words. Without a speaker's keen ability to listen, to feel, and to interpret the mood and circumstance of the people and times, their words would have failed to inspire. Their message would have lacked relevance. Empathic listening and deep understanding had to precede the great speeches of our past.

The Misunderstood Power of Listening

The speaking side of communication has undoubtedly been glamorized, which is fine, but unfortunately it's been at the expense of the essential skill that had to precede it – effective listening. Speaking typically represents action and power. Listening has been falsely perceived as weak and passive. A politician gave the "perfect" speech and swept the election. A sales-person gave the "perfect" sales pitch and overwhelmed the "helpless" purchaser.

The fact is that a salesperson without superior listening skills will never be a long-term sales success. It's simply not possible. A politician without a finely tuned ear will never effectively respond to the electorate.

Formal Speaking and Listening

If you're among a group of people listening to a speech, your individual power as a listener is limited. To listen to the speech effectively still requires your mental participation to absorb and reflect on the message, but your ability to impact the speaker and the subject matter is severely restricted as compared to two-way dialogue. I'm going to refer to this kind of speaking and listening as formal. Formal listening would imply that the listener must stay in the listening position and cannot assume the role of speaker.

Informal Speaking and Listening

In "informal" communication, which is where most of our communication takes place, the speaker and listener frequently switch roles from speaking to listening. This is where the listener can exert power and effectiveness through empathic, level-one listening or squander that power by interrupting, advising, judging and sharing similar experiences.

> *To listen well, is as powerful a means of influence as to talk well,*
> *and is as essential to all true conversation.*
> *~ Chinese proverb*

Listening Is Not Limited to Auditory Speech

Listening and communication is just as valid, and every bit as important, when it comes to non-auditory communication. Anytime someone is speaking (and that includes letters, notes, reading email and even Facebook posts), it's vitally important to really "hear them", and then, and only then, are you ready to respond.

The Real Power of Listening

It's a simple fact that a *listener* is always learning. You can't learn much with your own mouth open because it stands to reason that whatever you have to say, has to be something you already know!

Good listeners attract people like moths to a flame. They make us feel comfortable and valued. Have you noticed how a good listener affects your energy, comfort level, and enthusiasm? What about the opposite? Have you ever been excited to share some good news with someone only to find their disinterest drained your excitement and energy like a popped balloon?

Have you ever noticed how a poor listener can directly affect your energy, comfort, enthusiasm, or nervousness as you speak? Have you ever felt turned off by a speaker who drums his fingers, glances at his watch or looks anxious or bored? Have you felt your enthusiasm wane when you shared something exciting with someone who refused to share your excitement? Conversely can you recall sharing something exciting with someone who was caught-up in your excitement? Doesn't it add to your shared experience? Can you remember sharing a personal story, experience or intimate feelings with a person who really listened? If you have, you know that the listener had a powerful effect and a lasting influence on you. That is *real* power!

Silent Listening, a Wellspring of Information

If information is power, then listening is the conduit to power.

The next time you ask someone a question and you get an unsatisfactory answer try this … say and do nothing. Silence is a void that makes people extremely uncomfortable. Almost without fail a momentary pause, on your part, will cause the speaker to leap into the silence like a cat on a mouse. Just the simple act of silent listening will often produce a fountain of speech from the other person. When someone finishes speaking and you don't "go along" by immediately picking up your end of the dialogue, invariably the speaker will begin to elaborate. It may not be long before they eventually get around to saying exactly what you want to hear.

The power of holding your tongue is often overlooked, especially in sales. Remaining silent allows you to collect your thoughts and be more prudent in your reply. When working with international customers, one will often encounter a foreigner who erroneously claims ignorance of English. They will frequently bring along an interpreter even though they're perfectly capable of understanding and conversing with Americans. This tactic allows them to buy extra time to form a reaction and a response. It allows them to observe and *listen,* twice as much as they could without an interpreter.

Real Listening is Real Power

An effective listener can lead a conversation and greatly influence its outcome. When a listener begins to understand this little-known power they can wield silent listening with great force. A listener can use his observational powers to perceive a speaker's feelings and emotions. An effective listener will also hear volumes about things not said.

In a February, 2007 *Business Week* article, Carmine Gallo writes:

> *Only a small percentage of communication involves actual words: 7%, to be exact. In fact, 55% of communication is visual (body language, eye contact) and 38% is vocal (pitch, speed, volume, tone of voice). The world's best business communicators have strong body language: a commanding presence that reflects confidence, competence, and charisma.*

What does that say for a powerful listener with observational skills? The difference between what an effective listener would extract from a conversation (visually and audibly), and what a listener with a wandering mind would extract would be so strikingly different, it would almost suggest there were two separate conversations.

A capable listener can literally control a speaker through nods, subtle expressions and body language. A listener's silent communication can stop a speaker in his tracks or encourage him to open up and express his deepest thoughts and feelings. This type of listening isn't passive, weak or apathetic. In fact it's dynamic and requires a good degree of skill and energy to resonate with the speaker while absorbing words, feelings and emotions.

A disciplined listener's skills, strengths and perceptions continually grow stronger with practice. Through effective, empathic, level-one listening, you will quickly begin to deeply understand the important people in your life.

Now that's real power!

I love the story of effective listening that Jack Canfield shares in his wonderful book *The Success Principles*. He says that during his year of attending *Dan Sullivan's Strategic Coach Program*, he learned a powerful communication tool to establish rapport and create a feeling of connection with another person.

He learned a series of four questions that he applies in personal and business situations. He asks the questions one after another. He said the first time he tried it was with his sister Kim. He asked the first question and listened to her response. When she had finished he asked the next question, and then the third and fourth.

By the end of the fourth question over an hour had passed. Jack said that aside from the few words he used to ask each of the four questions, he himself never said a word. At the end of their conversation Kim smiled and said to him, "That's the best conversation I think we've ever had. I feel so clear and focused. I know exactly what I need to go and do now. Thank you."

The four questions Jack learned to ask were:

1. *If we were meeting three years from today, what has to have happened during the three-year period for you to feel happy about your progress?*
2. *What are the biggest dangers you'll have to face and deal with in order to achieve that progress?*
3. *What are the biggest opportunities that you have that you would need to focus on and capture to achieve those things?*
4. *What strengths will you need to reinforce and maximize, and what skills and resources will you need to develop that you don't currently have in order to capture those opportunities?*

I have asked some similar questions of my own to people in conversation and the results are always amazing. Not only will I always learn something about the other person, but by resisting the urge to jump in with "my story," or "my advice," I have a more meaningful conversation and a feeling of connection.

In his informative and entertaining book *Intelligence for Your Life*, John Tesh recalls the time he interviewed the master interviewer and anchorman, Ted Koppel. As John so beautifully phrased it:

> *Asking Mr. Koppel questions in a live TV interview is a bit like biking with Lance Armstrong. You're working, he's not.*

John said when he began his interview with Mr. Koppel, he had his first question all written out and perfectly phrased. He began with:

> *"Mr. Koppel, you've interviewed some of the most influential people in the world. What's the secret to being a great interviewer?" I waited for his answer. When it came, it took me completely by surprise.*
>
> *"I listen, John."*
>
> *"That's it?" I asked in horror.*
>
> *"Yes, that's it. I listen. I listen more than I talk."*
>
> *He then proceeded to dissect the basic questioning technique used by the rest of us. Ask a question. Get an answer. Ask another unrelated question, get another answer. And so on until it's time for the next commercial break.*
>
> *Koppel listens. Then he asks a follow-up question based on what he hears. Not only does he get great answers, but he honors his guest with his rapt attention.*
>
> *Mr. Koppel's point was this: most of us, whether we are on television or not, have forgotten how to listen to each other. We have an agenda, and we are not willing to let listening get in the way of it.*
>
> *Without the art of listening, you risk missing key information. What's happened to listening? It's been replaced by interrupting.*

If you ever watched the intensity in which Ted Koppel interviews someone, you should need no further proof of the power of listening.

Step 18 – At some point today begin to experiment with the powers of listening.

Remember: *If information is power, then listening is the conduit to power.*

If you have an opportunity today to listen to someone you care about, give that person your full attention for just two minutes. That's 120 seconds in which you fully, completely listen to that person. That means you do not allow your mind to wander, you do not form an opinion, you do not judge and you definitely don't interrupt or think of something to say. You just listen with rapt attention.

PROGRAM

Do your very best to find a listening situation today to put this exercise into practise.

DAY EIGHTEEN – P.M. MESSAGE

Welcome back. I hope you had the opportunity to observe the power of listening, or at least its effect on both you (the listener) and the speaker. If you did have the opportunity to become a totally committted listener for at least two minutes today, spend a few moments and reflect on that experience.

JOURNAL ENTRY

I'm on my way to permanent results!

To be an accomplished listener is not only an incredibly valuable skill, it is also an effective tool that can weild enormous power.

Today I spent a couple of minutes as a totally focused listener.

I was in conversation with _____ and while listening I learned the following:

_____

_____

_____

_____

How long did the two or so minutes *feel*?

_____

_____

_____

Was it really difficult to totally focus on the speaker and block out the usual distractions?

Why?

_____

_____

_____

_____

Was it difficult to suppress your opinion or thoughts? Why?

_____

_____

What were the results of your devotion to completely listen to the other person?

_____

_____

_____

_____

Practice this skill as often as you can. In a surprisingly short period of time it will become a wonderfully pleasant habit.

Remember the four questions that Jack Canfield used in the example he gave with his sister:

1. *If we were meeting three years from today, what has to have happened during the three-year period for you to feel happy about your progress?*

2. *What are the biggest dangers you'll have to face and deal with in order to achieve that progress?*

3. *What are the biggest opportunities that you have that you would need to focus on and capture to achieve those things?*

4. *What strengths will you need to reinforce and maximize, and what skills and resources will you need to develop that you don't currently have in order to capture those opportunities?*

Take a moment and think of a series of questions that you might use to encourage someone to express themselves. We all crave the opportunity to express ourselves, but only to people that we trust and feel will really listen to us in a non-judgmental, and empathic way.

We've said many times that one of the greatest gifts we can give another person is to truly listen and make them feel understood.

Take a few moments and think of a couple of questions that you could ask people that would help them to open up and consider the most important topic they can think of themselves.

For example:

- What do you think is your greatest asset? Why do you think this is so? What asset or trait would you most like to acquire? How could you go about getting it?
- What skill or trait do you most admire in other people? Do you feel you have this skill? If not, what would it take to acquire it? If you do have it, how did you acquire it?
- If you were to grant a newborn child two gifts or talents or character traits, what would they be? Why do you think these traits would be so valuable?
- If you could be any person in the world, past or present, who would it be? Why ...?

You get the idea. These types of questions can reveal a great deal about a person. Asking a question like any of the ones above, provided you're <u>not</u> doing so as a contrived exercise but one in which both you and the speaker can build rapport, can be a wonderful experience for both of you. Remember the response, and the outcome when Jack asked his sister those four questions. He didn't do it to get something out of her or manipulate her, he simply asked a great question and then he listened. He listened empathically and without interruption.

In most cases, people can solve their own problems and an attentive, silent listener seems to magically aid in helping the speaker find the solution. People pay thousands of dollars to therapists because they desperately want to be listened to.

Have a person or persons in mind and think of a couple of questions that you might like to ask them; suppose it's a business partner, your child, your spouse, your best friend, someone you meet on an airplane? Your questions might be quite different for each person but think of a question or two that might be particularly helpful for that person to think through. When the time and situation are appropriate, ask the question then sit back and LISTEN!

A couple of questions that I would like to ask people who I really care about are:

1. _____

2. _____

3. _____

4. _____

5. _____

6. _____

See you tomorrow.

29 DAYS . . . to becoming a great listener and communicator!

PROGRAM

DAY NINETEEN
I'm on my way to permanent results!

DAY NINETEEN – A.M.

Welcome to day nineteen. Yesterday we looked at the power of listening. Many people traditionally equate speaking and speech as being powerful, and listening as being weak, passive and submissive. We know otherwise. Knowledge is power, real power. Knowledge can only come from listening and learning. When you're speaking you can only be talking about something you already know.

Listening is not only a valued skill, but it's also the most overlooked position of power. Most of us jump at the opportunity to speak, to talk about our experiences, our feelings and emotions, our viewpoint. We want to hold the floor. The savvy listener grants others their wish.

Learning to listen will bring untold benefits. Learning to hold your tongue and listen will put you in favorable light with practically everyone, while at the same time giving you true knowledge, information and strength. So who wouldn't want all the benefits bestowed on the good listener?

There are a number of "knee-jerk reactions" most of us resort to that completely disengage our listening skills. In other words, there are a number of ways we *give away* our power by not heeding the rules of good listening.

How We Give Away Our Power – The Barriers To Listening

Picture this scenario. Your friend says to you:

> *"I'm really burned out. I'm so unhappy with my job.*
> *I can't stand my boss, she's always miserable and complaining."*

If you hear this type of gripe, do you immediately reach for one of these classic barriers to listening:

1. **Rescue, give advice, fix the problem, offer solutions:** "You should tell your boss blah, blah, blah," or "Why don't you get another job?" or "If I were you I'd ..." or "You should ..."

2. **Listen just long enough to tell your tale of woe, so you can talk about your problem:** "You think your boss is miserable, let me tell you about my boss ..." or "I was burned out like you until I ..." or "I know what you mean. Did I tell you about ...?"

3. **Take offense or get irritated:** "You're always griping at me, as if it's my fault." or "You're always complaining. I've got my own problems."

4. **Criticize, scold, rebuke the speaker:** "You say your boss is always miserable and complaining, try taking a look at yourself!" or "Burned out? How can *you* be burned out?" or "Your boss is complaining for a reason. Maybe you should take a closer look at your job performance!"

5. **Jump to conclusions:** "Don't tell me you're going to quit another job." or "Are you trying to tell me you're about to get fired?" or "You can't afford to stop working."

6. **Advise, placate, reassure:** "Oh I'm sure it's not as bad as you think." or "Forget about it, everything will work out." or "Things always look darkest just before the dawn." or "I'm sure you're making it sound worse than it is. Just hang in there." Blah, blah, blah.

Take a moment and review the above six responses. I'm sure you're quite familiar with these "typically" common reactions from either side: speaking or listening.

From a speaking perspective think about how annoying it is to receive any of the six responses from another person who you hoped would just listen? How do you feel when a "listener" uses one of these on something you've said?

Conversely, when you're "listening" to another person, how often do you resort to using one of these tactics?

I'm not suggesting that you should give your undivided attention to a chronic complainer. Steering clear of negativity is a simple act of self-preservation. All of us complain from time to time, and the reality is that the subject of complaint may have very little significance to what we really want to say or express. THAT is the key to listening. To hear what the speaker is trying to express, to hear beyond the spoken word. We've said many times in this program that people have a desperate need to feel listened to. If someone fails to have their need fulfilled, they may resort to complaining in their *unconscious* desire to be heard or understood. You may actually find that once a chronic complainer actually feels listened to, their need to complain completely disappears.

To be a skilled listener means to be aware. It means to be aware of people's feelings, emotions, and the circumstances that are driving those behaviors. Have you ever caught yourself complaining to someone about something and realized that whatever it was you were griping about really didn't matter to you all that much one way or the other? If you can recall an instance like this you know that you had ulterior motives. The complaint was simply a means of expressing yourself, of just wanting to be heard.

A number of months ago I came across this anonymous "request" on the internet. I think it perfectly describes this scenario.

Could You Just Listen?

When I ask you to listen to me and you start giving me advice, you have not done what I asked. When I ask you to listen to me and you begin to tell me why I shouldn't feel that way, you are trampling on my feelings. When I ask you to listen to me and you feel you have to do something to solve my problem, you have failed me, strange as that may seem.

Listen! All I asked was that you listen, not talk or do – just hear me.

When you do something for me that I can and need to do for myself, you contribute to my fear and inadequacy, but when you accept as a simple fact that I do feel what I feel, no matter how irrational, then I can quit trying to convince you and can get about the business of understanding what's behind this irrational feeling.

When that's clear, the answers are obvious and I don't need advice. Irrational feelings make more sense when we understand what's behind them. Perhaps that's why prayer works, sometimes, for some people – because God is mute.

He doesn't give advice or try to fix things. God just listens and lets you work it out for yourself.
So, please listen and just hear me. And if you want to talk, wait a minute for your turn - and I'll listen to you.

. . . Author Unknown

STEP 19 – Since this is action week let's continue to practice the skills of listening.

Today's step is to listen to someone beyond their words. If someone is complaining, a child is throwing a temper tantrum, or someone just seems to be rambling about some shallow incident, listen for a deeper meaning because in almost every case there is one.

The fact is, until you really listen it's not possible to know someone. To listen is to suspend the self. THAT is why it's so difficult. To suspend criticizing means to listen without judging, without an agenda, without labeling, criticizing or even agreeing. *It means to see the world through the other person's eyes.* To suspend ourselves is not an easy thing to do. To really listen is an act of faith and love. *Faith* in your ability that you can get back to "being yourself." *Love* in the sense that you're willing to go out on the limb. You're risking your cherished beliefs. You're allowing yourself to be open and vulnerable to change. Willingly exposing ourselves is not an easy thing to do.

To really listen to another means that you're willing, even encouraging the speaker to be themselves. That means you're going to accept them in the moment. They can be happy, miserable, irritable, sad, ill-tempered, whatever it is. If you're going to listen to another person that means to listen without any attempt to change that person. If they want to wallow in their misery then that is what you will hear and understand. A good listener then must accept whatever they hear.

Anyone can listen intently to a person tell a wonderfully entertaining story. It gets more difficult when you have to accept people for all their faults, moods and temperaments as well.

Your task for today is to listen to one conversation in which you hear and feel every word and nuance of someone's speech. Don't just hear the words, but hear what the person is trying to say. You will begin to sense the other person in a fuller realm. While doing so squash any attempt to judge, criticize or advise. Just listen.

PROGRAM

Week Three: Taking Action ~ 279

DAY NINETEEN – P.M. MESSAGE

Welcome back. I hope you had the opportunity to practice listening to another person at a level-one intensity. If the opportunity never arose, make a point of finding one tomorrow. If you did have a chance to listen to someone at a level-one, take a few moments to reflect on that experience.

JOURNAL ENTRY

I'm on my way to permanent results!

Today I practiced listening at level one. I didn't just listen to someone's words; I listened for what the person was trying to communicate. I did not judge, criticize or offer advice. I just listened.

I was in conversation with:

_____

While listening at level-one, were the words the person spoke and the meaning they were trying to convey the same?

_____

_____

_____

_____

By really listening at level-one, what did you learn about the other person that you wouldn't have heard, or noticed if you had listened at a level-two or level-three?

_____

_____

_____

_____

How did the speaker respond to you when you listened intently?

_____

_____

_____

_____

What other thoughts and observations do you have from your experience of listening to another person at level one?

_____

_____

_____

_____

_____

_____

I tell you everything that is really nothing,
and nothing of what is everything,
do not be fooled by what I am saying.
Please listen carefully and try to hear what I am not saying.
~ Charles C. Finn

See you tomorrow.

 . . . to becoming a great listener and communicator!

DAY TWENTY
I'm on my way to permanent results!

DAY TWENTY - A.M.

Welcome to day twenty. Yesterday you practiced listening to another person at level-one. You listened without judging, criticizing or condemning. While doing so you may have felt vulnerable or exposed. If you did feel that way it's perfectly natural. You chose to leave the sanctuary of your world and "your truth." To truly listen to another leaves us exposed. It can be a frightening experience. Congratulations for doing that. Many people never will.

Today we will examine some of the fears one may feel while giving another person our full listening attention.

The Natural Fear of Listening

A major barrier to listening to another person is the notion that silence may condone agreement. If someone is talking and we nod or indicate that we're listening by saying "uh-huh," our fear is that the speaker may confuse our failure to *object* with agreement. The speaker may even suddenly switch topics under the delusion that you share his view, which lays the setting for a future irresolvable argument. The speaker clearly "heard" your agreement because he mistakenly interpreted your "uh-huh" and "I see" response, with your "unequivocal endorsement" of what he said. You, on the other hand, were only indicating that you *heard* the message. You were particularly careful not to commit to anything. The future setting is now ripe for you to be accused of either changing your mind, or worse, lying!

An additional fear in silent listening is running into an abrupt end to a conversation. What would happen if we were listening to something we strongly disagreed with? What would happen if we were using the encouraging signs of "I see" or "Go on" for the speaker to complete his thoughts, but the conversation was suddenly disconnected or interrupted and we never got a chance to state our view?

These fears are valid because they're not at all uncommon.

I recently re-watched the timeless classic *12 Angry Men*. This movie is a masterpiece on so many levels, but one thing it so brilliantly demonstrates are the enormous communication challenges humans face.

12 Angry Men is about twelve jurors who must return a verdict in a slum kid's murder trial. In the early stages of the movie, eleven jurors are certain of the defendant's guilt. One isn't so sure and refuses to throw in a vote of guilty until he's *convinced* otherwise. As the drama unfolds we get a wonderful view of the twelve jurors, their personalities and peculiarities. Each juror heard the same trial, but each has heard a unique trial through the blurred vision of his own lens. Each juror has "innocently" arrived at his verdict through his personal filters, prejudices, and interpretations.

In one particularly poignant scene, juror number ten exposes his extreme bigotry through a hate-filled diatribe. During his vengeful rant, two of the jurors, unable to listen to his opinion, leave the room. The other jurors sit in twisted agony or stony silence as they fight their natural inclination to stifle this man's prejudicial rage with whatever means necessary.

As I watched that scene I reflected on the challenges each of the jurors were wrestling with. In the spirit of justice each man has the right to express his opinion, each has the right to be heard, but at what point does that right cross the line? I don't want to slip into a deeper discussion, but I think this point is a vivid example of the *same* challenges any skilled listener faces. It's not easy to listen to something we may not agree with, perhaps even violently disagree with, while battling the justifiable fear that even our temporary silence can be confused with acceptance of the speaker's view. In the case of listening to juror number ten, the other jury members listened and reacted in various ways. Although each juror managed to convey his vehement disagreement with what was being said, not all truly listened and certainly not at the same level.

Although the above example is extreme, it typifies the challenge a listener will confront when truly listening to another person. If the speaker says something that we find disagreeable, repugnant, or just plain ignorant, we naturally feel that our silence is either compliant or spineless in its lack of confrontation. Silence in the face of hearing something unpalatable is a very real challenge that any good listener *must* be prepared to confront. A good listener has to anticipate such a scenario in advance and know that he must not only hold his tongue, but he must make every attempt to see the world through the speaker's eyes. To become a skilled listener, this has to be a clearly understood and defined goal. Listening decorum does NOT mean we agree with the speaker's message, but it DOES mean we have risen to the lofty heights of practicing the fundamental human right of freedom of expression.

I disapprove of what you say, but I will defend to the death your right to say it.
~ Evelyn Beatrice Hall

Anyone, even a poor listener, can sit silently and listen to a speaker who says agreeable things. But it's when a speaker says something we cannot agree with that the very foundation of effective listening comes into play. It is precisely at that point that we must ask ourselves: "Can I listen empathically? Can I still try to see the situation through the speaker's eyes? Can I listen for the duration of the speech without judging or criticizing?"

If our desire to listen to another is only exercised when hearing an agreeable message, then we will never achieve any degree of listening skill. In fact, unless we're listening to "a string of facts," we might be very hard pressed to ever listen to another person without some disagreement. It is precisely at this point where our listening skills are required.

Listening empathically to someone say something we disagree with, to suspend our criticism and judgment, even temporarily, is the hallmark of maturity, wisdom and genuine listening skills.

STEP 20 – Today's step is to listen to, and then acknowledge, what you hear another person say. Even if you don't agree; in fact, especially if you don't agree! Listen first, then summarize what the person said. If the person confirms the accuracy of your interpretation, then, and only then, should you consider giving your view of the matter, or not! If the person corrects your interpretation, then restate your understanding of what was said until you both agree on what was said and heard.

Be very clear that *effective listening* is simply acknowledging what you heard, it does not imply approval, complicity or agreement. By restating what the person said, you are meeting a basic human need – the need to be heard.

If you confront a person in an emotional state, you can forget any chance of having a meaningful two-way dialogue. The emotionally charged person must release their emotions and feel listened to *before* there can by any conceivable chance of listening in return. Should you happen to find yourself listening to someone who is emotionally charged, try this. First listen, then acknowledge the other person by summarizing what you heard and how they might feel.

Joan: "I can't stand it anymore. I'm going to tell my boss to jump in the lake! Nothing's ever right. Nothing's ever good enough for him. All he ever does is criticize and complain!"

Response One: "Wow! You sure sound upset."

Response Two: "Wow! You sure sound upset. You're angry and frustrated that he never acknowledges anything positive."

In the first response you're restating what you heard. In the second response you're acknowledging how the person feels. Although you have acknowledged the person's feelings you haven't approved, agreed, given your opinion or advise.

When you acknowledge another person you have achieved one major goal in listening and communicating: you have let the other person feel heard and listened to.

We've said many times in this program that feeling listened to is a major human need. People want two things:

1. To be understood and acknowledged.
2. To be approved and agreed with.

Jane and Mary are sharing an apartment while finishing their graduate courses. Jane is meticulous and Mary is messy. They are constantly on edge with each other because of their differing views and habits. If Mary brings up the subject of Jane's meticulousness, Jane refuses to acknowledge Mary's feelings for fear that she will construe acknowledgment with agreement. As a result the more Jane refuses to acknowledge Mary's feelings, the harder she tries to have them acknowledged. It's a brewing volcano that's leading to an inevitable explosion.

In this case even if Jane doesn't agree with a single word Mary says, just *acknowledging* her feelings will diffuse the situation. If a person feels listened to they will correspondingly listen to your side as well.

Remember – acknowledging is one thing, sharing your story and advising is another matter. In the earlier example Joan complained about her ungrateful boss. In the second response the listener acknowledged how she must be feeling. If the listener had gone on to say; "If I were you I'd tell him a thing or two ...!" the listener would have left the realm of listening and have taken over the conversation. When you talk about your point of view, and feelings you have completely abandoned your listening post. It's important to learn to just listen and summarize.

Period. When you can achieve that, for even brief periods, you will experience the deep understanding and satisfaction that comes from truly listening to another person.

DAY TWENTY – P.M. MESSAGE

Congratulations on another great day. If you managed to listen to another person at level-one you really should be very proud of yourself. That simple act, even for a short duration, sets you apart from the vast majority of people.

JOURNAL ENTRY

I'm on my way to permanent results!

Today I continued my practice of listening to someone at level-one. I did my best to see the world through the speaker's eyes. I did not judge, criticize or offer advice. I just listened. When the speaker finished I summarized what I heard and acknowledged his/her feelings. I did not add my opinion nor did I give any advice. I just listened, summarized and acknowledged.

Note: If a listening opportunity did not present itself today look for an opportunity tomorrow or the next day. If it did present itself, jot down your thoughts to the following questions. Be as honest as you can in your assessment and answers to the questions. If you didn't do very well, admit it. Awareness is the first step to change! Don't get discouraged; you are in the process of reversing a lifetime of old listening habits. Awareness itself is a massive change! With desire and awareness you are on the path to becoming a great listener.

• Today I was in conversation with _____

While listening at level one I managed to encourage the speaker to fully express what they had to say. Even when I thought they might be finished speaking, I asked a relevant question or I waited silently for a moment to be sure they were finished expressing themselves. At that point I summarized what I heard and acknowledged what they said.

Was it difficult to summarize the speaker's message and thoughts? ☐ Yes ☐ No

Was it difficult to acknowledge how they felt? ☐ Yes ☐ No

Did it make you feel awkward? ☐ Yes ☐ No

Did you feel like you were trying to force an unnatural response by summarizing and acknowledging the speaker's thoughts? ☐ Yes ☐ No

Was your summary accurate? ☐ Yes ☐ No

Did the speaker have to reiterate what he/she meant? ☐ Yes ☐ No

What did you learn about the speaker?

_____

_____

_____

_____

What did you learn about yourself?

_____

_____

_____

_____

_____

How did the speaker respond to your summary and acknowledgment?

_____

_____

_____

_____

What other thoughts and observations do you have from your experience of listening, summarizing and acknowledging?

_____

_____

_____

_____

PROGRAM

Did You Know? Both business practitioners and academics listed listening as one of the most important skills for an effective professional, yet only 1.5% of articles in business journals dealt with listening effectiveness (Smeltzer, 1993).

Listening is an attitude of the heart, a genuine desire
to be with another which both attracts and heals.
~ J. Isham

See you tomorrow.

... to becoming a great listener and communicator!

PROGRAM

DAY TWENTY-ONE
I'm on my way to permanent results!

DAY TWENTY-ONE - A.M.

Can you believe it? You're seventy-five percent of the way there and today is reward day. You have come a very long way in the past three weeks!

You are so deserving of a reward that we no longer even need to mention why. I bet that by now, even your "doubting" inner-self will grudgingly go along with you in agreeing that you've not only earned your reward, but that you're well on the way to becoming a truly skilled listener and communicator.

STEP 21 – By now you're very conscious of listening and communicating. You're acutely aware of all the handicaps to attentive listening. You see, hear and feel the subtlety of communication. Your awareness is a huge step toward achieving the mastery of a skilled listener.

Today's step is to listen to someone for at least a total of two minutes at the skill of level-one. Listen for the meaning beyond the words. Put aside all judgment and criticism. Listen to the other person with the intent of seeing through their eyes. Check to see how well you've done by acknowledging their speech, and meaning. Your awareness and practice will have an immediate effect on the listener, and an even greater effect on you. Practice this step at least once today.

DAY TWENTY-ONE – P.M. MESSAGE

Way to go. Another great day!

The third week is complete.

PROGRAM

- Week One was about awareness and commitment. "I know I'm committed to becoming a good listener and communicator."
- Week two was about further commitment and embedding those neurological tracks into a new and powerful way of thinking.
- Week three was action week! You have successfully completed three full weeks. You are definitely in the minority when it comes to setting and achieving your goals. You have done things that most people couldn't imagine in their wildest dreams.
- You have set upon a course to learn the skills of listening and communicating – now by itself that may not be a great feat, but wait … there's more!
- You have taken the time and effort to mentally prepare yourself to become a good listener – now we're getting into much rarer territory … but wait, that's not all.
- You have written out your short-and long-term goals … this action puts you in a very, very small minority … but wait there's even more that you have accomplished.
- You have written affirmations, practiced visualization and made deep changes in your subconscious thinking toward your listening and communication habits. "Wow, all this is me?" Yep, and there's even more.
- You have begun to effectively incorporate the tools of great listener. You are aware of the bad habits of multi-tasking while attempting to listen. You acutely aware of a wandering mind while someone is talking. You are becoming aware of your acquired filters, and the myriad of sabotaging techniques that prevent effective listening. Very few people are even remotely aware of the importance of listening and the challenges that hinder that ability. You have come a great distance in understanding the barriers to becoming a great listener and communicator. You truly are a rare individual who should be very proud of all that you've accomplished!

JOURNAL ENTRY

I'm on my way to permanent results!

Today is reward day. For my reward I gave myself:

_____

In practicing these various listening skills the ones I find the most difficult to adapt to are:

_____

_____

_____

_____

The listening skills I find the easist to adapt are:

_____

_____

_____

_____

_____

Congratulations on such a successful journey. Let's keep on going!

See you tomorrow!

 . . . to becoming a great listener and communicator!

PROGRAM

— <u>WEEK FOUR</u> —

STAYING THE COURSE

<u>DAY TWENTY-TWO</u>
Staying the course!

DAY TWENTY-TWO - A.M.

Believe it or not, you're on the last leg of your *29 DAYS* journey. You should be proud of your efforts and commitment..

Last night we summarized all that you've accomplished so far. You curbed your habit of trying to multi-task; you put a short leash on your wandering mind when listening, you've become aware of your filters; you've managed to listen to someone empathically; you've begun to listen for meaning, not just words; and you've begun to listen and then acknowledge without judgment. You have begun to learn and practice a considerable number of skills toward becoming a good listener.

Although you are on your way toward becoming a good listener, it's most likely that you're not satisfied with your listening skills … yet, but you have built the proper foundation of awareness and desire to fulfilling your goal of becoming a good listener. This week is about further embedding those neuron tracks of "right-thinking" deep into your subconscious mind to take you to twenty-nine days and beyond. You took this program because you want to change your old listening and communication habits … for good. This week will firmly imbed those new habits.

The next part is on criticism and because it's quite involved, it's going to be spread out over the next three days. Today is part one.

Handling the Dreaded "C" Word: CRITICISM – Part One

Most of us are completely oblivious to how we are viewed by our family, friends and associates. We are so sold on our interpretation and beliefs of who we are, how we behave and what we are, we cannot conceive that we may be viewed by others in a considerably different light.

How many people do you know who would readily admit to being dishonest? Probably none. Since we all know of dishonest people, there's obviously a radical difference in perception.

If any of us were to point out, by way of example, someone's dishonest actions, you can bet the accused will have a detailed explanation that would conveniently absolve him (in his mind) from having acted in a dishonest manner.

So what's this got to do with criticism? Everything. For us to grow and mature it's imperative that we learn to properly recognize criticism, then depending on the type, either forget it or learn to accept and act on it.

If we're not open to criticism, it can only mean we believe we're living above it. If we're under the delusion we're above it, then it's literally impossible to change and grow. If we want to expand and develop as individuals we need to be open to criticism and put aside our natural tendency to defend or counterattack.

In fact, being able to accept criticism can be one of the most valuable tools you can acquire toward becoming the person you aspire to be.

- Accepting criticism doesn't mean you set yourself up to be a verbal punching bag for anyone to strike.
- Accepting criticism doesn't mean you have to completely agree with the comments and observations of the person criticizing.
- Accepting criticism really means holding your tongue, your emotions and your natural inclinations long enough to listen so that you can give yourself the opportunity for self-reflection and subsequent improvement.

Types of Criticism

I've broken criticism into three types: *constructive, casual* and *malicious.*

Constructive criticism is the kind given by someone with honorable intentions. They see someone doing something wrong or they see how a person can improve in some area and they offer the benefit of their caring, wisdom and experience.

Casual criticism might be something as ineffectual as an offhand comment. Someone might jokingly say, "You're such a slob!" and in the manner in which they said it our response might be equally offhand as we reply, "Yep, that's me!" Casual criticism might also be simple advice for improvement such as: "If you applied yourself toward your studies you would master any subject." This could be interpreted as a compliment as much as it could be interpreted as a criticism.

Malicious criticism is the third type. Its sole intent is to hurt.

Perceived Criticism

There is a fourth type of criticism, which I haven't listed among the three, because technically it's not a criticism, it's just *perceived* as criticism. This is the area that causes untold problems and is often the chief cause of misunderstanding and bitter feuds. We'll look at "perceived" criticism last.

Let's begin by examining the three types of criticism.

As was stated earlier, criticism is not only a part of life, it can be a vitally important part of life if we want to grow in wisdom and maturity. All of us have a natural tendency to avoid criticism, and if it becomes unavoidable we will often reject it with all manner of anger, excuses, and defenses … rational and otherwise. In some cases this reaction is perfectly justifiable, in most cases it isn't. So unless you're convinced you're perfect, let's begin to see criticism from several angles.

Malicious Criticism

For all intents and purposes, we're going to consider malicious criticism as just that … its intent is to inflict hurt. It's important to us only insofar as we need to properly recognize it and categorize it for what it is. When we receive this type of criticism think of the general rule of martial arts – deflection. When someone's intent is simply to injure, do not meet force with force, simply deflect the evil out of harm's way.

For example:

> John says: "I think you are one of the most ignorant people I have ever met. You come from white-trash and you'll always be white-trash. Why don't you just go back to the sticks you grew up in?"

Note: This type of criticism is void of any useful advice. In fact, all it does is expose John as an under-developed person with a lot of built-up anger. There is nothing to argue, defend or refute. Whenever someone serves us this type of malicious criticism do not serve it back; if you do, the game is in play. This type of criticism should be side-stepped and allowed to quickly die.

PROGRAM

You: There is only one reason that you would respond to such criticism and that is if you think it has some validity. If someone was to "spit" such venomous language at us, our natural reaction is anger. We will tend to violently lash out in our defense. In this case if you really believe that you are "so-called white-trash," then it might be best to have some internal discussions with yourself. It might be vitally important to try to understand why you are painting yourself with such a shallow, prejudicial brush.

In truth, no person without some serious internal issues, would voice such a thing as John had just said. When any of us hear such anger, whether it's directed toward us or someone else, we would be wise to consider the source, deflect the venom, and leave it at that.

Suppose John said this:
"You've got purple eyes! You've got purple eyes!"

How would you respond to such a statement? In all likelihood you would dismiss it for what it is. Although it's not easy, treat ALL malicious criticism in the same manner ... recognize it, deflect it and forget about it.

All famous people are "sitting ducks" to malicious criticism. Imagine being Bill Clinton, Martha Stewart, Oprah Winfrey or George Clooney for a single day. If they allowed malicious criticism to impact their daily lives they wouldn't come out of their clothes closet!

In fact, it's not surprising that George Clooney is a consummate master at deflecting criticism. In a March 2008 article in *People Magazine.com* by Christina Tapper, she asks the question:

> *"What do you do when Donald Trump pokes fun at your height and Fabio threatens to beat you up? If you're George Clooney you take it all in stride – and make a couple of jokes, of course."*

- When Clooney was asked about the rumor that Fabio once threatened to beat him up he admitted it was true and that getting beaten up by a big guy like Fabio would be rather painful.

- When he was accused of being "gay, gay, gay," he replied; "No, I'm gay, gay. The third gay – that was pushing it."

- In another example Donald Trump was on Larry King saying, "George Clooney is a very short guy. I mean he's a tiny guy." Clooney, who happens to be 5'11", responded by saying, "I've met Donald Trump once, and I was sitting at a table. He came over, shook my hand, and walked away. I guess I looked about three-foot-five sitting at that table."

How's THAT for deflection? Who comes out looking like the classier, more capable and likeable person? Who's more comfortable with himself?

We're all faced with the challenge of confronting "the cheap shot." It's nothing as overt and deliberately hostile as our earlier example of John and his white-trash accusation, but it's that snide comment or quasi-criticism that is intended to draw a reaction, or even better, an emotional reaction.

When we're confronted with this type of comment our natural inclination is to become defensive. We try to convince the other person they're wrong. Worst move you can make!

If you really want to disarm the snide comment or quasi-criticism then here's what you do … agree with it. That's right, agree with it. You will disarm the comment like a popped balloon.

1. Picture yourself making a presentation on the importance of Greenpeace and how we all need to pull together to ensure the health of our planet in the future. At the end of your presentation you allow for a question and answer period. The first questioner doesn't really ask a question but rather accuses you of being a hypocrite because he saw you arrive in a "gas guzzling" SUV.

2. You're a salesman for an electronics store. You have a great deal on plasma TVs that will not only give you a large commission, but the boss has asked you to really push this model. The customer says he's done his research and suggests that you should do the same. "It's obvious" he states, "an LCD TV is far superior to a plasma TV."

3. One of your co-workers at the insurance company you work for suggests that you should be a little more diplomatic with your customers.

The typical response to any of these statements is to get defensive and respond from an emotional level.

1. "So I drove here in an SUV. Do you expect me to walk? If I have to go to

PROGRAM

another country do you expect me to flap my arms? I think you're missing the whole point of my presentation. Try and see the big picture and how we all need to pitch in together for a healthy planet."

2. "I think YOU might want to do some additional research. Not only does plasma have a better picture, but compare the two side-by-side. On top of that, the price on this plasma is the best you'll find anywhere."

3. "What are you talking about? I'm diplomatic. Yesterday I stayed fifteen minutes late just to make sure I returned all my phone calls. I always ask my clients how they're doing and how I might be of service. A lot of them don't speak English 'good' which is maybe why it may sound like I'm not as friendly as I could be."

So, how did our defendants do? Do you think they were very successful at swinging their critics over to their point of view? In fact any kind of defensive tactic only serves to further reinforce the critic's point of view.

If we were to take a snapshot of what each of these people are thinking after your "defensive" reaction it would probably look similar to this:

1. "What an absolute blow-hard. You environmentalists are all the same. Do as I say, not as I do. What a loser!"

2. "Hey jerk, I think you've got our positions mixed up. I'm the customer. It's my money and I'll buy what I want to buy. Don't try and play the heavy with me!"

3. "Yeah, you're diplomatic all right. I can see your diplomacy in action right now."

What could each of these people have said that would have totally diffused the situation? They could have agreed with their critic.

1. Laughing or smiling you could say; "Yes, you're absolutely right. Ever since I've become an activist for Greenpeace I've been trying to live by example. As a result I'm advertising my SUV for sale at a huge loss. Our Greenpeace movement must be gaining widespread acceptance because I still haven't received a single offer!"

2. "It's nice to be able to talk to a knowledgeable customer. Most people think they prefer the vibrant colors of plasma, but you obviously have a discerning eye. Although the colors of an LCD aren't as vivid they really do look more natural."

3. "Hey thanks for the heads-up. Sometimes I get so focused on the details I forget to consider how I'm coming across."

If the malicious criticism really rankles you, consider the source. If it deeply hurts, perhaps you need to look a little deeper into yourself.

This is the end of part one.

STEP 22 — Today's step is to try and do a little memory recall. Can you think of the last time you got "sucked" into responding to malicious comments or criticism? Try to come up with at least one memory and then consider the questions in today's journal.

JOURNAL ENTRY

I'm on my way to permanent change!

I do recall a situation where someone made a deliberate malicious comment about me or my behavior. Very roughly this is what happened:

_____

_____

_____

_____

_____

My reaction to the malicious comment was:

_____

_____

_____

_____

_____

If I could go back into time I would have:

_____

_____

_____

_____

How do I feel about reacting "emotionally" to malicious comments?

_____

_____

_____

_____

_____

In the future I will try to do the following things to catch myself before I get sucked into reacting emotionally to malicious comments.

_____

_____

_____

_____

_____

PROGRAM

DAY TWENTY-TWO – P.M. MESSAGE

Way to go. Another great day!

I hope you have had a chance to really consider today's information on malicious comments and criticism. When you can rise above this type of criticism you not only immediately elevate your stature in your own eyes, but in everyone else's as well.

Remember, if you react defensively and emotionally to malicious criticism you will lose every single time. If you remember that you cannot win, you might be able to catch yourself the next time the situation rears its ugly head.

Your goal in this program is to become a great listener and communicator. Be conscious of communicating to others that *you* don't run on other people's agenda, and that *they* can't control you by pushing your buttons. Everyone is attracted to people who are calm, cool and collected ... especially under pressure. If you can consciously catch yourself, before you try a no-win defense to malicious criticism, you will communicate wisdom and maturity every time.

See you tomorrow.

... to becoming a great listener and communicator!

<u>DAY TWENTY-THREE</u>
Staying the course!

DAY TWENTY-THREE - A.M.

Welcome back. It's day twenty-three. Today is part two of our three-part discussion on how to recognize and handle criticism. We said that there are three types of criticism; *constructive, casual* and *malicious*. Yesterday we took an in-depth look at *malicious criticism* and we determined that our natural tendency is to react defensively against it, but if we do, we always lose. The only way to react against malicious criticism is to remember the basic rule of martial arts – do not meet force with force. Always deflect the force harmlessly away.

Today we'll look at the other two forms of criticism; *casual* and *constructive*.

Handling the Dreaded "C" Word: CRITICISM – Part Two

Casual Criticism

This type of criticism is often the type that is tossed out as a casual remark or observation. It's not meant to be malicious nor is it meant to be instructive or constructive. More often than not, it will be said in the spirit of an innocent comment.

> Example
> *"You look better in red than you do in orange."*
> *"You've had this car for quite some time."*
> *"You should get your eyes checked."*
> *"Stripes are more becoming on you than checks."*
> *"You should try and get some more sleep."*

Anyone of these comments can be taken as a mean-spirited, or it can be taken for what it was likely meant to be, a harmless comment that the speaker probably forgot about the moment after it was said.

I have been the recipient of this type of "innocent" criticism far more than once, and I've also caught myself dwelling on it for an embarrassingly long time … far more than once!

Whenever I catch myself lamenting over an innocent or offhanded comment, I can always trace it back to an unjustified insecurity. We all have a tendency to inflate such "innocuous" comments into gargantuan proportions.

The next time you're given – no better yet, you've *accepted* – one of these little "gems," ask yourself this: "Was it meant to be malicious?" If it was, then it's *not* a casual criticism and it doesn't belong in this category. It should be dealt with as instructed yesterday on dealing with malicious criticism.

If you think this type of criticism is *constructive*, then again it's in the wrong category and you will want to handle it in the manner we will discuss next on dealing with constructive criticism.

If you conclude that the criticism was indeed a casual comment that can be labeled as casual criticism, then give it as much attention as it deserves … dismiss it for what it is and move on.

Constructive Criticism

Believe it or not, constructive criticism is something we should welcome. It's often difficult, if not impossible, to see our own faults and shortcomings.

Since constructive criticism is neither casual nor malicious, you can think of it as a helpful critique. When anything is critiqued it's given serious examination and judgment. If we are critiqued by someone we admire and respect, we should not only take the criticism to heart, but we should be grateful. It would be pretty hard to improve your golf swing, your tennis serve or your personality and behavior without *receiving* and *applying* constructive criticism. The first step to change always begins with awareness. If we can open ourselves up to constructive criticism we become aware and we have completed the first step.

Constructive criticism, by definition, has to be helpful, after all, it's constructive!

Accepting Constructive Criticism

There are three simple steps toward accepting constructive criticism:
1. Determine that it is constructive.
2. Reflect on what was instructed.
3. Act on it.

Whenever you receive "advice" from a boss, co-worker, spouse or friend, and you know their comments are well-meaning, you would be wise to resist the urge to argue or react defensively. Hear them out. For the time being at least, accept their suggestion without getting your back up. You will need time to reflect on what was said, especially if you weren't aware of your particular shortcoming. If you weren't aware of your manner or behavior, don't protest or rebut the information, you will need time for self-reflection. In fact, respectfully ask your critic for specific examples to help you see the matter from their perspective. It may not be pleasant to hear, but it will be enlightening.

Since it's vitally important that you clearly comprehend the criticism, reiterate your understanding to be sure you and the speaker are in alignment. The speaker will respect you for listening and accepting the advice as opposed to most people's reactions of hostility, rejection and defense of their behavior. If the criticism is constructive, whatever you do, *don't* try to defend your actions. Bite your tongue, pinch yourself, or pace if you have to, but don't attempt to defend or justify. If you do, you will immediately lose face with your critic and later with yourself. If you know there's some truth to the criticism you may even want to fess up!

- *"Yes, I guess I haven't been pulling my weight lately."*
- *"Thanks, you're right. From now on I'll put the paper down when we're talking."*
- *"I didn't realize that I came across as being mean-spirited. I suppose I appear that way when my mind is elsewhere."*
- *"Do I really clench my fists every time I talk to you? Oh, look at that I'm doing it again!"*

You cannot grow as a person if you don't change. If someone you respect has taken the time, and yes risk, to help you improve your behavior or action in a positive way, there's nothing to get defensive about. The person offering constructive criticism probably doesn't feel overly comfortable with the task. They're offering their advice and opinion for your benefit. They're probably going out on a limb to tell you something that other people refrained from saying. Remember that!

After you've listened to and "accepted" the criticism, you may want to ask your critic a few follow-up questions to be certain you understand their suggestion for improvement. After that, thank them for their concern and get on with it. That's it!

STEP 23 – Today's step is to spend a few moments considering one of the most helpful, and ironically, one of the most rejected forms of self-improvement ... constructive criticism. If you should feel the need to be defensive, know that you are not acting in your best interest. You can consider the matter, perhaps analyze it later, but do your best to squash your defensive instincts. They can't help you nor can they actually defend you. When you get a whiff of criticism, try to identify it and then act accordingly. If you detect constructive criticism, welcome it. The reason constructive criticism is so vitally important for our personal development, is that very few of us can perceive ourselves. We need the view of an outsider to help us become aware of our faults and shortcomings.

Without awareness there can be no improvement!

JOURNAL ENTRY

I'm on my way to permanent change!

I recall a time when I received constructive criticism and I failed to accept it gracefully. Instead I reacted defensively. Briefly this is what transpired:

_____

_____

_____

_____

In retrospect, what I wish I had done, and what I learned from the experience was this:

_____

_____

_____

_____

PROGRAM

I can also recall a time when I received constructive criticism and I took the time to consider it, and to accept it, gracefully. Briefly this is what transpired:

_____

_____

_____

_____

_____

_____

DAY TWENTY-THREE – P.M. MESSAGE

I trust you had another great day!

As we saw today, constructive criticism should be received gratefully. In fact, you can even take the initiative and ask someone you trust and respect for advice or suggestions to help you do a better job or avoid undesirable behavior that you may not even be aware of. If you're concerned about becoming a more effective employee or just a better person, ask someone you trust for a performance review at work. If you want to become a better friend or spouse the next time you sense an appropriate moment, ask your friend or partner to expand on what they may have suggested.

Take a few moments and visualize the last time you received constructive criticism from someone. Recall how you reacted. If you reacted favorably then consider why you did and how you will do so in the future.

If you didn't react as best as you could have, reconstruct the scene in your mind only this time, respond favorably. This can be a great exercise to help you the next time you find yourself as the recipient of some constructive criticism.

Remember, the person offering the constructive criticism is subjecting themselves to a certain amount of risk and discomfort. They are probably telling you something that other people may have been afraid to say. Since this criticism is neither casual nor malicious, you should be grateful to receive it. Thank the person, consider what they said, and then follow through accordingly. That's the hallmark of a great listener and a wise and mature person.

See you tomorrow.

 . . . to becoming a great listener and communicator!

PROGRAM

DAY TWENTY-FOUR
Staying the course!

DAY TWENTY-FOUR - A.M.

Welcome to day twenty-four and part three of our discussion on criticism. During the past two days, we looked at the three types of criticism: *casual, constructive* and *malicious.* We said that constructive criticism, by its very nature is constructive and therefore should be welcomed, not defended. Of the other two, casual criticism should not be taken seriously, and malicious criticism should be deflected harmlessly away.

There is a fourth type of criticism which I call *perceived* criticism.

Perceived Criticism

The reason perceived criticism wasn't included with the three types of criticism is because *perceived* criticism wasn't meant to be critical, it was mistakenly "perceived" to be critical. This erroneous perception lies at the very heart of poor listening and poor communication. It is the chief cause of misunderstanding and feuds.

In many cases we confuse people's hurt feelings and need to be heard as direct criticism of *ourselves.* Our failure to listen, our tendency to jump to false conclusions, to defend ourselves against *nonexistent* charges, cause emotional reactions, anxiety, misunderstanding and untold damage to our relationships.

Example:

Bob is washing his car on his driveway when he notices the very early stages of rust around one of the fenders. He's thinking, "Great. I've just paid this car off last month and before long I'll have to start looking for a new one." Just then his son walks up the driveway and says; "Hey Dad, Mr. Wilson just bought a couple of new luxury cars for himself and Mrs. Wilson. She got a convertible and he got some exotic sports car. They are so cool!"

Bob hears: Mr. Wilson sure provides the best for his family. It's too bad we have to continue to drive this old rust bucket around.

Bob defends: "There's nothing wrong with our car. If you had to walk more often you might appreciate just how good you've got it."

Although this example might register with you as extreme, it's not at all uncommon for a perfectly innocent remark to cause a volcanic eruption, especially if a person is feeling vulnerable about a particular situation.

The very moment we become defensive, we've broken off effective communication. Verbal self-defense serves no useful purpose. As we pointed out in the section on malicious criticism, if the person meant to cause harm, and we pull out our defensive arsenal, that alone is proof of their success and our failure. If the person didn't mean anything, and we lash out in response, what have we done? What kind of venom did Bob spit at his son, an innocent victim? This is the antithesis of listening. It's the breeding ground for hurt, anger, misunderstanding and argument.

Why Do We Hear Criticism When It Isn't Even There?

We feel vulnerable, which causes us to automatically defend ourselves. Our focus isn't on the words, the intent, or the other person. Our sole focus is on "me," on self-preservation.

Example:

Greg and Mary attended his annual company Christmas party. Mary dreads going every year because it's always the same routine. As they're driving home Mary shares her feelings for the night.

Mary: "I wish you wouldn't invite me to your work parties and then ignore me all night. I really don't know anybody. I felt so awkward and uncomfortable. I think for a while I sat by myself for a full twenty minutes."

Greg: "What do you expect me to do? As company vice-president I'm expected to mingle with the staff. It's not as if I'm purposely avoiding you. I brought you several drinks and we danced. What more do you want? I can't be everywhere at once."

So, what just happened? Mary expressed her feelings and Greg jumped all over them. He refused to listen to anything Mary was trying to communicate. He refused to acknowledge how she felt. Greg wouldn't even take a moment to consider the fact that she may have felt lonely and uncomfortable. All he perceived was an attack that warranted a defense.

Does any of this sound familiar?

If Greg had bothered to listen he could have at least acknowledged Mary's feelings. In fact, he can try to justify his behavior until he's blue-in-the-face, but the reality is this; Mary felt the way she felt. She felt awkward, lonely and embarrassed. That's an irrefutable fact. Mary expressed her feelings in hope of receiving some compassion and understanding. What she got was a lot of defensive tactics, excuses and justification. How's that for listening and communicating?

Every one of us has been guilty of responding exactly as Greg responded. Instead of listening and acknowledging the other person's feelings, we hear criticism and respond with all the "human consciousness" of a komodo dragon!

We act defensively for only one reason; we hear a negative message about ourselves. In so many cases we completely miss the point. So often our spouses, bosses, friends, children are reaching out to us, trying to express their thoughts, feelings and needs, but because we failed to listen we hear an imaginary attack.

This is such an important point and a key to unlocking one of the major causes of feuds, misunderstandings and poor communication.

Earlier we said that there are three forms of criticism: constructive, casual and malicious. Properly handled, not one of these requires defensive action.

- Constructive criticism should be gratefully accepted.
- Casual criticism should generally be dismissed as irrelevant.
- Malicious criticism, if defended, makes the defendant look foolish.

Let me be the first to admit that this is easier said than done. I struggle with this from time-to-time, and I'm always sorry for it later. If there is one thing to try and remember it's this; anytime we find ourselves getting defensive we can safely bet it's the cause of poor listening. We're either misinterpreting or we're not listening … usually both!

Let's look at one final example and see the types of instinctual defenses we're all familiar with.

PROGRAM

Nancy and Bill have been married for almost twenty-five years. They have three children. Their youngest daughter has just left for her first year of college, and Nancy and Bill can't help but notice a huge void in their lives.

Nancy is especially concerned that she and Bill have grown apart, and without the binding agent of children in their lives, she's concerned for their future.

> **Nancy:** "Bill, I wish you wouldn't work late every evening of the week. On Saturdays you golf and on Sunday you spend the day reading the paper and watching sports. We need to spend some time together. I'm afraid we're becoming strangers."

Bill can choose a variety of responses. If he was really listening he would hear the concern in Nancy's voice that they have become strangers. Without the common bond of their children they hardly know each other. Bill can easily choose to get his back up and feel like his wife is unjustly criticizing him and he can resort to one of the old stand-by defensive techniques.

> **Bill decides to dispute Nancy's claim:** "How can you accuse me of not being around? I was home "on time" twice this week. I golfed Saturday morning and was home by mid afternoon, and I hardly take the whole day to read the paper. I need a little time to myself you know."

> **Or Bill decides to give Nancy a guilt trip:** "Nancy I'm sorry. I try my best to be a good husband, father and provider but it just never seems to be enough. Why do I work late? How do you expect to put three kids through college if I don't put in the hours I do? If you think I enjoy working so much think again. I don't know what I have to do to try and please you!"

> **Bill decides to deny Nancy's assertions:** "Nancy that's total crap. I did not work late every evening. I did not go golfing last week, and I can't even remember the last time I so much as glanced at the Sunday paper. Why do you try and lay a guilt trip on me with all these absurd accusations?"

Each one of these all-too-familiar replies are poster children for starting an argument and inflicting hurt. One person reaches out to express their feelings, emotions and concerns and the other person, in an unjustifiable act of defense, throws a grenade in response.

PROGRAM

Bill never bothered to listen. He only heard words. He never hear the underlying message. He never stopped to consider where Nancy might be coming from and what she was trying to express.

I won't bother to give you a laundry list of the "seven" or "ten" best things to do when you feel you're being criticized. Heck, when I feel like I'm being criticized, especially unjustly, I'm just trying to continue my intake of air!

When you feel yourself hauling out your usual defenses, try to remember that they will do you absolutely zero good. Not only will you be unable to successfully defend yourself, but you're misinterpreting the incoming message. IF it's one of the three criticisms, handle it in the manner prescribed.

There's only one thing to try and remember the next time you feel attacked, stop and listen. Really listen. Decipher the meaning. That's what listening's all about. If you can stifle the urge to react or defend, and instead just stop and listen, you will be doing yourself an enormous favor, and you will be extending the other person one of the greatest gifts you can give ... your full attention and respect.

STEP 24 – Today's step is to spend a few moments to consider the entire concept of *perceived* criticism.

Try and think of an example in your life where you jumped to a wild conclusion or assumption and felt the need to defend yourself from attack. How did you feel about it afterward? Can you recall defending yourself, but upon further analysis, your realize it was only *perceived* criticism?

You might also want to anticipate a future scenario when you can feel your defenses mounting in response to something your spouse, boss, child or friend has said. Decide in advance how you will deal with it.

JOURNAL ENTRY

I'm on my way to permanent change!

I recall a time when I reacted defensively to my boss, spouse, child, friend, family member, and now that I think about it, I know I misread the speaker's intent. Briefly this is what happened:

_____

_____

_____

_____

If I could relive that experience, I would have acted in this manner:

_____

_____

_____

_____

_____

I know that I will confront the desire to react defensively again. The next time I feel the urge to act defensively, I will try to do the following things to resist the urge:

_____

_____

_____

_____

_____

Example: You may want to take a moment and determine if it's criticism. If it is, you can respond in the ways that were suggested during the past two days. If you really listen to what the speaker says, you may hear a message that's deeper than the words. You may actually hear the person "crying" for help, for understanding or just a sympathetic ear. The next time I feel the urge to act defensively I will:

_____

_____

_____

_____

_____

_____

DAY TWENTY-FOUR – P.M. MESSAGE

Welcome back. It's the tail end of day twenty-four!

Today we took a good look at the major cause of anger, disagreements, feuds and misunderstandings ... the *perceived* criticism. Perceived criticism can happen so easily because we might be feeling vulnerable and someone says something that we *misinterpret* as a direct attack on ourselves. So often, the remark, or comment was given by the speaker in an attempt to express himself, but was taken by the listener in the wrong context.

Remember, we have a natural tendency to react to *what* is said rather than focusing our understanding on what the other person is *trying* to say. To compound the problem, as speakers we are hesitant to say exactly what is on our minds. We feel vulnerable so we couch our feelings and meaning.

Paul was invited to Rachel's family Christmas party. Rachel's close-knit family focused on enjoying each other's company, leaving Paul feeling left-out, awkward and ignored. While Paul was driving Rachel home he suggested that her social skills needed work. Paul, not wanting to appear weak, hurt or emotionally vulnerable, goes on the attack rather than expressing the real problem ... feeling lonely and awkward. Rachel, doesn't hear the meaning behind the words. She hears criticism. Rachel gets defensive and an inevitable argument breaks out.

This scenario plays itself out a billion times every day. Our true feelings, emotions and experiences are seldom revealed. We want the other person to "not only" listen, but *decipher* our meaning. Unfortunately that's the way most of us communicate.

Part of us desperately wants to make our thoughts and feelings known and the other part of us will do almost anything to keep them hidden. That's why it is so vitally important to listen for the message and meaning rather than the words.

Tonight, just before you fall asleep, visualize yourself listening to someone important in your life. See and hear them trying to express their feelings. See and feel yourself listening for the deeper meaning. Visualize the other person responding positively when you overcome your natural inclination to get defensive. See how a constructive discussion can result in place of an argument because *you* made the effort to hear the message rather than the words. If you can visualize a positive reaction, this will be an enormously effective aid the next time you instinctively reach for your defensive arsenal.

See you tomorrow.

29 DAYS . . . to becoming a great listener and communicator!

PROGRAM

DAY TWENTY-FIVE
Staying the course!

DAY TWENTY-FIVE - A.M.

Welcome to day twenty-five! Today you're going to look at the "me too" style of listening. Although we all do it, if we're supposed to be listening, it's highly inappropriate.

That's So Funny, the Very Same Thing Happened to Me!

Believe it or not, when someone is telling us a story, sharing their feelings or relaying an incident, to interject with a similar story or sentiment is not only NOT listening, it can be considered downright rude.

I don't know if the above statement came as a shock to you or not, but the first time I came across this suggestion it absolutely floored me. I had no idea. In fact, I thought that sharing a "me too" experience or "me too" feelings similar to the speaker's, was a positive sign of effective listening and communication skills. I thought it conveyed to the speaker that I not only heard the message and grasped the meaning, but even better, I could totally empathize since the exact thing happened to me!

Let's begin by making the following statement upon which today's discussion will be based:

To listen properly you must exist for the other person.

The listener must hold back the urge to interrupt, argue, or share a similar "me too" experience. The moment you do, you have shifted the focus from the speaker to yourself. THAT is not listening, that is stealing the show.

Characterizing a "me too" story as rude may seem rather forceful, but the world is full of poor listeners who constantly, and I mean constantly, share "me too" stories. The end result of a "me too" story is to take the focus off the speaker and direct it onto ourselves. I'm not suggesting that we do this consciously, or maliciously, but we do it all the same. The simple fact is, it's pretty hard to listen to another person if we're talking about an experience that happened to us!

Karen had only been working for her new employer for a few weeks. She found her work particularly enjoyable and she got along well with everyone in the office. Since she had recently transferred from another state, she was hoping to make some new friends. She felt especially close to Susan because they had so many things in common and Susan was always interesting and upbeat.

One day Karen arrived at work a few minutes late appearing disoriented and upset. She began to tell Susan about her unreliable car and how she seemed to have one problem after another. Susan was just about to share a similar car experience that happened to her that morning but instead she decided to let it go. She encouraged Karen to continue with her story and before long Karen was talking about how stressful the move had been for both her and her husband. She said that she had no idea that changing jobs, homes and states could be so emotionally draining. She talked for awhile about her family and the endless adjustments that she had never anticipated when they decided to move. Before long Karen was smiling and looking like her usual energized self.

Susan was grateful that she had not jumped in with her "me too" story of her car problems. She realized that Karen needed to talk to someone outside of her family about the stresses and emotions of moving. It wasn't the car she wanted to talk about, she just wanted someone to listen to her.

Susan's *gift* of silent listening allowed Karen to pour out her heart and feelings. Susan's ability to stifle the urge to respond proved to be just exactly what Karen had needed.

As you can see in the above example, suppressing the need or desire to share a similar feeling or story can mean the difference between genuine listening or listening just long enough to find an opening to flip the attention back onto ourselves.

If genuine listening can be so powerful, why do we so frequently disrupt the speaker's need to talk?

Because we erroneously think that sharing like experiences is a bonding agent. Since we've had a similar experience or feeling, who better could empathize with the speaker?

We would be wise to remember that no two people are alike. A father telling his son, "I know just how you feel because the very same thing happened to me when I was your age," is a blindly-presumptuous statement. Although the father may mean well, he has cut his son off. He has robbed him of the chance to express his thoughts and feelings. No two people are alike so therefore the very best we can do is get an approximation of the other person's feelings. Even if the father really did know how his son felt, it still doesn't negate the fact that his son needed to express his feelings. He needed someone to just listen. We all need to know that our thoughts and feelings are important. To interrupt another person with an empty platitude of, "Yeah, I know just how you feel," is emotional robbery and a far cry from listening.

How Can We Stop the Urge to Focus on Ourselves?

Practice, practice, practice. Eventually it will become as natural as our present bad listening habits.

STEP 25 – For the rest of today, look for opportunities to listen without offering a "me too" example. At the same time, and you'll have some fun with this, watch how often other listeners cut a speaker off with their own "me too" examples.

If someone says; "You won't believe my nosy neighbor ...," Our natural reaction is to say; "Man do I ever know what you mean. I had a neighbor … blah blah blah." But don't do it. DO NOT DO IT! Do not jump in with a story. Just listen to the other person and maybe ask them some additional questions. Then when the speaker is finished see what happens. Don't tell your story, just acknowledge the person and see what happens.

This is not to imply that it's wrong to follow-up with your story when the speaker has finished, but just for today, try this simple experiment. When a speaker has finished just acknowledge them and see what happens. Even if you have a great story to share with the speaker, that perfectly compliments their story, try something completely different … don't!

DAY TWENTY-FIVE – P.M. MESSAGE

Four more days to day twenty-nine! You're doing fabulous!

Today's assignment was to resist the urge to interrupt a speaker with a "me too" story. Perhaps you never came across a situation where you could have inserted a "me too" story even if you wanted to. If so, continue to look for an opportunity tomorrow. If you did find yourself in this situation take a few moments to consider the questions in your journal.

If the opportunity to offer a "me too" story did not present itself today, perhaps you had the opportunity to observe someone else. If you did you have a chance to see a speaker get cut short with someone else's "me too" story, use that example in your journal.

JOURNAL ENTRY

I'm on my way to permanent change!

Did you find yourself in a situation today where you could have interrupted a speaker with a "me too" story but you managed to resist the urge? If so, explain briefly what happened.

_____

_____

_____

_____

Did you find it difficult to suppress the urge to share your "me too" example?

_____

_____

How did the conversation go? Did the speaker appear to feel pleased, awkward, surprised by a lack of response from you?

_____

PROGRAM

_____

_____

_____

What are your feelings and observations about suppressing a desire to offer a "me too" response?

_____

_____

_____

What small step or action can you take to remind yourself not to *interrupt* a speaker with a "me too" story in the future?

_____

_____

_____

Just before you go to sleep this evening, spend a few moments reviewing the concept of one of the most common barriers to listening ... the "me too" *interruption.* If you can think of an example when someone pulled a "me too" on you, remember how it made you feel. If you can be aware of those feelings, they will go a long way to helping you stop the urge the next time it rears its ugly head.

Remember, *sharing* a "me too" story is not wrong, *inserting* a "me too" story IS!

See you tomorrow.

. . . to becoming a great listener and communicator!

PROGRAM

DAY TWENTY-SIX
Staying the course!

DAY TWENTY-SIX - A.M.

Welcome to day twenty-six! Yesterday we looked at the annoying, non-listening habit of cutting off a speaker with a "me too" story.

Today we'll take a look at another non-listening habit ...

Non-Listening's Deadliest Sin ... Giving Advice

We all have a tendency to spout advice:

> *"You should get more exercise."*
> *"You should stop smoking."*
> *"You should save more money."*
> *"You should, you should, you should ..."*

Advice like this doesn't help anyone. In fact, all it does do is make the advisor irritating.

> Gerald had enlisted the help of a real estate agent to sell his house. After being listed for two months he still hadn't had a single offer. One day while flying home from a business meeting, a man in the seat next to him mentioned he was going to be moving to Gerald's city and he was shopping for a home. Gerald mentioned his home was for sale, and lo and behold, two weeks later the man on the plane bought Gerald's home. It irked Gerald no end to have to fork over a five percent real estate commission to the sales agent who had nothing to do with the sale.

PROGRAM

Several days after the sale Gerald was at a family reunion and his brother-in-law, Jake, announced that he had just been given a promotion and a transfer to Chicago. He then mentioned to Gerald that he was wondering which real-estate agency Gerald had used to sell his home.

Gerald's Response: "Jake, let me give you a sound piece of advice, sell your house directly yourself. Real-estate agencies are a bunch of scam artists. They promise you the world and deliver nothing in return. If you're smart you'll take my advice and list the house yourself. Not only will it sell faster, but you'll save a full five percent on commission fees. I've been looking into the procedure for selling your own home and it's really quite simple. Whatever you do, don't use a real estate agency. Give me a call at the office tomorrow and I'll give you the details. If you're smart, you'll take my advice and do it all yourself."

- Does the advice Gerald just gave his brother-in-law Jake sound reasonable?
- Doesn't it sound like a guy who just wants to help?

So often this is exactly the type of advice we either *give* or *receive*. It's advice that is based on *our* experience. It's advice that is based on a whole lot of assumptions. Gerald was asked a simple question and rather than find out more about Jake's situation, he charges ahead with unsolicited advice.

Although Gerald's advice might be perfectly applicable, can you see how presumptuous it is?

- Gerald assumes he understands Jake's situation.
- He dives in with a solution based on his assumptions.
- He assumes that Jake wants to hear his solution to the question he never asked.
- He assumes Jake doesn't know anything about real estate, real estate agencies, or commissions.
- He assumes that Jake can and will find his advice useful and so on.

Jake: "Actually, Gerald, it doesn't matter all that much which agency I use. When my company initiates a transfer, they automatically purchase my house and set me up in another city until I find a new home there. I was asking for the name of your agency just to see if your agent new of a good sales "rep" in Chicago."

How often do we hear a perceived problem and install our solution? Gerald never bothered to ask Jake any questions, he just started advising. He never even thought to ask if Jake if he wanted his advice. He yapped on about real-estate agencies and their lack of moral conduct and ethics, and when he was finished he had still managed to avoid answering Jake's simple question; "Which real estate agency did you use?"

- Shouldn't we give people the benefit of our "hard-earned" wisdom?
- If I learned some lessons from the "school of hard-knocks," should I not try to help someone avoid the painful lessons I learned through first-hand experience?
- What parent can remain silent when they see their child making a decision that they feel certain will result in a painful conclusion?
- How could you consciously remain silent while your best friend told you he was going to invest in a company that you "knew" was a poor investment?
- On the other hand, how many times have you advised friends, or relatives to do, or not do something, and your advice turned out to be wrong?

To properly answer these questions we need to begin with our purpose and this begins with some honest, self evaluation. If our desire is to genuinely help another person then ultimately helping that person to help themselves is the best solution. When we can just listen, the speaker will more often than not arrive at their own solution. It's a solution that is uniquely suited to *their needs* because they're the only person privy to ALL of the details.

If we truly want to help we would be wise to withhold our prescription (advice) until we've been asked for it. Once asked, our advice should only be offered after we've made a thorough diagnosis. This may come as a surprise to you, it did to me, but when people share a problem with us, in almost all cases, they DO NOT want our advice. They just want us to listen.

When we can share our thoughts and concerns with someone who just listens, there is an energy, a force that begins the healing process. When we share a problem with someone who insists on giving unsolicited advice, it forces us into the uncomfortable position of either initiating the advice or explaining why it's not applicable.

Strange isn't it? I mean, why would someone share a problem with us, if they don't want our advice? The answer to this question is the basis of this entire program:

Because people just want, no they just NEED to be listened to.

People the world over just want someone to listen. They want to feel understood. Surprisingly enough, the moment a person feels listened to, they will often arrive at their own solutions which will be far more relevant and applicable than any off-the-cuff solutions the casual listener could have suggested.

STEP 26 - Today's step is to be aware of advice. Giving and receiving. Try to notice if you have a tendency to offer unsolicited advice. Can you catch yourself, or better yet, stop yourself from doling out unrequested advise? Can you "catch" other people's conversations and see how liberally they may serve unsolicited advice. Awareness is the beginning of change. "See" what you can "hear" for the rest of the day!

> *Remember that silence is sometimes the best answer.*
> *Dalai Lama*

DAY TWENTY-SIX – P.M. MESSAGE

Hey, welcome back. I hope you had an opportunity today to observe non-listening's deadliest sin ... Giving advice.

Most of us dread hearing someone say; "You should ...,"

Since *we* don't like to hear it, it's good to be aware of our own tendency to offer unsolicited advice to others. When we give advice, there's a subtle implication that the other person doesn't have the ability to solve their problem without the benefit of our wisdom. Our advice implies that the solution is so apparent, so obviously simple that the person with the problem might even be deficient.

Unless we are deeply immersed into the other person's situation, the advisor cannot know all of the ramifications of the other's problem. When people share their concerns with us, they seldom give us more than the tip of the iceberg. They will rarely go deep enough to share the details and complexities that make the problem so tenuous. In fact, unless we listen and probe, and listen and probe, in an attempt to unearth the myriad of issues – which seldom happens – our advice is generally going to be less than useless.

Please take a few moments to reflect on the following questions in your journal.

PROGRAM

JOURNAL ENTRY

I'm on my way to permanent change!

Were you involved in or did you witness any conversations today that contained unsolicited advice? If so, briefly describe what happened.

_____

_____

_____

_____

_____

How do you feel when you share thoughts, concerns and feelings with someone and they reply with advice?

_____

_____

_____

_____

When you receive advice, do you usually feel that the advisor fully understood your problem?

_____

If they didn't how does their advice make you feel?

_____

_____

_____

PROGRAM

Can you recall the last time that someone really listened deeply and empathically to you, asked and probed for further information, and then offered relevant advice?

_____

If so, how did this make you feel about the advice, and the advisor?

_____

_____

_____

You will constantly be confronted with the "opportunity" and "desire" to offer advice. As we have shown, it is seldom useful or constructive. It would be wise to consider how you will dispense advice in the future. Suppose a friend tells you that he is going to purchase a business that you happen to be quite knowledgeable about.

In a situation like this should you just listen to your friend tell you about this great opportunity and say nothing? What if your friend is making some assumptions about this new opportunity that you feel are wrong? With that said, how often have you said you're going to try something only to have everyone do their best to discourage you? These are rhetorical questions but ones that you must consider and internalize if you want to become a great listener and communicator.

If your friend began to tell you about his plans for something that you felt absolutely certain were wrong, should you, or could you, just sit there and listen?

If he never asked for your opinion do you not offer it anyway?

Suppose your friend said he was going to invest in a franchise. You have a great deal of first-hand knowledge about franchising and this franchise in particular. Because of your knowledge of both the franchise and your friend, you are certain that it's a mistake for your friend to get involved. If your friend doesn't ask for your opinion, do you have a moral or ethical obligation to offer your opinion?
Let's suppose you answered "yes" to the above question and you feel you simply _must_ give him your advice for your own peace-of-mind if nothing else. In this instance you should simply ask for permission.

You might say;

- ◊ "Since I've had some personal experience in this franchise, would you like to hear my views?"
- ◊ "May I give you some advise based on the limit of my understanding of this?"
- ◊ "I may be way off base, but I would really like to share my thoughts on some of the problems you may not be aware of."

Suppose you are the maid-of-honor at your best friend's upcoming wedding. You happen to feel strongly that your friend is making a huge mistake. You have witnessed her and her future husband quarrel endlessly. In fact, you just heard through the grapevine that he's seeing other women on the side. The wedding is set to take place in one week. Should you sit your friend down and tell her your feelings and share the rumors you heard?

This is a tough situation to be in. I certainly have my opinion on what you should do as the bridesmaid in this situation, and it's important that _you_ have a strong opinion as well – not necessarily about *this particular* issue - but you need to know how you will react in situations <u>like this</u> because they will crop up.

For example, suppose you have a personal policy that you will never gamble. Once you have that policy in place all your future decisions around gambling are simple. It doesn't matter if someone asks you to buy a lottery ticket for one dollar, or if they ask you to bet five dollars on the Superbowl, or you're asked to drop ten thousand dollars on an "inside tip" on the Kentucky Derby. You just say no to any offer because you have an entrenched philosophy you live by.

The same can be said for advice. Your policy might be that unless asked, you don't offer. Period. Your policy could be that I will offer advice to my children but other than them, I won't. Your personal policy could be any combination of things, but when you have your personal "advice policy" in place, it makes the future world of listening and advising infinitely easier to live by.

Many years ago I had a good friend (Jane) who was dating a married man. This man swore to Jane that he only stayed with his wife because of their children. He further assured her that all forms of intimacy between him and his wife had ceased years earlier. In spite of the promises and assurances, there was ample evidence that Jane wasn't his only female companion. To make matters worse, Jane managed his restaurant business which meant she worked seven days a week, from two pm 'till well past midnight. This arrangement had been carrying on for several years. Then one day another friend of mine reported seeing Jane's "man-friend" in another city walking into a hotel with his arm around another woman.

What should one do? I immediately went to Jane and told her the gory details of what I had heard.

Did Jane thank me? Did Jane go to her man-friend and confront him? No and no.

What she basically told me, in no uncertain terms, was to mind my own damn business.

Several weeks later she confronted her man-friend about the woman and hotel incident and amazingly enough, he had a perfectly acceptable explanation. Apparently it only "appeared" to be something untoward. He said that the matter was misunderstood by whomever saw him and that all his behavior was on the up and up.

As Jane relayed the story back to me I couldn't help but notice she was seething with anger for the embarrassment and sorrow I had needlessly put her through. We soon fell out of touch, I moved to another city, and I haven't seen or heard from Jane in over twenty-five years.

As a side note: I did hear that Jane and her man-friend did get married about five years after the "hotel incident," and at the time, they were enjoying their seven- year wedding anniversary.

It just goes to show you that unless asked ... keep out!

See you tomorrow.

DAY TWENTY-SEVEN
Staying the course!

DAY TWENTY-SEVEN - A.M.

Welcome to day twenty-seven!

Throughout this program we have said that being able to listen to another person at level-one requires far more than hearing words or even facts. It demands that one strive to listen empathetically. That one tries to see the world through the speaker's eyes, through their feelings and emotions. It requires that a listener suspend judgment and criticism.

Learning to listen at level-one is not a simple task, but the rewards for both the speaker and listener are enormous. As we have said many times in this program, listening to another with empathy is one of the greatest gifts one person can give to another. Learning to listen at this level takes total commitment and desire. It can be extremely difficult for most people, but it's the gold-standard of listening, which is precisely why it is so rare, and so appreciated, when given.

In many cases, level-one listening can be broken into further degrees of listening. A person may truly listen to another with either sympathy or empathy. People frequently assume that the two words are synonyms of each other. Not so. Not so at all!

What is the Difference Between Listening with Sympathy or Empathy?

Sympathy keeps the listener on the periphery. Empathy puts you in the shoes of the speaker. When you listen with empathy, you become one in sharing joy, turmoil, excitement or despair.

Most people can generate sympathy, very few can generate empathy.

Loss of a Job

Sandy calls her best friend to tell her that she has just been let go from her job. As she begins to share her feelings and emotions of anger, sorrow and fear, she begins to cry. As Sandy continues talking through her tears, she says that maybe this was the best thing. She has known for a long time that this was an unfulfilling dead-end job, and that by staying in it for so long she knew she was leading an unfulfilling life. Maybe this was fate's hand of helping her to a higher purpose.

Linda Responds Sympathetically

As Linda listens to Sandy she feels her pain. If Linda responds sympathetically, she will focus on Sandy's pain and fear and anger. She may even express it by saying she can feel the same pain and emotions as Sandy.

Linda Responds Empathetically

If Linda is to listen and feel empathy she will acknowledge and feel Sandy's pain, but she will also share in her hope and possibility for the future.

In this particular instance, the listener focusing on sympathy will put their attention on the pain the speaker is feeling. The listener who is committed to listening with empathy will feel all the emotions of the speaker; anger, fear and sorrow, as well as hope and excitement for the future. The empathic listener shares the speaker's experience in all its forms.

Religious Beliefs and Empathic Listening

Jim and Robert were almost inseparable friends through college. After graduating they each landed jobs, but at opposite ends of the country. At first they kept in touch but eventually the years and distance turned them into virtual strangers. Jim hadn't heard from Robert in well over fifteen years and then one day Jim received an email notice from Robert inviting him to hook-up on Facebook.

Jim responded and soon they were communicating regularly. When Robert and Jim began their dialogue, Jim was quite surprised to hear that Robert had adopted a Christian fundamentalist philosophy. It caught Jim by surprise because both had been "committed" atheists all through their college years.

Now that their friendship was renewed, Robert would frequently call Jim or write him long letters to express his Christian views.

Jim Responds With Sympathy

Responding to another person can be a case of sharing a similar view as much as in sharing an emotional feeling.

In this case, Jim *can* share Robert's passion and conviction in finding something to put one's faith in. He can *sympathize* with Robert's views. He may not necessarily agree on the same philosophy, but he can share the same *feelings of belief* in something. In fact, Jim might be a devout Buddhist who sympathizes with Robert's feelings but from a "slightly" different philosophy and perspective.

Jim Responds with Empathy

If Jim was to respond with empathy he might ask Robert to share his feelings and ask him to explain what his religion and philosophy mean to him. He will try to project himself into Robert's shoes and to inquire how other people such as his family and coworkers feel about his philosophy. He might inquire how his beliefs affected his work, his associates and his lifestyle. He would do his best to capsulize Robert's philosophy as much as possible to see if Robert would agree with his interpretation.

In this case, if Jim is a devout Buddhist, and Robert is a devout Christian, there is little chance of the two friends *agreeing* on each other's spiritual philosophy. Since Jim is listening to Robert empathically, his focus isn't on *agreeing* with him as much as it is on understanding Robert's view.

This is the key to understanding the difference between sympathy and empathy.

The strength and integrity of empathy is not about agreeing or disagreeing; it's about acknowledging and understanding the speaker's feelings. That is why it's so difficult to do. In this case, Jim completely puts aside his Buddhist feelings and philosophy, and he allows himself to psychologically walk unprotected and unarmed into Robert's world and Robert's philosophy. That takes real strength and real courage.

Differences Between Sympathy and Empathy

It's quite possible that one person can listen to another with sympathy, and still clearly be listening at a level-one, but empathic listening involves even higher states of listening.

Sympathy leads the listener to actively look for ways to become sympathetic to the speaker's feelings, beliefs and emotions.

PROGRAM

When listening empathically, the listener avoids looking for anything to sympathize with. It means the listener suspends counseling, judging, criticizing and evaluating. The empathic listener is not looking for ways to find common ground or an alignment of feelings and beliefs; his sole aim is to understand the world through the speaker's eyes.

The empathic listener is nonjudgmental. His mission is to understand. In fact, the empathic listener may vehemently disagree with the speaker, but while he is listening empathically, he sets aside his feelings and his views and gives his total commitment to seeing, feeling and understanding the world or topic through the speaker's eyes.

You can probably see why empathic listening is truly a rare thing, and why it is considered one of the greatest gifts one person can give another.

Both sympathy and empathy require the listener's total focus and commitment to listening, but the key difference is in the objective. The sympathetic listener will look for alignment, common ground and ways in which he and the speaker can agree. The empathetic listener tries to align with the inner feelings and beliefs of the speaker. Agreement or disagreement is neither the purpose nor the desire.

The person using empathy tunes into the entire inner world of the other person whereas the person using sympathy typically tunes into only those aspects with which he agrees. The empathic listener isn't concerned with attempting to cheer a speaker up. He isn't focused on praise or encouragement, his desire is to understand.

Have you ever felt listened to at this level? How do you think your spouse, child, friend or even a stranger, would feel if you were to give them that level of listening?

The greatest compliment that was ever paid me
was when one asked me what I thought,
and attended to my answer.
~ Henry David Thoreau ~

It's highly unlikely that one can simply decide to listen empathically to another without some degree of practice and diligence. Learning to suspend one's philosophy and feelings takes courage and total commitment. To listen to a loved one, friend or even a casual acquaintance is a great and powerful thing.

Even though we may not achieve this degree of listening in our first or second attempt, it can be one of life's most worthy goals.

Even though you love your family, your spouse, your child, unless you learn to listen, and ultimately to listen empathically, sadly, you will never *really* know them. You'll know many things about them, and you'll know their likes and dislikes and so on, but you'll never really know them until you can see the world, even for a few moments, through their eyes.

Remember, it doesn't mean you agree or disagree, but that you simply see their world, even temporarily, as they do.

STEP 27 – Today's step is to take a few moments and think about what it means to listen to another person with sympathy and empathy. Would you like to be able to acquire this ability? If you could learn to listen to people at this level, what would it do to your most important relationships? What effect would it have on your family, your career? Have you ever felt listened to by someone else at this level? If so, how did it make you feel? If not, what would it mean to you to have someone listen to you at such an elevated level?

Take some time to ponder these questions.

Have a great day.

DAY TWENTY-SEVEN – P.M. MESSAGE

Welcome back. I hope you had a wonderful day. You belong to a select group of people. You really have accomplished a great deal and you have proven to yourself that you have the mettle to achieve your goals of becoming a great listener and communicator. Congratulations!

I trust you took some time to ponder the concepts of sympathetic and empathetic listening. I hope you completely understand the differences between the two, and what it means to practice them. Both are necessary and highly valued forms of listening.

JOURNAL ENTRY

I'm on my way to permanent change!

• You have been focusing on becoming a great listener and communicator for nearly a month. Are you pleased with your listening progress so far? Whether your answer is yes or no, why do you feel that way?

_____

_____

_____

_____

• Becoming a great listener and communicator is a lifelong pursuit ... because you can always get better. Is there an area in your "listening world" that you feel needs particular attention? If so, what is it?

_____

_____

_____

_____

• Do you have any ideas on how to improve your listening skills? Think small, simple steps. A small step, practiced daily, becomes an enormous leap in a relatively short period of time.

_____

_____

_____

_____

• Reasons and motivation are vital to lasting change. What's the payoff for acquiring the rarified skills of becoming a great listener?

_____

_____

_____

_____

_____

See you tomorrow.

29 DAYS . . . to becoming a great listener and communicator!

DAY TWENTY-EIGHT
Staying the course!

DAY TWENTY-EIGHT - A.M.

Welcome to day twenty-eight! It's here again … reward day!

By now you know, and you know that you know, that you totally deserve a reward. You also know that the best reward is a small reward, because the reward is not the reason for doing what you do, it's just a really nice way to recognize and salute your achievements.

Please be sure you give yourself your reward!

STEP 28 – I imagine you're wondering how we're going to effectively deal with the second half of this program's title (becoming a great communicator), when we've used a full twenty-seven days on the first half (becoming a great listener)!

We all agree on the importance of listening, but we also said that everyone, even great listeners, need to be listened to … it's a basic human need. So how do we become great communicators and how do we get other people to listen to us?

Let's begin by examining the opposite side of the communication coin. Let's look at how we can be *absolutely certain* that we will be *ineffective* communicators and that people will *not* listen to us.

How to be an "Ineffective" Communicator

The first step to being an *ineffective* communicator is to assume that everyone is desperately waiting to hear your views, and that they will agree with everything you say … verbatim.

PROGRAM

You can choose from a wide array of openings. A particularly ineffective one is to barge into someone's space, office or life and start telling them whatever is on your mind. If someone happens to be engaged in another activity, or is speaking with someone else, pay no attention. Assume that the moment you begin imparting your words of wisdom, all those within earshot will immediately drop whatever they're doing and gratefully pay heed to whatever's on your mind.

Now that you have the "listener's" undivided attention, you can rest assured that everyone will instantly catch your "meaning and message" the moment you begin to convey your thoughts.

You may even want to begin your uninvited dialogue by telling the listener that he has several problems, and lucky for him, you have the solutions. Another "effective" beginning is to tell the listener that many of his present problems are a direct result of his past inability to listen to you and heed your advice. Listeners also respond exceptionally well to being blamed or criticized. When using this opening gambit, be sure to be very liberal with what the "listener" *should* or *should not* do. This always has them on the edge of their chairs.

Remember, you are always right, the listener is usually wrong, and you're doing them a huge favor by sharing your views and opinions. If you need to stop talking long enough to catch a breath, be sure it's not so long that someone else might have a chance to share their views. After all, this is not about them, it's about you. Since both you and your opinion are bang-on and completely correct, there's little point in wasting time and effort in listening to anyone else. Be sure to imply this, loud and forcefully if necessary, so that everyone can benefit. Most people don't know what's best for them, that's why you've been put on this planet, to help set them straight.

Further, never take the chance of clouding your mind by listening to the muddling thoughts of other people. Besides, what has listening to others have to do with you being heard? Nothing whatsoever!

One last thing to remember is body language. In order to get your points through the "thick skulls" of your listeners, feel free to shout, frown, scowl, fold your arms and sneer. Each are effective on their own and even better when combining two or more.

So there you have it. The basic no-fail techniques for being ignored, tuned-out and not listened to.

Okay, so now that we know how NOT to be listened to, how do we go actually go about being listened to?

How to be an Effective Communicator

Believe it or not, if another person truly feels listened to by you, they will invariably extend the same courtesy back to you.

The basic rule then is this: listen and understand first. Then in turn, you will be listened to, and with any luck, you will be understood as well.

You have invested the past twenty-seven days immersing yourself in the world of listening. You know that becoming a good listener is not a simple matter. It takes desire, focus, concentration, and the ability to suspend our needs in an effort to focus on the needs of the speaker. Not a simple task.

Basic Rules To Help Us To Be Listened To

Is the Listener Free?

How often do we call someone on the telephone, or enter their space, and begin speaking about whatever's on our mind without taking a second to ask the "listener" if it's an appropriate time? Just because someone answered their phone or stopped what they were doing does not mean they are actually free to give you the attention you deserve.

General courtesy, and common manners would suggest that you ask the other person if they have five or ten minutes to listen to what you have to say. If you think about it, it's extremely rare to hear someone make this inquiry and then flitter that time in idle gossip. When a speaker has the courtesy to inquire about your availability to listen, you can almost guarantee they have something important to say. If you request five or ten minutes of someone's time, then you should do your very best to honor that commitment. It can be very discourteous to ask for ten minutes and then drone on for forty-five.

If the listener suggests they have five minutes then be sure what you have to say can be said in five minutes. If you require more time than that, and that's all the time they have at the moment, then try and arrange a time that is more suitable.

So often people will fail to inquire if the speaker is available, then they compound their poor manners by overstaying their welcome, and then wonder why they don't feel listened to.

When people don't feel listened to, they will often blame a lack of courtesy and respect on the part of the listener, when in reality, it may stem from the complete disregard the speaker had for the rights of the listener. Even if someone appears to be available to listen, it's not your call to assume they are. The "intended" listener may be waxing his car, and appear to be completely available, but for all you know he may have judicially reserved this time-alone for some long overdue thinking time that he was looking forward to.

Remember, before you can expect someone to listen to you, be sure the time and place are appropriate.

Is Your Topic Relevant?

Another important factor in being listened to is to be sure the listener has an interest in what you're saying.

A friend of a friend of mine has an annoying habit of inviting himself to almost any social situation. This person may see my friend and me in a bar, or restaurant, and without asking permission he will pull up a chair.

After barging into the conversation with whatever pops into his mind, he will let us in on the most "spine-tingling" topics. We might learn that his neighbor is painting his house, his cat ran away from home, or that his second-cousin just bought a new motorcycle.

If you have a relationship with someone, a parent, a child, boss, close friend, it can be safely assumed that they will take a genuine interest in your thoughts, feelings and emotions … *provided* the time is appropriate.

Try To Understand How Things May Be Viewed by the Listener

David was organizing a community fund-raising drive for diabetes. He had begun to recruit a number of businesses and local celebrities to donate their time and money toward sponsorship. David had hoped to garner the support of Bill Smith, one of the town's leading citizens and employers. With the support of Mr. Smith, David knew he would be able to recruit many other sources of help and that he would easily reach his goal.

David wrote Mr. Smith a letter explaining the event, its purpose, the amount of money they were hoping to raise. He specifically outlined the various series of events they were staging, with the grand finale being a walk-a-thon in which they hoped the entire town would participate.

David spent several hours crafting his letter, and when he thought he had it just right, he showed it to Sally Stone, one of Bill Smith's senior managers. After reading the letter, Sally told David that Bill Smith was a "silent supporter" of Special Olympics, and that he was very close to his nephew who was confined to a wheelchair.

PROGRAM

After learning this new information, David re-wrote the letter to Bill Smith. In the re-write he outlined how they planned to involve the entire town, including several participants who were confined to wheelchairs. Those in wheelchairs would raise funds and would be teamed-up with runners who would ensure they could complete the course.

Was David's "new" letter underhanded or manipulative? I don't think so. He didn't do, or promise, anything that he wasn't already planning to do. He simply re-wrote his letter and highlighted the area that he thought would heighten the interest of the reader – in this case Bill Smith.

Understanding your audience, boss, child or spouse, and meeting their interests, can make the difference between being listened to … or not. If we try to persuade people to adopt our interests we are needlessly pursuing an extremely difficult task. Far too often, people will make the mistake of assuming that what is important to them will be important to the listener. To make such an assumption can often lead to a failure to be listened to.

Be Sure You've Been Heard and Understood

Just as a good listener will summarize and reiterate what he heard the speaker say, it is equally important for the speaker to occasionally summarize what he has said or ask the listener for his thoughts on what was said.

A good, communicative speaker, will never take for granted that the listener absorbed and understood exactly what was said. An effective speaker will make sure he was understood by asking the listener for his response and feedback. This will not only ensure that the speaker's message was understood, but it increases the likelihood of retention on the part of the listener because he will have actively participated.

Just as people overestimate their ability to hear and absorb what they heard, speakers overestimate their ability to communicate their message to the "listener." Without feedback, the speaker has no way of knowing if the message was received.

To become an effective communicator means to make certain you were successful at delivering your message. Making a point of receiving feedback will ensure your message was received and understood as intended.

If you can put into practice the lessons from the first twenty-seven days, you will become a great listener. If you genuinely listen to another person, remarkably and unfailingly, they will respond in kind, they will naturally listen to you.

JOURNAL ENTRY

I'm on my way to permanent change!

Today is reward day. For my well deserved reward I gave myself:

_____

The fourth week is complete!

- Week one was about awareness and commitment. "I know I'm committed to becoming a good listener and communicator."

- Week two was about further commitment and embedding those neurological tracks into a new and powerful way of thinking.

- Week three was action week! You took action by practicing your listening skills. You were willing to suspend your feelings and beliefs in order to listen to another person. Your listening skills have acquired a new energy and purpose.

- Week four is about staying the course. It's the week in which you built your resolve to make listening a life-long pursuit. You have made small, simple changes to your listening skils that are minor enough not to upset your amygdala, but major enough to radically change your life. For the past month you have sustained your focus and desire toward achieving your goal. You have enhanced your commitment to becoming that rare and cherished individual in life that can set aside, even temporarily, your feelings and needs in order to give another person the gift of your total attention and understanding.

When it comes to setting and achieving your goals, you are among the minority. You have traveled a great distance in understanding the barriers to becoming a great listener and communicator. You truly are a rare individual who should be so proud of all that you've accomplished!

DAY TWENTY-EIGHT – P.M. MESSAGE

You did it, you're here. We said earlier in the program that research confirms it takes between twenty-one and twenty-eight days to form a habit. Well whether it's twenty-one or twenty-eight, you've made it!

You have indelibly changed your thoughts and habits toward becoming conscious and aware of listening. You will never again be able to embrace your old bad-

PROGRAM

listening habits. Your conscious and subconscious minds will constantly remind you to listen and communicate effectively.

Giving and Receiving the Gift of Praise
To listen empathically to another person is one of the greatest gifts we can give. Another rare, and valuable gift is the gift of praise.

You may be surprised to learn that not all praise is accepted gratefully.

When we praise another person we should strive to be genuine and specific. To say to Sally, "You're such a good girl," is not nearly as effective as saying "That is so kind of you to you help your little brother clean up his toys."

The second statement clearly lets Sally know what you're appreciating.

Praise should not be focused on a person's personality but rather on his achievements and actions. Look at the difference between a *meaningful* and *specific* compliment versus broad-based and sometimes "meaningless" praise.

- You're a really nice person.
- That was so nice of you to help your neighbor shovel the driveway.
- You're a good worker.
- I really like the way you clean up the construction site at the end of the day. We get a lot of compliments and extra work because of it.
- You're always so friendly.
- Your genuine concern and response to our customer's problems has really improved our company and brought lots of new sales.
- You're a good soccer player.
- Your focus on defensive play has really improved our team.

You can probably see the two kinds of praise. The first examples are broad, general and often meaningless. The second versions are specific. They let the receiver know specifically what it is we value. It shows that we have noticed a particular action or behavior and the recipient is likely to accept it as a meaningful compliment.

Have you ever listened to someone praise you but wish they hadn't bothered?
It might come as a surprise to you, but praise can be harmful as much as it can be inspiring and helpful. If you're not sure what that means read the following sentence and see how much you would relish this type of praise.

"You're always so helpful, you're such a good friend. I love spending time with you. Oh, by the way, I finally found a new apartment. Would you help me move this weekend?"

Although the above could be construed as a compliment – if one was desperate for a compliment – in most cases it could be interpreted as crass, manipulative or even malicious.

When we praise another person there are only two rules to follow;
1.   Make sure our praise is genuine.
2.   Make sure it is specific.

Although we usually like to be complimented or praised, how often has our praise given to someone else been rebuffed? Suppose you say to someone,
 "I really admire you for being so good to your parents. You're a really good son."

How often might we hear this type of a compliment rebuffed or brushed aside with remarks like the following;

- ✧   "Oh I'm just doing what any son would do."
- ✧   "It's nothing. It's the least I could do.
- ✧   "I don't do anything anybody else wouldn't do.

Suppose you changed that compliment or praise to:

- ✧   "I really admire you for the way you look after your parents. Getting them up in the senior's home and then cheerfully visiting them three times a week shows such love and concern."
- ✧   "You've really set a great example of caring for your parents. I'm going to try to be as good to my folks as you are to yours."

The more specific the praise the less likely it is for someone to brush it aside. After all, if we give someone a gift or a compliment, ideally we would like the person to accept it, and value it. The more genuine and specific the compliment and praise, the easier the acceptance becomes.

Do You Rebuff Praise?
How often you caught yourself responding to someone's compliment or praise with phrases like the following:

- ◊ "Oh it was nothing."
- ◊ "Anyone could have done that."
- ◊ "You thought my talk was good? I don't think so. I should have mentioned this and that and blah blah blah."

Try to remind yourself that genuine praise from another person is a gift. Don't deny other people the chance to give the gift of praise. When you brush praise or a compliment aside with phrases like, "It was nothing," you can leave the giver feeling embarrassed and awkward.

There's absolutely nothing wrong with accepting the gift of praise with a simple "Thank you."

Tonight, when you get into bed, and just before you fall asleep, picture yourself giving and receiving praise. See yourself giving the gift of a genuine compliment and notice the result.

Also, vividly imagine someone giving you praise. How do you react? Do you accept their gift? If you accept their gift with a simple acknowledgement how does the giver react to your acceptance?

Remember, the last thing you think of before you go to sleep is what your subconscious mind has to work with all night long.

See you tomorrow.

 . . . to becoming a great listener and communicator!

DAY TWENTY-NINE
Staying the course!

DAY TWENTY-NINE - A.M.

You made it! You stuck with it all the way. You must be feeling very proud of yourself … and you should be.

For the past twenty-nine days you have willingly immersed yourself into the world of listening and communicating.

STEP 29 – In *29 DAYS … to a habit you want!* as in this program, we talked about the importance of daily focus and awareness toward creating a new habit. We also said in this program that becoming a great listener and communicator would be a lifelong task because it's one skill in which everyone can always improve. This *29 DAYS* program on listening began with understanding your old thought patterns and listening habits, and then using the rest of the program to overwrite those old patterns into new habits that you desire.

On days one and two of this program, you filled out two listening questionnaires. The purpose of these two questionnaires was to get a benchmark of your listening skills, habits and tendencies.

Undoubtedly, you are not the same person today that you were a month ago. You have a far greater awareness of listening and communicating. You may not always put your new awareness and skills into practice, but nonetheless, you will always be aware of them.

I would like you to take those two tests from day one and two again. This time you'll know the "best" answer – the answer that will produce the highest score – but you know that's not the purpose. You want to see the changes you've made. You want to notice where you've improved and where you need more focused effort.

PROGRAM

When answering these two questionnaires, use your listening habits from the last seven days to consider your answers.

HOW WOULD YOU RESPOND?

1. You're at home watching TV when the phone rings. You pick up the phone to hear your best friend, a newlywed, with exciting news. "Hey guess what? I just got the promotion I've been after! It comes with a raise, profit sharing and a company car. The only problem is I have to move out of town to the big city. I'm not sure how well I'd fit in there."

   _____ a) "Are you kidding? Take the job. It's what you've been after for the past two years. You'll love city life."

   _____ b) "I can't believe you wouldn't jump at this opportunity. You need to be more confident in yourself."

   _____ c) "What city is the job in? What concerns you about moving?"

   _____ d) "Congratulations on the opportunity, but it sounds like you've got some concerns about moving."

2. Your wife was having lunch with one of her friends and she comes home in a melancholy mood. "I don't know why I bother getting together with Joanne. All she ever does is brag about who she knows and how much money she's worth. She's not even remotely interested in my life."

   _____ a) "It sounds like you don't feel very valued as a friend. Are you considering ending your relationship?"

   _____ b) "You need to be more assertive. You should say what's on your mind. Don't worry about it, you've got lots of other friends."

   _____ c) "If I were you I'd blow her off. Why should you sit and listen to her honk her horn all the time?"

   _____ d) "If you make a point not to see her any more what are the ramifications?" How will it make you feel?"

3. Your close friend tells you that her boyfriend has just asked her to marry him. "I've been waiting for him to ask me for over a year. Now that he has, I'm not so sure. I think I really love him but he has such a violent temper. Sometimes he frightens me."

_____ a) "Are you kidding me? You need to be a little more aggressive. If you're afraid now you'll feel a lot more frightened when you're married."

_____ b) "What has he done that scares you and makes you feel so uneasy?"

_____ c) "If you're not sure, then you've got the only answer you need. Under no circumstances should you say yes unless you feel absolutely certain."

_____ d) "It sounds like you might be afraid to say *yes* and just as fearful to say *no*."

4. You come home from work to see your son in a bad mood. When you ask him how his day went he replies; "I had an awful day. The teacher yelled at me in front of the whole class for no reason. Then later we were playing soccer in gym class and I accidentally scored on my own goal."

_____ a) "Wow, that's a tough day, but you've got to just shrug it off and forget about it. I've had a few days like that. I remember one time ..."

_____ b) "That's some day. You must be feeling like the whole world's out to get you."

_____ c) "Come on son, you were obviously doing something wrong. The teacher isn't going to yell at you for no reason. As for scoring on your own net, that's got to be one of your bigger screw-ups don't you think?"

_____ d) "That's a rough day. What got your teacher so excited that she yelled at you?"

PROGRAM

5. A fellow employee enters your office and says; "Since you know my boss pretty well, I'm wondering if you wouldn't mind listening to my problem. He's always taking on every new assignment asked of him so he can look good to senior management. The problem is, he's always dumping every-thing on my desk and I can't keep up. Whenever I don't get my work completed he insinuates that I'm incompetent."

_____ a) "Have you talked to him about your work-load and how you might handle it in the future?"

_____ b) "Perhaps you're not being as efficient as you could be. After all, he should know how much work you can handle."

_____ c) "Don't worry about it. Just do the best you can. If you don't finish an assignment because he's overloading you, it's his fault."

_____ d) "You must feel like your in a no-win situation?"

6. Your son was one of the city's top Little League football players the previous year. It seems like every boy, except your son, sprouted up over the past year. Your son will now be the smallest player on the team and he's clearly worried. It's the last day to sign up and he says; "Dad, I don't think I'm going to play this year. I think I'm too small and besides, I'm not that inter-ested in football any more."

_____ a) "Son, you've got to face your fears. You can't run and hide from them. I was a couple of years behind the guys when I was your age. I caught up, and so will you. Sign up, Son, when you catch up to the others in size, you'll be glad you didn't quit playing."

_____ b) "Son, you haven't lost interest in football, you're just scared. You can't go through life being afraid. If you do you'll regret it."

_____ c) "You must be feeling like you can't compete on the same level as you did last year."

_____ d) "Why do you think you're too small? Do you think you might want to try another position? Would you like to try playing another sport?"

7. Your father calls you on the phone and says there's something on his mind. He tells you that shortly after your mother died he met another woman. He's considering asking her to marry him but he's just not sure how the rest of the family will take it. He loves this woman but he doesn't want anyone to be upset.

_____ a) "You can't be serious. Mom only died eight months ago. You shouldn't be so selfish. You've got to wait a while."

_____ b) "Why don't you let everyone know that you met another woman. That will soften the blow. Then in a few months time you can propose to her and the 'fall-out' ... if there's any at all, won't be nearly as bad."

_____ c) "You must be feeling a whirlwind of emotions and uncertainty."

_____ d) "So who is she? How did you meet her? What's she like? What does her family think?"

8. Your wife comes home from the office in a strange mood. She excitedly tells you that she was chosen to give the key sales presentation in Hong Kong later in the year. Just as you begin to join her in celebration she turns all melancholy and says she's not so sure that she's up to the task.

_____ a) "It seems like you're feeling a little overwhelmed with this new responsibility."

_____ b) "You're always selling yourself short."

_____ c) "What makes you feel unsure about your ability?"

_____ d) "You should be proud of yourself. The company wouldn't have picked you if you weren't up to the task. Don't worry, you'll be fine."

9. Your daughter has just finished her third year of a four-year BA program. She's still not sure what she wants to do. She tells you that she feels going to school for another year is a waste of time and money.

_____ a) "If you don't go back to school do you know what you want to do?"

_____ b) "It's only one more year. You've gone this far. If you don't finish it's like wasting three years. Get your degree and then see what you want to do."

_____ c) 'You must be feeling a little lost and uncertain."

_____ d) "You can't go through life starting and stopping things. If you commit to something stick to it and finish it. You're just not applying yourself enough."

10. A colleague at work storms into your office and says: "Can you believe it? They just replaced my boss with a woman from another firm. I thought it was company policy to hire from within. The president as much as told me that job was mine if it ever opened up. I don't know what I'm going to do yet, but I'm going to do something!"

_____ a) "I'm sure there's a perfectly good reason you didn't get the job. It probably opened up earlier than expected and the president knew you weren't ready for the responsibility just yet."

_____ b) "You must be feeling really let down, especially since you were practically promised the job."

_____ c) "I wouldn't take that. You should go and talk to the president and clear the air. After all, the least he owes you is an explanation."

_____ d) "Your boss left suddenly? What do you know about this new person? Do you think her assignment might just be temporary until they can get you properly trained?"

At the end of each question/scenario, you were given four answer choices. Please check the listening/answer choices you selected.

Questioning Response: You seek additional information before committing to a response. If you ask too many questions it could be construed as being grilled.

PROGRAM

1 - c, 2 - d, 3 - b, 4 - d, 5 - a, 6 - d, 7 - d, 8 - c, 9 - a, 10 - d **TOTAL** _____

Critical Response: This response tends to be judgmental and critical. It closes the door on continued discussion.

1 - b, 2 - b, 3 - a, 4 - c, 5 - b, 6 - b, 7 - a, 8 - b, 9 - d, 10 - a **TOTAL** _____

Empathic Response: This response is nonjudgmental. It encourages the other person to open up and to feel safe enough with you to explore their deeper feelings and to find their own solutions.

1 - d, 2 - a, 3 - d, 4 - b, 5 - d, 6 - c, 7 - c, 8 - a, 9 - c, 10 - b **TOTAL** _____

Advice Response: This response suggests that the solution is rather obvious. It does not invite discussion or evaluation. It simply slams the door on further exploration.

1 - a, 2 - c, 3 - c, 4 - a, 5 - c, 6 - a, 7 - b, 8 - d, 9 - b, 10 - c **TOTAL** _____

After you've circled your choices, notice which response is most dominant. Do you have a tendency to 'Ask Questions,' 'Give Advice,' 'Feel Empathic' or 'Offer Criticism'?

How do your present answers stack up to your answers from day one?

How Well Do I Listen?

	Almost Always	Often	Occasionally	Almost Never
1. I will listen to someone speak to me even when I'm not interested in what they have to say.	_____	_____	_____	_____
2. I remind myself when listening that I can learn something from everyone.	_____	_____	_____	_____

PROGRAM

	Almost Always	Often	Occasionally	Almost Never

3. While a speaker is talking, I like to think about what I want to say so I can respond intelligently.

_____   _____   _____   _____

4. I pretend to be listening even when I'm not so I don't hurt the speaker's feelings.

_____   _____   _____   _____

5. While someone is telling me their problems, I concentrate on what advice I can give them.

_____   _____   _____   _____

6. I don't mind interrupting the speaker if I have something important to say.

_____   _____   _____   _____

7. When people complain to me about their problems I don't argue I just listen and allow them to vent.

_____   _____   _____   _____

8. While a speaker is talking I like to think of a similar experience that I can share with them.

_____   _____   _____   _____

9. I try to listen well enough so I can give my opinion and advice as soon as the speaker is finished talking.

_____   _____   _____   _____

PROGRAM

	Almost Always	Often	Occasionally	Almost Never
10. When someone is finished speaking I try to ask questions that will encourage the speaker to elaborate further about what's on their mind.	___	___	___	___
11. I will focus on what the speaker is meaning and feeling and not just on the words they use.	___	___	___	___
12. I will encourage people to go on when they have stopped talking.	___	___	___	___
13. I can anticipate what a speaker will say before they finish, which allows me the chance to think of something else without getting bored.	___	___	___	___
14. When I'm talking to someone on the phone, my listening skill is good enough that I can multi-task (check email, read short notes) while they're speaking.	___	___	___	___
15. When someone is explaining how upset they are, I will attempt to soothe their feelings by telling them I know exactly how they feel and that everything will turn out alright.	___	___	___	___

PROGRAM

	Almost Always	Often	Occasionally	Almost Never

16. As soon as a speaker pauses, I will share similar experiences of my own rather than encourage the speaker to elaborate.

_____ _____ _____ _____

17. If a speaker has something important to say and I'm not in the mood or the timing isn't right, I'll suggest that we schedule another time.

_____ _____ _____ _____

18. I try to make people feel that I'm interested in them and in what they have to say.

_____ _____ _____ _____

19. I try to acknowledge what the speaker said before I respond with my point of view.

_____ _____ _____ _____

20. I focus on what the speaker is trying to communicate not just on the words they're using.

_____ _____ _____ _____

21. I wait until the speaker is completely finished speaking before forming my opinion.

_____ _____ _____ _____

22. I will often paraphrase what the speaker said so I know I've understood the message.

_____ _____ _____ _____

PROGRAM

	Almost Always	Often	Occasionally	Almost Never

23. Whenever it's appropriate, and I need to remember certain points, I will take notes while the speaker is talking.

_____ _____ _____ _____

24. I can accept criticism without getting defensive.

_____ _____ _____ _____

25. When people tell me their problems I give them my helpful opinions and advice.

_____ _____ _____ _____

26. I consider good listening to be more instinctive than a skill that requires effort.

_____ _____ _____ _____

27. If a speaker is interrupted and then asks me a short time later "where he left off," I can tell him where he left off.

_____ _____ _____ _____

28. I can tell in the first few seconds if someone is worth listening to.

_____ _____ _____ _____

29. While listening, I use body language (nodding my head, eye contact) to encourage the speaker to continue.

_____ _____ _____ _____

PROGRAM

	Almost Always	Often	Occasionally	Almost Never

30. If a speaker gets a little lost
in finding the right word or words
to express how they feel, I will
jump in with the right words to
help them out.

_____   _____   _____   _____

Please circle the answer you chose in the numerical list that follows. For example; if you chose *Occasionally* for question number 1, then you would circle number 2 under *Occasionally* in that column. When you have finished circling all 30 answers add the totals in each column.

	Almost Always	Often	Occasionally	Almost Never
1.	4	3	2	1
2.	4	3	2	1
3.	1	2	3	4
4.	1	2	3	4
5.	1	2	3	4
6.	1	2	3	4
7.	4	3	2	1
8.	1	2	3	4
9.	1	2	3	4
10.	4	3	2	1
11.	4	3	2	1
12.	4	3	2	1
13.	1	2	3	4
14.	1	2	3	4
15.	1	2	3	4
16.	1	2	3	4
17.	4	3	2	1
18.	4	3	2	1
19.	4	3	2	1
20.	4	3	2	1

PROGRAM

	Almost Always	Often	Occasionally	Almost Never
21.	4	3	2	1
22.	4	3	2	1
23.	4	3	2	1
24.	4	3	2	1
25.	1	2	3	4
26.	1	2	3	4
27.	4	3	2	1
28.	1	2	3	4
29.	4	3	2	1
30.	1	2	3	4

TOTALS

_____ _____ _____ _____

Almost Always = _____
Often = _____
Occasionally = _____
Almost Never = _____
GRAND TOTAL = _____

What's your Grand Total?

How did your answers stack up to your day two results? You may want to take these two simple tests from time to time to track your progress and to continually align your focus.

JOURNAL ENTRY

I'm on my way to permanent change!

On day eight you were asked to write out two goals: one was your goal for the rest of this program, and the other was a lifetime goal. I'm going to ask you to look at that lifetime goal, and make a slight adjustment. Very often when we think of a goal it becomes a target, an end in itself.

For this reason why not change your lifetime goal from a goal to an intention? Goals represent a finish line, but intention represents achievement and mastery.

Intending to live your life a certain way is infinitely more powerful and lasting, than setting a goal. You see, there really is no goal when it comes to a lifestyle because it's so much more than that.

PROGRAM

It becomes something that you are. It's an intention to live your life the way you choose to live it. Please review the lifetime 'goal' you wrote down and reshape it as the way you intend to live the rest of your life.

On day eight I wrote out my lifetime goal. I now change my lifetime goal to my lifetime intention.

I intend to live the rest of my life by these principles:

_____

_____

_____

From here forward, my listening and communication intention is to live my life in the following manner:

_____

_____

_____

_____

_____

DAY TWENTY-NINE – P.M. MESSAGE

You now have the knowledge to understand what a great and powerful thing it is to listen to another person. You have witnessed its magnetic power and the unseen forces that true listening can have on those around you.

Each day that you listen to someone you help them to reach their potential. That is why listening is the ultimate gift. It says to the other person that he is important, that what he says truly matters. For some inexplicable reason we are able to discover our abilities, and true potential, when someone really listens to us. It magically calls forth our inner resources and creativity.

Your commitment and dedication to becoming a great listener and communicator will positively change your world and the world of those to whom you grant your gift.

If we fail to listen to others we live in isolation. It's a great tragedy, but most people actually *do* live in isolation. Oh sure, they talk and converse, they speak and hear words, but they never hear the message, that deeper form of communication that each of us craves.

Remember, it's not the talker but the listener who becomes the sanctuary we seek. The listener is more powerful, more effective and more cherished. Listen to those in your world and you will witness miraculous happenings.

Loving your spouse, your family, your friends is, of course, a wonderful thing, but if you cannot listen to them, truly listen, you will never really know them. *You will never <u>really</u> know them.* To listen to another person is not easy, but it's a gift that will be remembered for a lifetime.

Your old listening thoughts, patterns and habits have been replaced by new thoughts of your own choosing. From here on in you are living your life with the unlimited power of intention. Your intention.

Congratulations for all that you've accomplished!

You really are special!

Good luck!

May you continue to enjoy your lifelong journey to becoming a truly great listener and communicator!

... to becoming a great listener and communicator!

PROGRAM

About the Author

Richard Fast, the author and creator of more than thirty toys, games, puzzles and books, has devoted the past twenty years to the research and development of the *29 DAYS* program(s).

He, like the rest of us, had always been told, "If you want to change your life just change your thoughts." That was the challenge.

Richard discovered that we *can* change our fundamental thoughts into desirable new habits by following the same cognitive procedure that we used to create our existing habits.

Richard's *29 DAYS* template for change uses proven scientific techniques, technology and online coaching, to guide you through a step-by-step process toward changing your thoughts and acquiring desirable new habits ... permanently.